LEWIS: A HISTORY OF THE ISLAND

LEWIS

A HISTORY OF THE ISLAND

DONALD MACDONALD

GORDON WRIGHT PUBLISHING
55 MARCHMONT ROAD, EDINBURGH EH9 1HT
SCOTLAND

© Donald Macdonald 1978

Copyright leased to the publisher. No part of this publication may be reproduced, stored in a retrieval system, or transmitted, in any form or by any means electronic, mechanical, photocopying, recording or otherwise, without prior permission of the publisher.

S.B.N. 903065 23 1

Published with the financial assistance
of the Scottish Arts Council

Printed in Scotland by Macdonald Printers (Edinburgh) Limited.
Bound in Scotland by James Joyce & Duffin Ltd.

CONTENTS

To
My wife Marion
and my daughters
Catriona and Christine

PREFACE

About twenty-five years ago a series of articles appeared in the *Stornoway Gazette* recalling various aspects of past life in North Tolsta, a Lewis village. It was an absorbing account which aroused tremendous interest and I only wish that the same could have been done for every other community in Lewis.

Donald Macdonald, the author of these articles, has recently completed this new history of the Island, an arduous task which has taken him many years of study to complete.

The last detailed history of Lewis was published in 1932 and formed part of W. C. Mackenzie's *History of the Western Isles* so the need for a new account has been apparent and frequently expressed for a long time.

Here in this volume that need has been met, and met in splendid fashion. The people of Lewis can now read with well-founded pride the story of their forebears, and those outwith the Island who express an interest in our affairs and way of life can learn how we became the people we are.

Donald Macdonald's researches have produced a book which will greatly benefit present and future generations and he is to be congratulated on an outstanding service to the community.

Rt. Hon. Donald Stewart M.P.
Stornoway, 1978.

ACKNOWLEDGEMENTS

I am indebted to the many people who have helped and encouraged me to write this book and special thanks are due to the following:

Messrs. Alexander Fenton, Gavin Sprott and Hugh Cheape, National Museum of Antiquities of Scotland, Country Life Section. Mr Donald Campbell, Edinburgh. Dr I. F. Grant, Edinburgh. Mr Angus M. Macdonald, Stornoway, Lewis. Mrs Christina Macdonald, Tolsta, Lewis. Miss Jo MacDonald, Ness, Lewis and Edinburgh. Mr Norman Macdonald, Tong, Lewis. Mr Norman Mackenzie, Stornoway, Lewis. Mr Angus Macleod, Tolsta, Lewis. Dr Finlay Macleod, Shawbost, Lewis. Mr Murdo Macleod, Luerbost, Lewis and Edinburgh. Rev. William Matheson, Edinburgh University. Mr George Morrison, Tolsta, Lewis and Glasgow. Mr Alex M. Morrison, Barvas, Lewis. Dr Thomas Murchison, Glasgow. Mr Henry Murray, Stornoway, Lewis. Mr J. Macleod Nicol, Edinburgh. Dr Michael Robson, Hawick. Mr Donald M. Smith, Stornoway, Lewis. Prof. T. C. Smout, Edinburgh University. Mr Donald Whyte, Kirkliston.

Permission to reproduce copyright material was granted as follows:

Mr Andrew M. H. Matheson, Brahan, Conon Bridge, Ross-shire, for the Seaforth Muniments in the Scottish Record Office, Edinburgh.

Rev. D. F. M. Macdonald, Principal Clerk to the General Assembly of the Church of Scotland, for the Reports on the General Assembly Schools.

Dr Horace Walker, Secretary to the Church of Scotland Home Board, for the Reports of the Edinburgh Free Church Ladies' Highland Association Schools.

Rev. Colin I. Maclean, Clerk to the Church of Scotland Presbytery of Lewis, for the old Stornoway Presbytery Records.

Controller of H.M. Stationery Office for Crown Copyright Records in the Scottish Record Office:

    Agriculture and Fisheries Report Ref. AF67

    Customs and Excise Reports, Stornoway. Ref. CE86.

    Lord Advocate's Papers. Ref. Box 181.

    Privy Council Records of Scotland.

John Bartholomew and Son Ltd., Edinburgh, for the map of Lewis.

The Archaeological Dept. of the Ordnance Survey, Edinburgh, for notes on the Lewis Survey, 1848-52.

The Secretary of the Society of Antiquarians of Scotland, for the various topics on Lewis.

I would also like to thank the staff of the National Library of Scotland; Edinburgh University Library; Edinburgh Central Library; Register House, Edinburgh; St Andrew's House, Edinburgh; The School of Scottish Studies, Edinburgh University; The Western Isles Library, Stornoway, and the editors of The Stornoway Gazette, The Scotsman and the Oban Times.

I am also grateful for permission to reproduce the photographs used in this book which have been credited individually wherever possible.

Donald Macdonald

INTRODUCTION

This book is the result of many years' research by a Lewisman who has lived most of his life in Edinburgh.

It was not of his own choosing that Donald Macdonald left Lewis to work in the city; as with so many other islanders looking for employment, the opportunities were not available in Lewis when he qualified as a teacher and he had to seek a post elsewhere.

In 1933 he married a Lewis girl he had known since his childhood and they set up house in Edinburgh where they raised a family of two daughters.

During all these years in Edinburgh his love for the Island of his birth never diminished, and each summer the family would "go home" to Lewis when he would explore different parts of the Island on foot, collecting local lore wherever he went.

His memories of life in North Tolsta during his youth compelled him to write various accounts of life in Lewis during that period, particularly for the benefit of his daughters, and these were published in the *Stornoway Gazette* in the early 1950s under the name Tolastadh bho Thuath. These fascinating accounts of shieling life and boats being launched from open beaches brought many letters of appreciation from interested readers and he was greatly encouraged to write more.

In one particular respect Donald Macdonald was fortunate in having settled in Edinburgh, for there he had access to a wealth of information which enabled him to delve into the history of Lewis so far largely neglected.

The documentation of Lewis' past stored in places like Register House, The School of Scottish Studies and the National Library of Scotland in Edinburgh, is considerable, and over the years, Donald Macdonald has investigated many a dusty volume, record and manuscript.

It is typical of many rural areas and islands that the records of their past are held in centralised archives in the major cities and are not readily available to the people whom they particularly concern. Such documents tend to become academic material and little of the knowledge gleaned from them is ever fed back to the place of its origin. In this instance, the tide has changed.

As a schoolmaster, it is not surprising that Donald Macdonald became interested in the papers of the various Gaelic school societies of the nineteenth century, and it is no accident that the longest chapter in this book deals with education. The role bilingualism plays in education has never before been such a live issue in Scotland as it is today, and Donald Macdonald's unique contribution is in examining how the various bodies who aimed to educate the people of Lewis dealt with it in their time.

The first five chapters give a concise account of events in Lewis during different periods in its history, but throughout, there is a tendency for the discussion to gravitate towards the eighteenth and nineteenth centuries.

As a source book of events during this time, the book is special in that it is well documented and the author does not attempt to introduce many of his own analyses but prefers to let the documents speak for themselves.

The documentation of the Macleod period tends to dictate a history in terms of kings and queens, but the remarkable documentation of the Seaforth family and of the Matheson period means that life in Lewis as reflected by events surrounding these proprietors becomes the foundation of this book.

The series of themes which have a chronological trend, tend to settle down to events in the Seaforth and Matheson period, and these are often strengthened by the author's personal experience of Lewis and its culture. His use of Gaelic tends to be confined to this latter strand in his writing, such as his description of clothing, houses and croft implements. Each chapter is an essay in itself, but taken together, they form a rich weave which gives a varied and comprehensive picture.

It is inevitable that the theme of land should dominate this history, particularly when the proprietor's family papers are taken as starting points and perhaps the greatest impact this book will have is in the way it demonstrates the power and influences wielded by the proprietors and their factors over the poverty stricken people. It is hoped that the readers will acquire a greater understanding of the present question of land use in Lewis and be able to contribute to serious discussion on the matter.

The reader may be surprised to find that massive areas of land are still being purchased by individuals who have no direct link with the islands, and the pellets from the landlord's guns are still as likely to fall around the crofter's ears as they did in his grandfather's day. In the meantime, Comhairle nan Eilean has a difficult task in discovering who owns the various estates in the Western Isles, and the people who successfully strive to remedy the situation will be those who know something of events in the past, for they will have a perspective to help them in their understanding of the present.

For many different reasons we have tended to know very little of our own history and heritage. The oral tradition was truncated by imported influences, and education was confined to the customs and history of others.

The importance of Donald Macdonald's work in altering this situation cannot be overestimated, and he himself would be the first to admit that this book is only a beginning and that others must now take up the fruits of his labours and transform them into forms suitable for people of different ages and backgrounds. This book is an important contribution to an ongoing process of a people's rediscovery of their own confidence and it is in this way that the book is to be evaluated.

The work of the young Ness Historical Society indicates one way in which the study of the Island's past may be revived and developed. With the aid of cassette recorders, a group of local young people are at present collecting the memories of the older people in the area. The material gathered is then made available to the people themselves through exhibitions and other events, rather than being lodged in a city archive, and it is likely that it will eventually be published in book form. This development is most akin to that part of Donald Macdonald's writing which draws on his own early experiences.

As tape recorders have facilitated certain developments, so have the introduction of photocopying techniques, and this means that unique documents need no longer be isolated outwith the Island.

It is hoped that information gathered in this book will encourage others to refer to the source material and generally expand on the various themes. Already as a result of information in an early draft of this book, young children from Point in Lewis have staged a play portraying Lt. John Munro of Uig and the soldiers blinded in Egypt.

Now retired in Edinburgh, Donald Macdonald always loves to hear news from Lewis, especially from others who have visited his favourite secluded places. Few realised how much it meant to him when he was invited to open the new primary school in Tolsta in 1977. His complete involvement and continuing interest dominates his life and few people know Lewis better than himself.

Until recently, virtually every summer was spent tramping in Lewis, setting off into the hills in his frayed kilt and faded balmoral. "If anyone should ask you where you are from," said his brother, on one such occasion, "speak to them in English so that they will think you are from Skye."

Throughout this book, the passion for education pervades, in spite of his doubts about the kind of education being offered; his pride of achievement in war is there in spite of knowing how regiments such as Seaforth's originated; his ambivalence towards proprietors such as "Sir Seumas" is there in spite of his painful awareness of the empty townships.

For all his time and work involved in producing this book, the people of Lewis are greatly indebted to Donald Macdonald. A lively mind and a strong light step brought the work to fruition.

Finlay Macleod
Shawbost
Spring 1978

PRE-HISTORIC LEWIS

Lewis, with Harris, forms the most northerly portion of the hundred-mile long string of islands called the Outer Hebrides, or the Long Island. Lewis is most mountainous where it adjoins Harris. The mountains of Mealasbhal in the parish of Uig, and Beinn Mhor, in the parish of Lochs, rise to over 1,800 feet, while the rest of the Island consists chiefly of a low, undulating, mossy plain, where peat may lie to a depth of twenty feet in places on top of boulder clay.

The Island has been fairly accurately described as being "an immense peat, with notches of the moss cut away here and there, to afford a sure foundation for the inhabitants, and produce for their bodily wants". (1) However, on the east and west coasts, where the soil is fairly fertile, there are sandy tracts which have been cultivated for thousands of years.

It is evident from the numerous tree stumps found embedded in the peat, that the surface of the island was once totally different from its present brown, heathy, unprepossessing condition. It is difficult to picture Lewis forested, with alder, birch, ash, rowan and hazel, where now lies only bogland.

Lewis tradition blames the marauding Norse for destroying these forests, by setting them on fire, as part of their scorched earth policy to harass the native population. Magnus Bareleg's punitive campaign of 1098, when "fire played fiercely over Lewis", (2) may account for this belief, there being little else to burn except trees and very primitive houses. The real enemy of the forests, however, was the peat, which gradually formed as the warm climate changed to the cool conditions we know today.

There was probably very little peat in Lewis when the Callanish Stones were set up, between 3,000 and 4,000 years ago, and yet, when Sir James Matheson had the site excavated in 1856, the peat was five feet deep. In an Iron Age kitchen midden excavated in Galson (estimated to be about 1,500 years old), were found the bones of wild-cat and blackbird, both creatures of woodland and tropical grasslands. (3) In the Tolsta crannog, in Loch Osabhat (found when the loch was drained in 1870), it was discovered that the outer rim of this artificial island, which had contained three houses, was formed of an outer and inner row of wooden stakes five or six inches in diameter. (4)

The Norse devastation therefore, only hastened the process of woodland deterioration which had been in operation for centuries. Finally, only small patches of hazel scrub were left in sheltered places such as Swordale, on Keose Glebe by Luerbost Loch, and in Garry, and rowans on odd islets in moorland lochs.

There is ample evidence that people lived in Lewis thousands of years ago. *Tursachan,* or *Fir-Bhreige Chalanais,* the Callanish Stones, with their neighbouring stone circles, and the Neolithic relics found in old habitation sites and quarries are sufficient proof. Who these early settlers were, it is now impossible to say, but they were not Celts, for the Celts did not arrive in Scotland until about 500 B.C., and the previous inhabitants were Stone and Bronze Age people. The Island, as it stands, on the north-western periphery of Europe, must also have been the final place of refuge for displaced persons, as well as many sea-rovers, using the western sea-routes.

From an examination of the many excavated kitchen middens, all on machair lands, we can determine that the Islanders earned their livelihood by hunting, fishing and agriculture. The most favoured sites were in Uig, round the shores of Loch Roag, and it is in this area that so many relics of antiquity have been discovered, including the afore-mentioned Callanish Stones, erected by Neolithic invaders from the Mediterranean, who came sailing northwards. The purpose of these stones has been the subject of discussion for many years. The local people, at one time, were firm in their belief that the Stones were used for religious ceremonies, in which human sacrifices, at the tall, central pillar, played an important part. These standing stones, second in importance in Britain only to Stonehenge, form a most impressive sight. They are forty-two in number, of undressed Hebridean gneiss, in the form of a circle, with approach avenues, and they range from three and a half to fifteen and a half feet in height.

There are other stone circles in the Loch Roag district, and more monoliths throughout the Island. There is a *Clach Stein,* Standing Stone near Bayble, and one in Eoropie. There are also Standing Stones called Steinacleit and Clach Stei Lin in Airidhantuim, and Clach an Tursa in Carloway. Pride of place however, must be given to Clach an Truiseil, in Balantrushal, which is eighteen feet ten inches above ground, six feet wide, with a maximum thickness of three feet nine inches, and a girth of fifteen feet seven inches at its base. From about halfway up, it begins to taper until, at the top, it is only one foot thick. (5) According to island tradition, this monolith was once a man, who, for some reason, had been turned to stone, for did not a benighted passer-by once hear a voice issuing from it, proclaiming in sepulchral tones:

> *Is Truisealach mis' an deigh nam Fiann;*
> *Is fhad' mo thriall an deigh chaich;*
> *M' uilinn anns an Aird an Iar,*
> *'S mi gu m' dha sgiath an sàs.*

> A Truisealach am I after the Fiann;
> Long is my journey behind the others;
> My elbow points to the west,
> And I am embedded to my oxters.

Not all the dwellings were above ground, though some were partially so. The souterrains, or earth houses, were wholly underground. Of those discovered, three were in Uig, one in Mealista and two in Valtos; one in Ness on the Habost machair, and one in Gress. They were all built to the same design with a long underground passage leading to a circular central chamber, from five feet to nine feet in diameter, like a miniature underground broch. Unfortunately, they are not easily identified today.

The Gress souterrain was well preserved. A slightly curved passage, about two feet square, led to a circular chamber nine feet in diameter, and on each side of the entrance to the chamber, there was a recess two feet six inches wide. The whole structure was built of unhewn stones, with a stone pillar in the centre of the chamber to support the flag-stones which formed the roof. (6) In other instances the roofs were corbelled.

A Stone Age settlement was discovered in Eoropie, Ness, in September 1977.

In addition to the Tolsta crannog already mentioned, there were others in Loch Oransay on the Arnish Moor, in Loch Airigh na Lice, outside Stornoway, and probably in Loch Shiavat, in Borve, as the dun there, rising as it does from the loch bottom, may have originally been a crannog.

Bronze Age swords have been found in Aird Dell, in Ness, dating from the eighth century B.C., and a treasure trove from 600 B.C. was found at Adabrock, Ness, in 1912. (7) Other objects found include stone implements of all kinds, horn objects, fragments of pottery, arrowheads, combs, bronze pins and brooches.

Nothing testifies more to the uncertainty of life in these far off days than the numerous duns or forts, whose ruins, dating from the Iron Age, can still be traced.

There were two types of fortification, the broch and the ordinary dun. The brochs were drystone circular buildings formed by two concentric walls, the inner one perpendicular, and the outer one inclining inwards, fastened together with flags at varying heights by means of which galleries were formed in the inter-space, connected by stairs. There were no openings in the wall except a low door at the entrance to a passage to the inner court which was open to the sky. There was a guard cell in this passage.

There were four of these brochs in Lewis, at Dun Carloway, Bragar and Borve, on the west coast and one, at Cromore on the east coast. Of these, the best preserved is at Dun Carloway, which will always be associated with the daring exploit of the seventeenth century Uig hero, Donald Cam MacAulay, who is said to have climbed the forty foot high outer wall with the aid of two dirks which he used as stepping stones to get at his enemies trapped inside. Dun Bhragair also had its own hero, the formidable John Roy Macphail or Mackay, who is said to have fled from Dornoch in 1608. (8) He and Donald Cam were arch-enemies, and it was from here that he was dragged by twelve MacAulays (and they needed all that man-power) to be executed at *Cnoc 'na Mi-Chomhairle,* The Hillock of Evil Counsel, near Kirkibost on the Island of Bernera.

Of the other duns, simple forts, as distinct from brochs, there were seventeen in the parish of Barvas, eight in Uig, ten in the parish of Stornoway, most of them in the Point district, and three in Lochs. Other forts were built on the east coast, probably after Norway's cession of the Hebrides to Scotland, in 1266, when Lewis became part of the Earldom of Ross. These were at Stornoway, Dun Eistein and Dun Eoradale in Ness, and the Mormaer's Castle in Garry.

The inhabitants of Lewis at the beginning of the Christian era were Picts. However, even before the establishment of the kingdom of Dalriada and the arrival of St Columba in Iona in 563 A.D., the Scots from Ireland had begun to move up into the Hebrides, for according to an Irish manuscript of 1150 A.D., the Ulster hero Donald Cearnach, is recorded as levying toll in "The territories of Leodus", about 1 A.D.. (9)

From the sixth century onwards, Columban missionaries ventured northwards in their frail boats, some as far as Iceland. The two Lewis people best remember are St Ronan and St Moluadh, who lived at the beginning of the eighth century. They seem to have spent most of their time in Ness, but there were obviously many other priests, judging by the number of small chapels found all over the Island, not all of which are post-Norse. The island of Pabbay in Uig (Priest's Island) and the village of Bayble (Priest's Village) in Point, (10) must have been so named by the Norse.

The Scots would not only bring their Gaelic language with them, but also the tales of the Fianna (a legendary band of warriors led by Fionn), tales which are still remembered. The story of the giant Cuitheach, who lived in Dun Bhorranais, near Crowlista in Uig, has even Fionn, the Celtic hero himself, visiting Lewis.

According to local traditions, Cuitheach and his three equally gigantic brothers, who lived in the duns of Carloway and Tidiburgh and Baile Glom, in Bernera, oppressed the people in the vicinity. On hearing of this, Fionn came to Lewis with his army to fight Cuitheach, the strongest of the brothers.

The Fianna took up their position on a ridge near the village of Penny-Donald. Since they believed in fair play, they did not move to attack Cuitheach in a body as the fight had to be a man to man affair. Cuitheach however, ignored the Fianna as he strode past them each day on his way to spear flounders on the beach.

One day, Fionn's grandson, Oscar, asked him if he could borrow his famous sword "Mac Luinn" as he wanted to go hunting. "What shall I do if the giant comes out to fight me while you are away with my sword?" asked Fionn. Oscar replied that he would only hunt on the nearest hill and if the giant came out to fight, they had only to blow the strongest whistle and he would be back in a moment. He was given the sword and he departed. That very day, the giant came out to meet the Fianna. His appearance was so terrible, that they all fell back a step, including Fionn, the only time he ever did such a thing before the enemy.

The next day, Fionn and the giant faced each other, and the fight began, Fionn without his famous sword. The strongest whistle possible was blown and Oscar came rushing back to find his grandfather had been brought to his knees by the giant's sword-play. Oscar shouted to Fionn "Come out of there and let me engage him with the never-failing weapon "Mac Luinn". They exchanged places, and Oscar, with his third stroke, cut Cuitheach's head off. What is supposed to be Cuitheach's grave, fourteen feet in length, can still be seen near the sands of Uig.

THE NORSE

When the Norsemen colonised Lewis in the eighth and ninth centuries, it led to the practical extermination of the existing population and its replacement by ruthless, heathen foreigners.

These invaders, called Vikings, as they came from the viks or creeks of Norway, were grouped into two nationalities. These were the *Fionn-Ghoill,* White Foreigners who came from Norway and Sweden and the *Dubh Ghoill,* Black Foreigners from Denmark. There was nothing to choose between them, for both were equally barbarous and largely devoid of moral scruples. Pity or remorse were emotions practically outwith their comprehension. They committed fearful atrocities, not only against foreigners, but also against their own people, and the Sagas are full of instances of men being blinded, mutilated and burnt to death in their own homes.

No wonder the sight of the dragon-ships on the horizon struck terror into many a heart. Safety lay in instant flight.

The Vikings rounded up men and animals alike. The men were often quickly dispatched, while the women, especially the young and sturdy, were kept for future use or abuse, and many of these unfortunates were eventually sold in Baltic slavemarkets. All the captives were kept bound on the beach, sometimes for days, until the animals were slaughtered and the galleys provisioned.

Before the Norse decided to settle, they were only interested in plunder, monasteries being their favourite targets. The raiding season began after the corn was planted and lasted until harvest time, but later, with improved vessels and an increased knowledge of geography, some of these piratical expeditions went much further afield and lasted for years.

The first mention of Viking activities on British shores is given in the Anglo-Saxon Chronicle, which records the arrival of three of their ships on a Northumbrian beach in 787 A.D.. When the local sheriff went to investigate, he was promptly murdered.

The Orkney and Shetland Isles (the Nordereys), and the Western Isles (the Sudreys), must have suffered from these raiders long before they were recorded as having arrived in these parts. In 795 A.D., Iona was ravaged for the first time, and suffered again in 798 A.D. and 802 A.D.. In 806 A.D., the whole community of monks, sixty-eight in number, was murdered, a deed which was to be repeated in 825 A.D., when the Abbot, Blathmac, and his company were put to death. (1)

As Lewis was the first Hebridean island on the Viking western route, its inhabitants must have been constantly harassed by these pirates both on their outward and homeward journeys. Unfortunately, there is no Lewis Saga, like the Orkneyinga and Heimskringla Sagas, to tell how the people fared in these days, but there is no reason to suppose that they were any better off than the Orcadians and Shetlanders.

Until about 853 A.D., the Western Isles were still regarded as part of what we now know as Scotland, but by this time, permanent Norse settlements were being formed in Lewis as elsewhere throughout the Hebrides, Galloway, Man and Ireland. A new race of people, the Gall-Gaidheil, of mixed Norse and Celtic ancestry had come into existence who were every bit as ruthless as the Norse.

For a long time, Norway was divided into numerous independent states, each with its own kinglet, eager to enlarge his territory at the expense of his neighbour, but in 872 A.D., after the Battle of Haversford, Harold the Fair-haired appointed himself sole king. He gave his former rivals the choice of submitting to his will or exile. Many chose the latter course, and sailed away to make new homes in the Northern and Western Isles, Man, Ireland, and distant Iceland. This emigration must have increased the number of permanent settlers in Lewis.

These new settlers, anxious to avenge themselves, combined with the other Vikings to harry the coasts of Norway until finally King Harold sailed in force to the west in 880 A.D. and either killed or drove them out of their island strongholds.

Harold's conquest of the Hebrides was short-lived, for he was no sooner back in Norway than the Vikings were back in their old haunts and at their former practices of plundering and killing.

On Harold's way home, he offered the Earldom of Orkney (which included the Hebrides), to Earl Rognvald, who declined the offer. Harold then gave it to his brother Sigurd, but on the latter's death, trouble broke out in the Northern and Western Isles.

To quell the disturbances in the Hebrides, Harold sent over one of his nobles, Ketil Flatnose. This task Ketil performed so successfully that he decided to discard his allegiance to the King and take control himself. His rule does not seem to have lasted long. (2)

Unfortunately for Lewis, there was seldom stable government in Orkney for any length of time. Sometimes there were three earls sharing the earldom. The most outstanding of these were Torf Einar, who is credited with the introduction of peat burning into Orkney, Sigurd the Stout, and, perhaps the most capable of all, Thorfinn, whose rule brought a modicum of peace to the Western Isles, chiefly owing to the exertions of his lieutenant there, Kalf Arneson, an able, ruthless man.

> From Thurso-skerry to Dublin,
> All people hold with good Thorfinn—
> All the people love his sway,
> And the generous chief obey. (3)

On Thorfinn's death, the Hebrides lapsed once again into a state of anarchy, sometimes being ruled from Orkney, sometimes from Man, and sometimes from Ireland.

There were some outstanding Norwegian kings, such as Hakon the Good (934-961 A.D.) who tried, with little success, to introduce Christianity into his scattered kingdom. King Olaf Tryggvason (968-1000 A.D.), at one time a noted Viking, was baptised into the Christian faith in the Scilly Isles in 994 A.D. and became a zealous proselyte. On his way home to Norway he surprised Earl Sigurd in the Orkneys and ordered him to turn Christian or else suffer instant death. Sigurd refused, preferring death to baptism, but when Olaf seized his young son and prepared to behead him, he relented and allowed himself to be baptised. However, he did not remain a Christian for very long, and soon reverted to his old religion worshipping Odin and Thor.

Sigurd was killed at the Battle of Clontarf in Ireland in 1014, when he led one of the three divisions of the combined Norse and Danish host against the forces of the Irish King, Brian Boru. Sigurd's men were levies from all the isles from Shetland to Man, including some from Lewis. They were described as being a fierce, barbarous lot, senseless, uncontrollable and unbiddable.

Little is known of the happenings in Lewis for a period after this. Christianity became the national religion of Norway about 1000, but the old religion, with its sacrifices to the gods, continued for a long time. it is strange to think that Odin, Thor and Freya, were once worshipped in Lewis, but no stranger than the fact that Thor's name is still perpetuated in names like *Tormod,* Norman, and *Torcuill,* Torquil.

The year 1066 is always associated with the Battles of Stamford Bridge and Hastings, when the Normans conquered England, but this date is also of importance to the history of Lewis and the other Hebridean islands. One of the Norse leaders who escaped the slaughter at Stamford Bridge was a certain Godfrey Crobhan (White-handed). He made his way to the Isle of Man where he repaid hospitable treatment with three attempts to take control of the island. At his third attempt he was successful and became a strong and capable ruler whose kingdom extended from the Butt of Lewis to Dublin. His power was such, that not one of his subjects dared to build a vessel with more than three bolts in it, or above three strakes high.

Godfrey was still supposed to be a vassal of the King of Norway, a fact he was inclined to forget. When Magnus Barefoot (1093-1103) came to rule Norway, he wanted complete control of his scattered kingdom, so in 1098, he sent one of his nobles, Ingemund, to bring his unruly island subjects to allegiance. This, of course, brought him into conflict with Godfrey.

Ingemund, like Ketil Flatnose before him, liked his new appointment so much that he decided to be his own master. He set up his headquarters in Lewis, from where he sent messengers to all the Isles' chieftains calling them to an assembly in Lewis to confirm him as king. (4) While awaiting their arrival, Ingemund and his boon companions spent their time plundering, drinking and outraging the womenfolk. When the chiefs assembled as requested and were informed of Ingemund's excesses, they were so furious that one night they set fire to the house where he and his companions were staying. They exterminated them all, partly by fire and partly by the sword as they tried to escape. (5)

King Magnus was not the type of man to tolerate such actions, so he set off with a large fleet, first to the Orkneys and then on to Lewis, where he gained a victory. (6) He devastated the island before proceeding to Skye, where he had a strand-slaying, "strand-hug" of captured stock before foraging southwards as far as North Wales. People fled before him in all directions, some out into Scotland Fiord (The Minch) and others as far as Ireland.

Biorn Cripplehand, the king's skald, gives a vivid account of Magnus' southward progress:

In Lewis Isle with fearful blaze
The house-destroying fire plays;
To hills and rocks the people fly,
Fearing all refuge but the sky.
In Uist the king deep crimson made
The lighting of his glancing blade;

The peasant lost his land and life
Who dared to bide the Norseman's strife.
The hungry battle-birds were filled
In Skye with blood of foeman killed,
And wolves on Tiree's lonely shore
Dyed red their hairy jaws in gore.
The men of Mull were tired of flight;
The Scottish foemen would not fight,
And many an Island girl's wail
Was heard as through the Isles we sail.   (7)

Although Magnus visited Iona, he did not ravage it as he considered himself a Christian. He peeped into the Abbey, but immediately closed the door and locked it.

On the arrival of the fleet in Man, Godfrey Crobhan was expelled by the King who appointed his own son Sigurd in his place. Lagman, Godfrey Crobhan's son, who tried unsuccessfully to intercept the royal fleet, was captured off Scarba as he tried to escape.

Unsafe was every hiding-place that Godfrey's heir possessed:
the men of Trondhjem's king had him banned there from the land.
The able young king of Agdir has taken the despoiler of the snake's
bed (Wales) beyond the headlands; there where the swords'-blades whined.

On his return journey, Magnus had a boat hauled across the Tarbert Isthmus with its rudder shipped, and himself at the tiller, and so claimed Kintyre as one of his island possessions from King Edgar of Scotland. The adoption by the king and many of his followers of a form of kilt as an article of dress led to him being called "Barelegs".

Magnus was killed in Ulster in 1103, and his son left Man to return to Norway. Godfrey Crobhan returned to Man, but died the same year. He was a man described as "a Prince fortunate in war, prudent in peace, and merciful after victory". (8) His *birlinn,* galley, still sails from Man to Islay in the song *Birlinn Ghoiridh Chrobhain,* Godfrey Crobhan's Galley.

Godfrey left three sons, Lawman, Harold and Olaf. Lawman succeeded his father, but his brother Harold was a constant menace to his power, so he had him seized and mutilated, as a result of which he died. This deed preyed on Lawman so much that he abdicated and went on a pilgrimage to Rome where he died in 1075. (9)

As Olaf the Red, the surviving brother, was so young, Murchadh O'Brian, the King of Ireland was asked to send someone of royal descent to rule until Olaf came of age. A certain Donald MacTade was chosen for the task but he abused his position so much that he was expelled after three years and Olaf began to rule. Olaf was a man of peace, and he enjoyed the trust and friendship of all his neighbours. The Hebrides enjoyed a tranquility they had not experienced for centuries.

After a reign of almost forty years, Olaf was murdered in 1142 by his nephew Reginald, a son of his brother Harold, and lawlessness returned.

About this time there lived the most famous and perhaps the last of the Vikings, Swein Asleifson of Gairsay in the Orkneys. There was no crime he had not committed; murder, theft, house burning, abduction, yet he was on friendly terms with many important people. He spent much of his time in Lewis and it is possible that Swainbost retains his name, as it was his place of refuge when things grew too hot for him in Orkney. Swein had taken his mother's name after his father Olaf was cremated by Olvir Rosta, another Viking who frequently took refuge in Lewis. Swein met his death in an ambush in Dublin on what was to be his last raid.

Olaf the Red had one legitimate son, Godfrey the Black, who succeeded him, three natural sons, Reginald, Harold and Lawman, and many daughters. One of these, Ragnhildis, married Somerled, the formidable ruler of Argyll around 1140, and it is from this marriage that the dynasty known as the Lordship of the Isles emerged. (10)

This Somerled, egged on by some of the Hebridean chiefs, laid claim to the Kingdom of Man, including the Western Isles, on behalf of his eldest son by Ragnhildis. As the result of a drawn battle between Somerled and Godfrey the Black, his brother-in-law, all the islands south of Ardnamurchan Point passed into Somerled's possession, with Godfrey retaining Man and the Northern Hebrides, including Lewis.

Two years later, Somerled invaded Man which was still nominally part of the Kingdom of Norway and defeated Godfrey who was forced to flee to Norway where he remained until Somerled's murder in Renfrew in 1164. Godfrey then regained possession of Man and the Northern Hebrides which Somerled had ruled for the past six years.

On Godfrey's death, the Kingdom of Man, which included Lewis, was seized by his illegitimate son Reginald at the expense of the lawful heir, Olaf the Black. In 1207, Olaf was given the island of Lewis for his maintenance as it was more extensive than any of the neighbouring islands. However, because of its mountainous nature it was almost impossible to cultivate and it was very sparsely populated. (11) Olaf found that the island's limited resources were not sufficient to maintain himself and his followers in comfort, so he returned to Man where he reminded Reginald that he was the lawful heir and demanded some land where he and his retinue could live in becoming state. Reginald promptly ordered Olaf to be seized and sent to William the Lion of Scotland where he was kept in irons for seven years, only being released on the death of King William and the accession of Alexander II to the Scottish throne.

Olaf then returned to Man, where he was forced to marry Lavon, the daughter of a Kintyre noble and sister-in-law of his brother Reginald. So back to Lewis he was sent again. He was not long back in Lewis when he had a visit from his nephew, another Reginald, the Bishop of the Isles, who declared the marriage null and void on the grounds that Lavon was too near a relation of his former concubine. (12) The Queen was so annoyed with this slight to her sister that she sent a letter in her husband's name to their son Godfrey Donn, then in Skye, ordering him to cross to Lewis to murder his uncle Olaf, who was now married to Christina, daughter of the Earl of Ross. This Christina is believed to be the mother of Leod from whom the Macleods of Lewis and Skye are said to be descended.

Olaf, being fore-warned of the plot to kill him, fled in a small boat to his father-in-law on the mainland, while the frustrated Godfrey Donn laid Lewis waste before returning to Man.

About the same time, Paul Balkasson, the Sheriff of Skye, had also to seek refuge from Godfrey Donn at the home of the Earl of Ross. With the aid of these two men, Olaf later gained possession of Man, while Godfrey Donn was given the Western Isles. Godfrey Donn met his death in Lewis. (13)

Back in Norway, King Hakon decided to take action to preserve his island possessions which Alexander II of Scotland wanted to add to his kingdom. He assembled a large fleet under the command of Uspak, whom he appointed King of the Hebrides and on whom he conferred his own name, Hakon. However, this new King of the Hebrides was killed in the Island of Bute and the expedition achieved nothing, although Lewis was raided on its homeward journey in 1231.

Olaf the Black died in 1237 and he was succeeded in turn by each of his three sons, Harold, Reginald and Magnus. However, the failure of the Norwegian attempts in 1230 and 1263 to retain control of Man and the Northern Hebrides, combined with Alexander III's determination to make all the Western Isles part of the Kingdom of Scotland, meant that the Kingdom of Man was doomed. King Magnus, who preferred being a vassal of the Norse king rather than the King of Scotland, died in 1265, the last of the race of Godfrey Crobhan (14) and the Island of Man became part of England.

Lewis and the rest of the Western Isles were ceded to Scotland in 1266 by the Treaty of Perth, which also provided a general amnesty in the Hebrides where this union with Scotland was not universally popular. All those who so desired, were allowed to return to Norway with all their possessions, while those who opted to become Scottish subjects were exhorted by the King of Norway to be loyal to their new ruler.

The islanders who decided to return to their former homeland were, no doubt, those who had been in the habit of keeping slaves or sgallags, who worked for their masters from dawn till dusk when they were then allowed the privilege of working on their own small plots of land.

The Norse occupation of Lewis has left its mark on the topography of the Island as well as on its people. The dals (vales), bhals (hills), bhats (water), so common in place-names, are all of Norse origin, as are the names of many villages with sta, bost, or shader added to the name of a previous occupant, e.g. Grimersta, Swainbost and Grimshader.

Lewis seems to have been thoroughly colonised, for there are only two or three townships without Norse names.

The MacLeods, MacAulays, Morrisons and Nicolsons all claim to be of Norse origin and a few personal names still linger on; Tormod (Norman), Torcull (Torquil), Amhlaidh (Aulay), Raghnailt (Rachel), Raghnall (Ronald), and Gormul (Gormelia).

Apart from the clan's ancestor Leod, the Macleods seem to have some connection with a man named Oliver, whether the Viking Olvir Rosta (turbulent, not roasting, though both terms could suit him equally well), is unknown, as the following lines seem to indicate:

Sliochd Olbhair sin nach d'fhuair baisteadh tha buan masladh;
Ta Tormodaich, agus Torcuil, Teah agus Tescuil.

On the race of that Olvir who never received baptism, there is everlasting reproach; they were the children of Norman and Torquil, Teah and Tesquil. (15)

Many Lewis people have the fair hair and blue eyes of their Norse ancestors, while their sailorly qualities and roving instincts have carried them to every corner of the world.

THE MACLEODS

With the cession of the Hebrides to Scotland, Lewis experienced many changes apart from the change of nationality. New overlords and numerous immigrants arrived from the mainland, bringing with them their own language and customs. However, it is not known when the Norse language ceased to be spoken in Lewis.

King Alexander III granted the island to the Earl of Ross as a reward for his efforts to rid Scotland of the Norwegians and it remained in his family (except for a short period around 1303) during the Scottish Wars of Independence when the Earl of that time, like so many of his contemporaries had traitorous dealings with England.

In 1292, Lewis was included in the sheriffdom of Skye. then established by King John Baliol of Scotland. From 1315-29 King Robert the Bruce brought peace to the land, peace which quickly vanished on the accession of his young son to the Scottish throne in 1329, when England renewed her attacks on Scotland.

The Earl of Ross was killed at the Battle of Halidon Hill in 1334 when the English defeated the Scots. The following year, Edward Baliol granted Lewis to John of Isla (the future Lord of the Isles) for his allegiance. This grant was confirmed by King Edward III of England in 1336. (1)

On the return of David II from his enforced exile and the expulsion of the Baliol party from Scotland, King David reaffirmed the grant of Lewis to John of Isla in order to gain his allegiance.

In 1382, King Robert II granted to his son, John Stewart, Earl of Buchan, the baronies and lordship of Lewis and Skye which Euphemia, Countess of Ross had resigned on entering a convent. (2)

Euphemia's daughter Margaret, married Donald, the second Lord of the Isles (a Lordship established in 1357), who claimed through her the Earldom of Ross, a claim which led to the battle of Harlaw in 1411 which involved men from Lewis. Among the casualties, were the Red Priest of Carloway and a Lachlan Macmillan. (3)

The Lords of the Isles later regained the Earldom, but in 1475, Lewis and the other isles were forfeited by John, the last Lord of the Isles, restored to him in 1476, and finally forfeited by him again in 1493. (4)

Meantime, the Macleod chiefs of Lewis, who had held their lands successively from the Earls of Ross, the Stewarts, the Macdonald Lords of the Isles and the Crown, were steadily gaining in importance. They regarded themselves as being of royal descent through Leod, a son of Olaf the Black, the King of Man who died in 1265 and Christina, a daughter of the Earl of Ross. Leod was fostered in Skye by his father's friend Paul Balkasson and may have acquired Lewis from his brothers to keep him as far away from the Isle of Man as possible to avoid fratricidal disputes about the kingship there. This had happened to his father at one time.

Leod, who lived during the reign of Alexander III when the Hebrides became part of Scotland, was married to a daughter of Macraild Armuinn of

Skye. It is said they had two sons, Torquil, from whom the Macleods of Lewis derived their patronymic *Siol Torcuill,* the race of Torquil and Norman, the progenitor of the Macleods of Harris and Dunvegan, the *Siol Tormod,* the race of Norman. Leod died about 1280 and was succeeded as the second Macleod chief of Lewis by his son Torquil (Norman being given Harris and Dunvegan). Torquil married Dorothea, daughter of William, Earl of Ross, who bore him a son called Norman, who lived during the reigns of Alexander III and Robert the Bruce. (5)

Little is known of Norman the third chief, who was followed by his son Torquil, the fourth chief, who is recorded as having received a charter of Assynt from King David II. Torquil obtained this barony through his marriage to the MacNicol heiress, Margaret, but Lewis tradition has it that this only happened after the Macleods had murdered all the male members of her family. These MacNicols or Nicolsons are said to have had their stronghold, Caisteal Mhic Neacail, on the shore near Garrabost. (6) Torquil died in the reign of King Robert II. (7)

It is thought that there may have been, as fifth chief, a man named Malcolm, (8) or Roderick, and if this was so, then the sixth chief was the Roderick who witnessed a charter of John, the Lord of the Isles in 1449 and was married to his daughter. Their sons were Torquil and Norman, the latter to whom he gave the Barony of Assynt.

The seventh and eighth chiefs, Torquil and Roderick respectively, were loyal subjects of the Lord of the Isles, a Lordship which, unfortunately came to an end in 1493.

Roderick's eldest son was mortally wounded at the Battle of Bloody Bay, near Tobermory, in 1480, between the forces of John, Lord of the Isles and his natural son, Angus Og. Of his two other sons, Torquil succeeded him as ninth chief and Malcolm became the tenth chief in 1511.

Of all the Macleod chiefs in Lewis, this Torquil was the most outstanding. He was married to a daughter of the Earl of Argyll, a sure indication of his social position. In a poem, "Moladh air Torcul MacLeoid, Leodhuis", in the Book of the Dean of Lismore, he is described as being like his father, and praised for his courage, loyalty and unfailing generosity. (9)

Torquil's forfeiture was caused by his support of his wife's nephew, Donald Dubh in his attempt to regain the Lordship of the Isles. James IV led the first of two expeditions to the Isles to suppress the rebellious chiefs of whom Torquil seems to have been the most prominent. He was not one of those who submitted to James, but during the second expedition under the Earl of Huntly in 1506, Stornoway Castle was captured and destroyed and the lands of Lewis ravaged. Torquil vanished without trace during this operation, possibly under the ruins of his castle.

In 1508, King James IV commissioned the Bishop of Caithness, Ranald Alanson of Clanranald and Alexander MacLeod of Dunvegan, to let for five years to approved tenants, the lands of Lewis and Waternish in Skye which had been forfeited by Torquil. They were to act under the direction of the Earl of Huntly. (10)

In 1511, the king granted these lands to Malcolm, Torquil's brother, to the exclusion of the latter's son, John. Like his father and brother before him, his support of the House of the Isles led to trouble with the crown. He took part in the battle at Creag an Airgid, where MacIan of Ardnamurchan and his two sons were killed in 1518. After this incident, he seems to have led a quiet life. He died about 1528, and is buried in the church at Eye, near Aignish.

Malcolm had three sons, Roderick, who became the eleventh, last, and worst MacLeod chief of Lewis, Malcolm Garbh, from whom the MacLeods of Raasay were descended, and Norman, ancestor of the MacLeods of Eddrachilles. (11)

On the death of Malcolm in 1528, his nephew, John mac Thorcuill, whose father had disappeared without trace in 1506, took possession of his father's lands though he had no legal claim to them owing to his father's forfeiture. His death in 1532 was greatly mourned by his people. (12)

Roderick, better known as "Old Rory", took over as the eleventh chief, and from the very beginning, seemed bent on self-destruction. Like the rest of his race, he was a supporter of the Clan Donald claim to the Lordship of the Isles, and along with Donald Gorm of Sleat, the latest claimant, invaded Trotternish in Skye and the Mackenzie lands of Kintail. Donald Gorm was killed at the seige of Eilean Donan Castle in 1538. In 1540, Rory was one of the chiefs who were forced to accompany King James V on his tour of the Northern and Western Isles, but he was released soon afterwards, and in 1541, was granted a new charter for his lands, erecting them into the free Barony of Lewis.

From about 1545-55, Rory was engaged in treasonable activities, being at one time a member of the Council of the Isles who sought to transfer their allegiance to the King of England.

Rory's domestic life was no more peaceful than his political one. He married, when young, the flighty Janet Mackenzie of Kintail, the widow of Mackay of Reay, (13) a woman whose morals were on a par with his own. Rory accused her of having committed adultery with Hugh Morrison, the Brieve (Hereditary Judge) of Lewis and refused to acknowledge her son Torquil (usually named Torquil Conanach from having been reared among his mother's people) as his heir. The Parson of Barvas later made public what was purported to be the Brieve's death-bed confession, in which he admitted the truth of the allegation.

After Janet's elopement with John Mac Gille Chaluim of Raasay, Rory divorced her and married Barbara Stewart, the daughter of Lord Avondale, by whom he had a son, Torquil the *Oighre,* Heir. This Torquil seems to have been a promising young man, for in 1563, Queen Mary sent him the following letter:

Torquill McCloyd, we grete you wele. We ar informit that sum of the Ilis ar desirous to have you allyat to thame be mareage; and becaus ye have that honor to be of the Stewarth blude, we thocht expedient to gif you advertisement that it is our will and pleshour that you allyat yourself to na party in mareage without our advyss, and quhillwe declair our opinioun to yourself thairin. (14)

Unfortunately, in 1566, Torquil was drowned, along with his companions, while sailing from Lewis to Trotternish, in Skye.

Rory was again without an heir, so he married as his third wife, Jeannette, the daughter of Maclean of Duart, who bore him two sons, Torquil Dubh and Norman. He also had five illegitimate sons, Tormod Uigeach, Murdo, Donald, Neil (usually known as Niall Odhar) and Ruairidh Og.

Meantime, Torquil Oighre's drowning raised Torquil Conanach's hopes of gaining Lewis, and with this end in view, he landed there secretly one night and having captured his reputed father, kept him prisoner for over two years "in maist miserable captivitie in mountanis and cavernis of craigis far

25

distant from the societie of men, almaist pereised wt cauld and famine", (15) until he agreed to acknowledge him as his lawful heir. This agreement Old Rory immediately revoked on obtaining his freedom.

The Macleod fratricidal squabbles now increased in ferocity. The chief had the support of three of his illegitimate sons, Donald, Neil and Ruairidh Og, while Torquil was aided by Tormod Uigeach and Murdo.

Donald murdered his half-brother Tormod Uigeach, and in return, Torquil Conanach, aided by Murdo, captured him, but he managed to escape and before long, had Murdo imprisoned in Stornoway Castle.

Torquil Conanach, on learning that his ally was in peril, crossed from Kintail to Stornoway, captured the Castle, and set Murdo free. Once again, he had Old Rory in his power, but he left him in the charge of his son John, to whom he gave control of the Island. (16) Soon afterwards, John was murdered by his uncle Ruairidh Og at Sandwick Loch, a deed which was soon avenged when Torquil Conanach executed Donald at Dingwall. (17)

When Old Rory died about 1595, at the age of ninety-five, he left the problem of his succession unsettled, and the "Clanleyid of the Lewis" listed as one of the broken clans in the Highlands and Islands, along with the Clan Gregor and a few others. (18)

Torquil Dubh succeeded his father in the over-lordship of Lewis, to the exclusion, for the second time, of Torquil Conanach, and the deep chagrin of the Mackenzies of Kintail who wanted to add the Island to their extensive mainland territories. (19)

Torquil Dubh, for some reason or other, quarrelled with his half-brother Ruairidh Og, and handed him over to his mother's people, the Macleans of Duart. While making his escape from them, Ruairidh Og died in a snow-storm leaving a family of three sons, Malcolm, William and Ruairidh. (20)

When Torquil Conanach captured Stornoway Castle, he seized the writs and charters for Lewis and handed them over to Mackenzie of Kintail. Mackenzie believed he had a claim to the Island, since Torquil Conanach's two sons were dead and his daughter married to his brother, Rory Mackenzie. However, he knew that this would never be possible as long as Torquil Dubh was still alive, so the problem became how to dispose of him. (21)

Mackenzie found two willing accomplices in John Morison, the Brieve, and Murdo Macleod, one of the two surviving illegitimate sons of the old chief. (22)

The Brieve managed to entice Torquil Dubh aboard a captured Dutch vessel where he was immediately seized and taken across to Coigeach and executed. (23) He left three sons, Ruairidh, William and Torquil.

With Torquil Dubh out of the way, the Mackenzies' next move was to take his younger brother Norman from his school in Perth and keep him in close custody.

Neil Macleod, the redoubtable Niall Odhar, now took charge of the Island affairs, fully determined to pursue the Brieve and his Morison clansmen and exact vengeance for their treachery. For some time the Morisons held out at Dun Eistein in Ness, but they were forced to flee across to Assynt where the Brieve met his death at the hands of John Macleod (Iain mac Dhomhnuill mhic Uisdein), who also captured the Brieve's eldest son Malcolm, in Coigeach, and brought him across to Stornoway, where he was executed on Gallows Hill. (24)

The *iorram*, rowing song attributed to Allan Morison, another son of the

Brieve, testifies to the implacable hatred that existed between the Macleods and the Morisons.

> O's truagh nach robh mi fhein 's Niall Odhar
> An lagan beag air cul Dhun Othail,
> Biodag 'nam laimh is esan fodham:
> Dhearbhainn fhein gu'n deidheadh i domhain

> Pity that I and sallow Neil were not
> In a small hollow behind Dun Othail,
> A dagger in my hand and he under me:
> I would make sure that it would go deep.

Allan Morison and two of his brothers were pursued and killed by the Macleods while fleeing across the Minch, but only after a desperate struggle, which did not end until the gallant Allan's sword had stuck in his boat's gunwale as he broke an assailant's oar to which a sword had been attached.

As if Lewis had not suffered enough from the fratricidal strife of the Macleods, the machinations of Mackenzie of Kintail, the vendetta between the Macleods and the Morisons and the constant feuding between the Morisons and the Macaulays of Uig (under the leadership of the doughty Donald Cam, so often thwarted by the equally redoubtable John Mackay or Macphail of Bragar), more trouble was to come from a totally unexpected quarter.

The reputed fertility of the soil, and the undoubted riches in the surrounding seas attracted the attention of the greedy and impecunious James VI. This sudden interest in the Island's resources arose from a report published c. 1577-95, which stated:

This Ile of Lewis is very profitable and fertile alswell of corns as all kind of bestiall wild fowl and fishes, and speciallie of beir, sua that thair will grow commonlie 20, 18, or at leist 16 bolls yeirlie eftir ilk bolls sawing. It is 40lb. land of auld extent and payis yeirlie 18 score chalders of victuall, 58 score of ky, 32 score of wedderis, and ane great quantitie of fisches . . . (25)

All these riches in the possession of unappreciative savages! The treasury was empty. Drastic action was called for.

With the ostensible object of introducing the benefits of Lowland civilization to this rich yet backward portion of his kingdom (its exploitation for his own profit being at first discreetly hidden), James had several Acts passed by Parliament, two of which brought consternation to the Highlands and Islands. (26)

An Act of 1597 made it compulsory for all who owned, or thought they owned land in the Highlands and Islands, to present themselves before the Lords of the Exchequer, by 15 May 1598, to show their titles and give some suitable security for their future behaviour. Failure to comply with either of these stipulations meant the immediate forfeiture of their lands. (27)

The fate of Lewis was never in doubt, for its writs and charters could not be produced as they were still in the hands of Mackenzie of Kintail. Torquil Dubh had already been declared a rebel for his non-appearance before the Privy Council in Edinburgh to account for his devastating raids in Coigeach. (28)

The island, now at the King's disposal, was granted to a group of men

27

from Fife, who undertook to colonise and civilise the Island at their own expense. These Gentlemen Adventurers were to have Lewis, Rona Lewis and Trotternish in Skye, rent free for a period of seven years, after which they were to pay a rental of 100 chalders of bear for the first two places and 400 merks for Trotternish. They were also expected to replace with Lowland settlers, the wicked and rebellious natives, who were to be transported to the mainland, where, it was hoped, they would learn the rudiments of civilisation. (29)

Late in October 1598, the expedition, consisting of about six hundred mercenaries, a large number of artisans and some volunteers (including a minister), with all the equipment necessary for a plantation, arrived in Stornoway. Their disembarkation was stubbornly resisted by Murdo Macleod. (30)

There was great disillusionment when the new settlers realised just how "fertile" the island really was, and the constant harassment by the natives under the combined leadership of the two half-brothers, Murdo and Neil Macleod, did not improve matters. A shortage of provisions also lowered the morale of the invaders.

Two months after their arrival, one of the leaders of the settlers James Learmonth of Balcomie, set sail for Fife. Not far off Coigeach, his ship was becalmed, and he was attacked by Murdo Macleod and a small fleet, consisting of a galley, with Murdo at the tiller, two birlinns and a boat. (31) Balcomie was captured after a desperate struggle and held prisoner. A year later, he was released, after promising to pay a ransom of 3,000 merks. Unfortunately, he died in the Orkneys on his voyage home and the ransom was never paid. (32)

Although Murdo and Neil Macleod were united in their opposition to the settlers, they were never on friendly terms. Neil had not forgiven his brother for his part in Torquil Dubh's capture and execution and shortly after Balcomie's death he ambushed him and took him prisoner, killing his twelve Morison followers. (33) The invaders promised Neil that they would give him a portion of land and ask the King to pardon him for all his misdeeds if he handed Murdo over to them. Neil agreed to this, and Murdo was submitted to the tender mercies of the settlers with as little compunction as he himself had shown when he delivered Torquil Dubh to the equally tender mercies of the Mackenzies two years before. (34)

Neil proceeded to Edinburgh with his new-found friends, carrying the heads of the twelve slain Morisons in a sack, and Murdo under close arrest.

Neil received the promised pardon, but Murdo's fate was sealed from the moment he was surrendered to the settlers. He had to be punished for Balcomie's death, although he renounced all claims to the promised ransom. The King ordered his immediate trial in St Andrews, the royal letter making it perfectly clear what the verdict had to be.

As Murdoche McLewd of Sebuste and brother to Torquil McLewd of Codzeache has been apprehended for the treasonable capture and detention of the late James Learmonth of Balcomy and putting him to ransom, and for being in the cruel murders of Arthur Hamilton of Bothwellhaugh, Joseph Learmonth and David Short, and various other persons who were in the company of the said James, and for various other crimes of sorning, piracy, theft and reafe, to be contained in his indictment, is to be brought to immediate trial in St Andrews for the said crimes. It is our will and command that justice be administered to McLewd without delay, notwithstanding any precepts to the contrary, and if found guilty of the crimes mentioned, or any of them, that you pronounce sentence on him to be hanged, quartered and drawn, and his head to be fixed above the Nether Bow of Edinburgh, as an example to others, to abstain from the like treasonable, barbarous and heinous attempts in future. (35)

Murdo Macleod was duly executed for forcibly resisting the settlers' plans, (36) but during the trial he revealed Mackenzie of Kintail's schemes for gaining possession of Lewis. As the result, Mackenzie was imprisoned for some time in Edinburgh Castle but managed to escape before being tried.

The settlers now felt that the worst of their troubles were over, with Murdo Macleod dead and Neil Macleod kindly disposed towards them. They began to build and to partition the land among those Islanders who were willing to guarantee obedience. Before long, however, Neil Macleod and Sir James Spence of Wormiston quarrelled and the peace of the Island was once again shattered. An ambush was set for Neil, but he was informed in advance and killed sixty of those sent to arrest him. (37)

This turn of events pleased Mackenzie of Kintail immensely. He set Norman Macleod, the brother of Torquil Dubh, at liberty, knowing that the Islanders would rally to him, and this they did. The settlers "prettie town" near Stornoway was caught in a surprise attack, many of its inmates killed, and the encampment set on fire.

After eight months' captivity, the settlers were released after promising never to return again and that the Islanders would obtain a pardon from the King for all their past crimes, and that all rights previously invested in the settlers would be transferred to Norman Macleod. To ensure fulfilment of these conditions, Sir James Spence and Thomas Monypenny of Kinkell were detained as hostages. (38)

Norman Macleod then ruled the Island for a time, and during this period, Torquil Conanach who was in his power, explained how he had given the writs for Lewis to Mackenzie of Kintail. Norman allowed Torquil his freedom much against the wishes of his followers who wanted him executed since he had been responsible for so much trouble on the Island. (39)

However, the King and his Privy Council had no intention of honouring the pledges given to Norman Macleod, and shortly after the release of the hostages, a royal proclamation was issued on 17 July 1602, for the mustering of all men between sixteen and sixty, in the shires of Aberdeen, Banff, Nairn, Inverness, Caithness, Orkney and Shetland. They were to be "weill bodin in feir of war", at certain specified places, with forty days' provisions, for the re-conquest of Lewis. (40)

The measure of humiliation suffered by the King on the ignominious expulsion of the settlers may be judged by the violence of his denunciation of the Lewis people. He described their lack of knowledge and fear of God, their disloyalty to the King, their love of murder, stealing and oppression (and many other crimes never even thought of by the Turks and other infidels), although they lived in the most fertile part of the kingdom, rich in corn and fish, which brought no prosperity to the rest of the country, owing to the barbarity of its inhabitants. (41)

However, this proposed invasion did not materialise as it was decided to postpone it for another year. (42) In 1603, King James, now King of Great Britain, issued a similar proclamation to that of 1602, in which he again accused the Lewismen of all manner of crimes. The Commissioners in command of the new muster from the Northern Counties, were given powers of fire and sword for the complete subjection of "sic ane tyrannous byke of rebellious lymmaris". (43) The Hebridean chiefs were forbidden to give any aid to these rascals, irrespective of age, sex or need, nor to hold any communication with them. Their galleys, lymphads and birlinns were to be handed over to government officials in Lochbroom. (44) As a special concession, the natives of Lewis were permitted to carry blunt knives to cut their meat.

In the summer of 1605, to the dismay of Norman Macleod, a large force landed in Lewis, and in spite of his uncle Neil's advice to the contrary, he submitted to the invaders in return for a promise of safe conduct to London. This was agreed, and in addition, the invaders promised to use their influence to obtain him a royal pardon and secure some means for his subsistence.

When they arrived in London, Norman made such a favourable impression on the King while giving him an account of the Island and his right to its overlordship, that he was transferred to Edinburgh Castle where he was imprisoned until 1615. He was then granted permission to go to Holland where he later died.

In spite of being rid of Norman, many of the new invaders became so depressed at their lack of success and the steady strain on their resources that they decided to withdraw from the undertaking. (45) Mackenzie of Kintail, ever ready to seize an opportunity to further his own ends, produced Torquil Conanach's conveyance of the Island to himself and, with the help of his friend the Lord Chancellor, made a gift of the Island to himself under the Great Seal. (46)

On hearing of this transaction, King James was furious and forced Mackenzie to resign his rights in favour of the Crown. These were immediately transferred to the colonists, now only three in number, Lord Balmerino, Sir James Spence, and Sir George Hay.

In 1609, the men from the northern counties were again mustered and transported to Lewis to help the colonisation scheme and, if possible, capture Neil Macleod. (47)

The crafty Mackenzie of Kintail pretended to help the colonists while secretly assisting Neil to capture a shipload of provisions he was sending them. The colonists were thus deprived of much needed supplies. This unexpected loss, combined with the failure to capture Neil Macleod and the subsequent scarcity of food, made Hay and Spence so weary of the whole operation that they dismissed the men from the northern muster while they themselves returned to Fife for men and supplies, leaving a small party to guard the fort. (48)

Meanwhile, Neil Macleod, assisted by his nephew Malcolm and a strong party of followers, promptly attacked the fort, captured it, and sent the survivors of the garrison back to Fife. This ended the attempt to colonise Lewis, and Sir George Hay and Sir James Spence sold their title to the Island to Mackenzie of Kintail (49) for 10,000 merks in 1610. (50)

Lord Kintail crossed to Lewis to take possession, and the majority of the inhabitants willingly submitted to him.

The Lords of the Privy Council were annoyed that Neil Macleod, with his nephews Malcolm, William and Ruairidh (the three sons of Ruairidh Og who had perished in a snow-storm), Torquil Blair and thirty-four others refused to surrender. They appointed Lord Kintail His Majesty's Justice and Commissioner for Lewis, "and thair with fire and sword and all kind of hostility, to search, seik, hunt, follow and persew, the said Neill his

30

complices, assistaris and pertakers by sea and land, quhairever they may be apprehendit". Any damage done to man or property during this operation was not to be considered a crime on the part of the Justice. (51)

Neil and his small band were forced to retire to the island of Berisay, off the coast, where they held out for three years. In 1611, Lord Kintail died, and as his son and heir was still a minor, his brother Rory, the Tutor of Kintail, had the commission formerly held by Lord Kintail, renewed on his behalf. (52)

The Tutor of Kintail was a much more ruthless man than his late brother. His name is still held in execration in Lewis where it used to be stated that the three worst evils which could afflict a tenant were May frost, July mist, and the Tutor of Kintail. (53)

During the time of his retreat in Berisay, Neil Macleod became friendly with an English pirate, Peter Love. After some time, Torquil Blair (one of Neil's followers) and his four sons, captured Love, and Neil sent him, his crew, and his ship, the *Priam,* to the Privy Council, who hanged them. It is thought that the reason for this action was to help obtain a pardon for himself and gain Norman's release from prison. (54) In due course, he did receive a pardon and was invited to Edinburgh but, considering what had happened to Norman and others of his race, he decided not to go. (55)

Tradition has it that Neil was forced to leave Berisay when the Mackenzies gathered the wives and relatives of the men on this island and placed them on a rock which was submerged at high tide. There they threatened to abandon them unless the fort was vacated. To save the lives of these innocent people, Neil and his followers went to Harris (56) where Neil finally surrendered to his kinsman, Rory Macleod. Rory promised to take him to the King in London but, on their arrival in Glasgow, Rory Macleod was ordered by the Privy Council to bring Neil and his son Donald to Edinburgh. This was done, and the two men were handed over on 2 March 1613. (57) Neil was brought to trial on 30 March 1613, charged with fire-raising, burning, murder, theft and piracy. (58) He confessed to all the crimes listed in his long indictment and was sentenced to be taken to the Mercat Cross to be hanged, "and thaireftir, his heid to be strukin frome his body, and affixt and set upone ane priket" above the Nether Bow Port, (59) where his brother Murdo's head had been stuck twelve years before. The sentence was duly carried out in April, 1613, when it was stated that he died "verie Christianlie". (60)

Lewis tradition has it that Neil was expecting a reprieve up to the very last moment, and that one of the officials, wanting to finish the job, said to his victim, "Hurry up, you old *bodach,* old man" to which Neil replied: *"Nam bithinn air deck luinge far am bu duilich do fhear seasamh, stiuireadh na mara gu tric, cha bhodach dhuit mis' a mhacain."* "If I were on a ship's deck, where it was difficult to keep one's footing, while steering over the billows, you would not call me a *bodach,* laddie" and promptly knocked the fellow down. (61)

Neil's son Donald was released on condition that he banished himself from Scotland, as was his brother Ruairidh Dubh later on, but both returned to Lewis, where Ruairidh was killed near Arnol. Donald escaped to Holland.

Little more is known of the sons of Torquil Dubh. Ruairidh, the eldest of the three, was in the custody of the Mackenzies for a while, William was a student at Glasgow University, while Torquil resided for a while with his uncle, Sir Rory Macleod of Harris, (63) who had been knighted after handing over Neil Macleod to the Privy Council.

The Tutor of Kintail executed two of Torquil Og's sons, but the third, Malcolm, escaped, and was for a long time a thorn in the flesh of the authorities.

In 1616, a fresh commission was given to the Tutor of Kintail owing to a rebellion in Lewis led by Malcolm Macleod with the support of some of his uncle Neil's old colleagues. (64) Malcolm also engaged in piratical activities in the Minch, attacking merchants and fishermen. The Harris men gave him much assistance, guiding him on one occasion to an anchored vessel, on the promise of a share of the spoils. Malcolm captured the ship and on landing in Ranish, attacked a John Mackenzie's house and killed him. The men from Harris later sold their share of the spoils openly at Dunvegan. (65)

Malcolm supported the rebellion of Sir James Macdonald of Dunyveg, Islay, but when it was suppressed, he went to Spain. In 1621, he was back in the Minch harrying the merchants and fishermen. (66) He is supposed to have died in Holland.

The following assessments of the Macleods seem to be fairly correct:

The Clan Torkil in Lewis were the stoutest and prettiest men, but a wicked bloody crew, whom neither law nor reason could guide or moddell, destroying one another, till in the end, they were all expelled that country and the Mackenzies now possess it. (67)

As a poet expressed it:

'S e mo bharail air Clann Leoid, gur cosmhuil iad ri poir an uisge.
An te is sine, mas i is mo ithis i an te is oige dhiubh.

It is my opinion of Clan Leod, that they are like pikes in water.
The oldest of them, if the larger, eats the younger. (68)

THE MACKENZIES

Colin, Lord Mackenzie of Kintail, received official possession of Lewis in 1610. His death in 1611 encouraged the Macleods and their supporters to continue their struggle. However, it was not until the execution of that loyal and daring son of Lewis, Niall Macleod (Niall Odhar) at the Mercat Cross in Edinburgh in 1613, that effective resistance to the Mackenzies may be said to have ceased. Stornoway Castle was captured by the Mackenzies in 1613, "although it had bidden the cannon by the late Earl of Argyle of old, and the Gentlemen Adventurers of late", (1) otherwise only sporadic outbreaks (chiefly instigated by Malcolm Macleod) occurred until 1625.

It is believed that the Mackenzies had their headquarters at Seaforth Head, on Loch Seaforth, before Seaforth Lodge was built across the bay from the village of Stornoway. (2) Shortly after their conquest of the Island, they built a dyke called *Garadh an Tighearna,* Laird's Dyke, between the heads of Loch Erisort and Loch Seaforth to enclose the Deer Forest of Park, where it was once believed two-tailed deer and four-footed fish were to be found. (3)

The Macleods also used to hunt deer in this district, but it was not until the erection of this dyke, the remains of which can still be seen between Balallan and Arivruaich, that the people of Uig were forbidden to shiel there in the summer. The ruins of numerous shielings are still to be seen in Park, including one that bears the name of Donald Cam Macaulay, the Uig warrior chieftain. The milch cows were kept on pastures between Morsgail and Loch Resort, when the rest of the stock was driven to Park, swimming across a shallow part of Loch Langabhat on the way.

The importance that Seaforth and other lairds attached to sport is shown by an agreement, drawn up in 1628, for the preservation of game and the penalties to be imposed on poachers. A gentleman poacher was to be fined 100 merks and his hagbut, an old fashioned hand-gun, confiscated. Tenants were to pay £40., and have their hagbuts confiscated, while common or "stragling" persons were to be deprived of their hagbuts or bows and their bodies punished. (4)

It was natural that the Mackenzies should reward their kinsfolk and friends for their services by leasing them tracts of land. These lessees were called tacksmen, with purely nominal rents at first, and the obligation to perform whatever services their chief demanded.

The tacksmen let most of their land to sub-tenants, living on the proceeds of their labours and doing practically no work on the land themselves. The sub-tenants, in the course of time, became the crofter class.

The people disliked this new system of land tenure intensely, for they were now at the complete mercy of these tacksmen who looked on them as an inferior race and treated them accordingly. Unfortunately, they had no means of redress, since the Mackenzies left the management of their Lewis estate in the hands of their factors or chamberlains, who, ably assisted by the tacksmen and the four ground officers (one for each parish), ensured that their sub-tenants' lives were far from pleasant.

There were, perhaps, some good tacksmen. However, during the whole of the Seaforth regime, proprietor and tacksmen alike exploited the people with little or no consideration for their welfare.

In the Judicial Rental of Lewis in 1718, there are nineteen Mackenzie tacksmen, eleven Macivers, ten Morisons, ten Macaulays, four Maclennans, three Macleods and two Mathesons. (5)

Tacks were formed where the soil was most fertile, with the rest of the land (as in the old parish of Cladach on the west side, and in Ness) given to conjoint tenants who held it directly from the proprietor.

In 1628, Colin Mackenzie, the first Earl of Seaforth, received the royal assent to erect Stornoway into a royal burgh, providing the Convention of Royal Burghs agreed. This they refused to do, as such a privilege would allow Stornoway to compete for a share of their trade in the North. (6)

The Earl did his utmost to develop the Island fisheries with the assistance of the Dutch, the early exploiters of Hebridean fishing, some of whom were then living in Stornoway. (7) In 1629, the Earl was censured by Parliament for encouraging foreign fishermen. (8)

George, the second earl, was a lukewarm supporter of Charles I during his unhappy reign. For this, the Island of Lewis paid dearly. Out of the three hundred islanders who fought at the battle of Auldearn in 1645, only three, according to tradition, survived. (9)

The third earl, Kenneth, was equally devoted to the House of Stuart and raised a force to fight for the royal cause. With Glengarry, he travelled all over the north of Scotland, rallying men to fight against the Commonwealth. He also prepared to defend Lewis, but with limited resources, was unable to afford the necessary arms. Kenneth's hostility to the new government had Cromwell both annoyed and alarmed. Besides his activities in the North and the West, he also gave the Dutch the opportunity to interrupt the trade in the Isles.

To prevent Lewis from becoming a base from which the Dutch fleet could operate against Britain, and to teach Seaforth a lesson, Cromwell dispatched a body of soldiers to the Island under the command of a Colonel Cobbet. They landed in August 1653 without meeting any opposition, and began to fortify the town of Stornoway by building a fort on Goat Island and (from excavated remains) probably a larger one between the present Cromwell St. and James St. (10)

Early in 1654, between four and five hundred men made a determined attack on the Cromwellian garrison but the fort could not be taken due to the lack of artillery. (11)

That the attack was well planned, is confirmed by the writer "Indweller" believed to be John Morison of Bragar, the tacksman of Gress, a man said to possess "Ladies' modesty, Bishop's gravity, Lawyer's eloquence and Captain's conduct", (12) who spent the night previous, drinking with the garrison, and noting the likeliest places of assault, while his brother Allan was rallying the Islanders. The attack took place at midnight, with Seaforth leading one of the two columns and Norman Macleod of Raasay the other.

Shortly after, there was more trouble in which some of the garrison were killed, and in return, the soldiers slaughtered many of those who were known to be supporters of Seaforth. In this operation, they had the assistance of the "old natives", probably the Macleods. The losses on both sides seem to have been severe, resulting in the withdrawal of the Cromwellian occupation forces (13) who destroyed the castle before they left.

Seaforth's opposition to the Commonwealth led to his exclusion from Cromwell's Act of Grace and Pardon in 1654, and to the forfeiture of his estates, including Lewis. On his submission, there was the further punishment of imprisonment, from which he was released at the Restoration in 1666. (14)

It was about this time that Coinneach Odhar, the Brahan seer, is said to have prophecied the doom of the Seaforth family. Coinneach Odhar was under sentence of death on the orders of Lady Seaforth, who was angered by his disclosure (at her insistence) of how her absent Lord was disporting himself in Paris. As he was being led to his execution, it is traditionally related that he peered into the hole in the white stone which had been miraculously gifted to his mother in Baile na Cille cemetery, in Uig, Lewis, and said:

I see into the far future and I read the doom of the race of my oppressor. The long-descended line of Seaforth will, ere many generations have passed, end in extinction and sorrow. I see a chief, the last of his house, both deaf and dumb. He will be the father of four fair sons, all of whom he will follow to the tomb. He will live care-worn and die mourning, knowing that the honours of his line are to be extinguished forever, and that no future chief of the Mackenzies shall bear rule at Brahan, or in Kintail. After lamenting over the last and most promising of his sons, he himself shall sink into the grave, and the remnant of his possessions shall be inherited by a white-coifed (white-hooded) lassie from the East, and she is to kill her sister. And as a sign by which it shall be known that these things are coming to pass, there shall be four great lairds in the days of the last deaf and dumb Seaforth—Gairloch, Chisholm, Grant and Raasay, of whom one shall be buck-toothed, another hare-lipped, another half-witted, and the fourth a stammerer. Chiefs distinguished by these marks shall be the neighbours of the last Seaforth: and when he looks around him and sees them, he may know that his sons are doomed to death, that his broad lands shall pass away to the stranger, and that his race shall come to an end. (15)

The fourth Earl, another Kenneth, learnt nothing from his father's misfortunes and followed the dethroned James VII to France in 1688 and then to Ireland. In recognition of his services, James created him Marquis of Seaforth and Lord Fortrose. On his return to Scotland, he was imprisoned and on his submission to the Government, he went to France where he died. (16)

Kenneth's son, William, the fifth Earl, was probably the staunchest Seaforth adherent of the ill-fated Stuarts. He took part in the 1715 Rebellion, and fought at Sheriffmuir before fleeing to France. By the Act of Attainder of 1716, he forfeited both his title and estates.

William later returned secretly to Lewis, where, in conjunction with the Marquis of Tullibardine and the Earl Marischal, he made plans for the abortive rising of 1719 when he was badly wounded at the Battle of Glenshiel. His clansmen carried him aboard a ship back to the Isles from where he made his way back to France. (17) He remained in France until he was pardoned by George I, then returned to Lewis where he died. (18) During his exile, the rents of Kintail and probably of Lewis were remitted to him. (19)

The next proprietor of Lewis was William's son Kenneth. Because of his father's attainder, he was known as Lord Fortrose. He did not follow the example of his predecessors, but gave his full support to the House of Hanover. He was a Member of Parliament for twenty years and spent most of his life in London. Kenneth had very little interest in Island affairs and unlike his predecessors failed to give financial assistance to the Parish School in Stornoway. His attachment to the Hanoverian dynasty probably explains why Prince Charles Edward Stuart met with such a cool reception in Lewis after his defeat at Culloden in 1746. (20)

The second Lord Fortrose was also a Member of Parliament and strongly supported the Hanoverians, which led to his being created Baron Ardelve and Viscount Fortrose in 1766, and Earl of Seaforth in 1771, in the Peerage of Ireland. (21) In 1778, he raised the 78th Regiment of Foot, later to be numbered the 72nd., embodying 1,130 men, of whom 500 came from the Seaforth estates. As Commander-in-Chief of the regiment he sailed with his men to India, but he, along with 230 of his soldiers, died on the passage. (22)

Before leaving Britain, Seaforth had sold his estates, including Lewis, to his cousin, Lieutenant Colonel Thomas Mackenzie Humberston of the 100th Foot, a great grandson of the fourth Earl of Seaforth, although he did not inherit the title. He had taken the additional surname of Humberston on succeeding to his mother's property in Humberston in Lincolnshire. (23)

In 1783, Colonel Mackenzie Humberston died of wounds at Geriah, in India, after an engagement with a Mahratta fleet off the Malabar Coast, (24) and his estates passed to his youngest brother, Francis Humberston Mackenzie.

It now seemed as if Coinneach Odhar's alleged prophecy might be fulfilled, for the new laird had become deaf at the age of twelve after an attack of scarlet fever. He latterly became dumb as well. In spite of his disabilities, Mr F. H. Mackenzie was able to hold many important posts. He was a Member of Parliament, the Colonel of the 78th Regiment, and after his elevation to the British Peerage in 1797 (with the title of Lord Seaforth, Baron Mackenzie of Kintail), he held the post of Governor of Barbados from 1800-1806. (25)

Seaforth and his wife spent most of their time at Seaforth Lodge. Lady Seaforth taught the women of Lewis spinning, knitting and weaving, while his Lordship was keenly interested and actively involved in the fishing industry. In 1791, he was also responsible for the first attempts at road-making and completed four miles in six years. (26)

Lord Seaforth was the first of his race who tried to improve the condition of his tenants, for his predecessors had merely looked on Lewis as a source of revenue, and, when required, manpower for their martial exploits.

In spite of his physical disabilities, Lord Seaforth also liked soldiering and practically denuded the Island of its male population for this purpose.

The Seaforth family certainly lived up to its motto *Cuidich An Righ,* Helpers of the King.

Stornoway grew steadily in importance during this time. In 1695, there were only sixty families in the village, (27) but by 1791, it was a town which was a pattern of neatness and cleanliness, with over a hundred houses. The roofs of the houses were mostly slated with a few still thatched. (28)

Soon after his arrival on the Island, Lord Seaforth realised "the folly as well as the inhumanity of lending out the people of his Island to imperious tacksmen for the purpose of raising fortunes to themselves on the ruins of the unfortunate sub-tenants." (29) He examined means of removing the tacksmen but found they were extremely well rooted. Indeed, his own factor George Gillanders, was the most important tacksman of the lot, holding the lands of *Gearraidh Chruaidh* (Castle Grounds), Aignish, Knock, Swordale, Sulishader, Nether Bayble, Arnish, Grimshader, Soudenish, Branahuie, Aignish Mill, Garrabost, St Columba's Island and Gravir.

Lord Seaforth was also keenly interested in the lucrative kelp industry, and even more so as his financial situation worsened. He made a start with the lotting of the Island in 1811, before which the whole Island was in runrig.

As the Brahan Seer foretold, Lord Seaforth's four sons died before him, and on his death in January 1815, his title became extinct while his estates passed to his eldest daughter, Mary Frederica Elizabeth, Lady Hood, whose husband, Admiral Sir Samuel Hood, had died eighteen days earlier. Admiral Hood had been Commander-in-Chief in the Indies, and so as the alleged prophecy had predicted, "the white-coifed lassie from the East", Lady Hood, inherited the Seaforth possessions. Some years later, while out driving with her sister, the Hon. Caroline Mackenzie, in a pony carriage, the horses bolted, and the two ladies were thrown, Lady Caroline suffering a fatal injury. (30)

Lady Hood married James Alexander Stewart of Glasserton in May 1817, after which, Mr Stewart assumed the additional surname of Mackenzie.

The Hon. Mrs Stewart Mackenzie, as Lady Hood became, the last of her race to possess Lewis, was a most outstanding person and possibly the ablest of the Mackenzies.

Circumstances afforded full play to her peculiar talents and graces of manner and deportment, whether accompanying her father during his government of Barbados, or as wife of Admiral Sir Samuel Hood, when commanding on the Indian Station, or enjoying the personal dignity of chief of a clan, or moving in the higher circles of society. . . . Her talents and influence were devoted, like those of her sisters, to works of Christian benevolence. (31)

Unfortunately, her period of tenure of the entailed estates was marred by a lack of money, recurring famines, the failure of the kelp industry, unemployment, an ever-increasing population, and a husband whose imaginative ideas for increasing his rapidly diminishing income were not matched by his power of accomplishment.

The complete Island of Lewis, with the exception of the Parish of Stornoway, was sold by auction in the Parliament House of Edinburgh in 1824, (32) and bought by Mr Stewart Mackenzie, a gross mistake on his part, as it led him further into debt. Perhaps he should have listened to his sister-in-law when she suggested that he turn the Island into Gas or Glauber Salts, either of which was likely to be more profitable than beef or kelp. (33) He adopted neither of these suggestions, and after the failure of the kelp industry, he tried to recoup his losses by concentrating on fishing and sheep farming, unfortunately without much success. The many deserted townships in Lochs and Uig are reminders of his sheep farming policy that caused untold misery to so many defenceless people. By 1833, the administration of the estate was in the hands of Trustees as had been the case with Lord Seaforth from 1810-15.

Finally, a benevolent Government appointed Mr Stewart Mackenzie to the Governorship of Ceylon, and later, Lord High Commissioner of the Ionian

Isles. He died in 1843, and in 1844, his widow sold Lewis to Mr James Matheson, a merchant prince, for £190,000.

The long occupation of Lewis by the Mackenzies, and its subsequent loss, can be summed up in the old Gaelic proverb:

'A n rud a thig leis a' ghaoith, falbhaidh e leis an uisg'

'What comes on the wind, the floods will sweep away'.

THE MATHESONS

Mr James Matheson who purchased Lewis in 1844 was a native of Sutherland. Early in life, he entered upon a business career, first in London, then in Calcutta, before going to China, where he amassed a considerable fortune. He returned to Britain in 1842. (1)

James Matheson could not have bought Lewis at a more unfortunate time, for during the previous eleven years it had been administered by the Seaforth Trustees, and practically nothing had been spent on it. In addition, the Disruption of the Church of Scotland in 1843, when a band of ministers left it to form the Free Church, caused much confusion and bitterness throughout the Island. The famine years of 1846-50, strained his financial resources to the limit, and later, land hunger and tyrannical factorial oppression so embittered relations between himself and the people, that his many good deeds came to be disparaged and forgotten.

Although the Mackenzies had owned Lewis from 1610 till 1844, the welfare of the country people had not materially improved, although the village of Stornoway had become a town with many neat houses and had a small library. In 1825, Mr and Mrs Stewart Mackenzie had granted the burgh a Charter with power for the feuars and burgesses to elect nine of their own number to be magistrates and councillors. Two of these were to be bailies, one a treasurer, and the other six councillors for the administration of all burgh affairs. (2)

Matters were different in the rural areas, where, according to a report of 1841, (3) the people's idea of comfort was to possess a house, with plenty of peat, some grain, one to five cows, and a few sheep. The houses, all self-built, were small, cheerless and chimneyless, with only holes on the wall-tops for windows. One or two of the houses had panes of glass in these holes, but apart from this, the houses were similar, with the occupants and their stock sharing the same roof, unpartitioned.

The backwardness of the Island presented a challenge to the new proprietor, who saw an opportunity to make his new property worthy of his position and to exploit, to his financial advantage, its natural resources, however limited.

Mr Matheson, who had little interest in the fishing industry, believed that the future prosperity of the Island depended on the development of the land, and for this purpose, he chose as factor, John Scobie from Sutherland, who had some knowledge of the methods of "Improvement" in that county.

It was decided to build a castle, with policies, on the site of Seaforth Lodge, but before he could do this, the inhabitants in the vicinity had to be removed. The citizens of Stornoway who had been in the habit of keeping cows were deprived of their winter pastures when the areas between the Lochs Road, the River Creed and the harbour, were enclosed, and afforestation begun. (4) The building of the Castle commenced in 1847.

During the first few years of Mr Matheson's proprietorship, the town flourished: new houses were built, Gas and Water Works Companies were formed; a gaol and a ragged school were built; (5) harbour facilities were improved; the New Quay was built at the western extremity of South Beach Street, the Big Quay (attached to the Macpherson and Mackenzie Quays) at the north west extremity of the North Beach, and the Esplanade Quay between these two quays, connecting North and South Beaches, were all built at Mr Matheson's expense. (6) By 1849, the townsfolk were enjoying the benefits of all these undertakings. (7)

The failure of the potato crop in 1845 lent an added impetus to the work being carried out both in the town and in the country, and the years 1845-50 saw unprecedented activity throughout the Island.

In spite of the proprietor's efforts, the famine years of 1845-50 were difficult for everyone. Not only was there disease in the potatoes, but the grain harvests were also poor, fish was scarce, and cattle prices low. By 1850, many of the people had disposed of most of their livestock to stay alive.

For the first three years of the famine, Mr Matheson avoided applying to the Highland Relief Board for assistance and aided his tenants by providing work in road-making and repairing, building quays, erecting dykes to protect the cultivated land from animals, trenching to increase the arable land, and in the planting of bent on sandy shores. In addition, he offered free transport on his boat *Mary Jane* to anyone from the Western Isles who wished to seek work in the Lowlands.

During these four years, the proprietor bought supplies of oatmeal which he sold to his tenants at 25% of the market price. (8) Seed potatoes were also imported and distributed, the cost of both of these being debited to the crofters and added to their rent bill to be paid for later in labour or in cash.

Mr Scobie, the factor, was just and generous in all his dealings with the crofters, and on his departure in 1848, he was succeeded by Mr Munro Mackenzie. On discovering that most of the tenants were in arrears to the Estate, the new factor changed the method of meal allocation and introduced piecework, which was measured and paid for each month, after the cost of any meal provided had been deducted. (9) Mackenzie was so very strict in all his dealings with the crofters, especially with regard to the payment of rents, that when he left Lewis in 1854, only about six months' rental was outstanding.

The Highland Relief Board supplied large quantities of oatmeal to the proprietors of the Western Isles, including Lewis, but the meal was issued in return for labour, much of it for the benefit of the proprietors who thus had their properties improved at no expense to themselves. (10) At no time was the land improved without the crofters having to pay for it. (11)

To advise him on his Lewis projects, Mr Matheson then engaged a Mr Dean who had the reputation of being an expert on land reclamation, but his experiment with deep peat land near Lochganvich was not a success, although a great amount of money and labour was expended on it. (12) It was then decided that future reclamations would take place on the "skinned" land near the existing villages, where the peat had been removed for fuel.

With the assistance of £30,000 borrowed under the Drainage Act, 890 acres were reclaimed and brought under cultivation. Of this total, 520 were in Stornoway parish, 50 round Loch Roag, 140 in the Galson area, 60 in Achmore, 40 in Carloway, 40 in Barvas, and 40 in the Shawbost district. (13)

When the crofting lands were surveyed, enclosed and relotted between 1849 and 1851, less than half this acreage was added to crofters' lands or made into new crofts. The greater portion was added to the farms. (14)

In 1849, 791 men, 832 women and 3,125 dependents were receiving aid from the Highland Relief Board, (15) numbers which rose to a total of 12,829 souls when, in 1850, the improvement scheme which had employed so many people ceased. (16)

In the same year, a baronetcy was conferred on Mr Matheson for his untiring efforts for the relief of his people during the years of famine.

Things looked so gloomy in 1851, that the four Parochial Boards of Stornoway, Barvas, Lochs and Uig, sent a Memorial to Lord John Russell, Secretary to the Treasury, stating that conditions were such as to render Government action imperative to save human lives. Although since 1844, the proprietor had spent an average of £12. per annum on each family paying rent, had reclaimed and improved wastelands, formed roads and bridges, built an extensive brick and tile works, a large patent slip, and established steam communication with the South, all the work had proved unremunerative and had done little to benefit his tenants. The Island had not provided food for more than six months of the year over the past four years, necessitating the annual importation of £25,000 worth of provisions.

As Sir James had suspended his operations and the Relief Committee funds were exhausted, it was expected that famine would ensue before the next crop was due. To avoid this catastrophe, the Boards asked for Government aid, to organise emigration to the Colonies, and secondly, to give all necessary assistance to those left behind. (17)

In forwarding the Memorial, Sir James commented:

attention cannot fail to be excited by the fact set forth in the Memorial of the inhabitants being still so helpless and so incapable of earning a livelihood after the large alms that have, for some years, been expended in every mode that was considered the most conducive in placing them in a position to maintain themselves from the fruits of their labour. (18)

It was this Memorial which led to the McNeill Inquiry of 1851, but the aid requested was not required. The herring industry, in which Sir James had shown little interest, came to the rescue of the impoverished inhabitants. The expansion of the Caithness fisheries brought such prosperity to the Lewismen who went there for six weeks every July, that by 1854, practically all arrears of rent had been repaid and household plenishings were more plentiful than ever before.

This seasonal visit to *Gallaibh,* Caithness, engendered a new confidence in the men, widened their horizons, and developed their ability to deal with strangers.

In spite of their poverty over the years, the population of the Island steadily increased, so Sir James (probably influenced by the financial implications of the new Poor Law Act of 1844, and perhaps, other more humane reasons) offered to pay the passage of all destitute people to any place in Upper or Lower Canada, Ontario or Quebec, where they might wish to settle. He also offered to forfeit all arrears of rent, to relinquish his right to hypothec (the legal claim to their property until their arrears were paid) over their stock, which he was willing to buy from them at a fair price if they could not dispose of it themselves, and to give clothing to those in need.

41

(19) Not as many took advantage of this offer as he had hoped, but between 1851 and 1855, 1,772 people emigrated.

In a memorandum of expenditure which Sir James Matheson incurred in Lewis, the following items were listed:

1.	Building houses and reclaiming land	£99,720
2.	School buildings and teachers' salaries	11,680
3.	Roads and bridges	25,593
4.	Bulls for the improvement of the crofters' stock	1,200
5.	Meal and seed for crofters in the destitution years	33,000
6.	Emigration	11,855
7.	Patent slip at Stornoway	6,000
8.	Fish-curing houses at Stornoway	1,000
9.	Steamboat Quay	2,225
10.	Chemical works	33,000
11.	Loss in establishing steam communication	15,000
12.	Loss on improved mail service	16,805
13.	Brickworks	6,000
	Total	£263,078 (20)

ADDITIONAL EXPENDITURE

14.	Castle buildings and offices	£100,495
15.	Shooting lodges at Morsgail and Uig	19,289
16.	Stornoway Gas Company	350
17.	Stornoway Water Company	1,150
	Total	£121,284 (21)
	Grand Total	£242,568

This expenditure however, was not all loss, nor was much of it spent directly for the benefit of the crofters. Of the £99,720. spent on the building of houses and land reclamation, nothing was spent on the housing of crofters, as was all too evident, and up to 1853, only £8,471. 10/- was spent on their lands with a further £3,000. later on. (22) All of this was eventually repaid. (23)

Education certainly benefited from Sir James' generosity, and the expenditure on roads and bridges benefited all sections of the community, even if they seemed to lead to manses, farms and shooting lodges. In 1844, there were only 44 miles of road to be found in the whole of the Island, but by 1883, there were 200 miles, with bridges where necessary. (24) It was intended to have a road encircling the Island, but this was never done. Even today, roadless gaps still exist from Mealista to Aline, Eishken to Lemreway, and from Skigersta to North Tolsta. Until 1923, South Lochs had only township roads and footpaths.

The £30,000 spent on meal and seed for the crofters was not all loss, as the cost was added to their rents and repaid, more or less in full. The Estate therefore, had the benefit of their labour in return for the meal which was in fact supplied by the Highland Relief Committee.

The sum of £11,000 spent on emigration was partly off-set by the increased rental received from the new farms which replaced the cleared townships of Reef, Carnish, Dun Carloway (later given to the Mangersta tenants), Dalmore, Melbost Borve, North Galson and North Tolsta (now New Tolsta).

The fish-curing houses proved to be a very profitable investment. The rental for the store houses in 1883 was £38., and that of the fish-curing stations £145. (25)

The patent slip more than paid for itself, but the experiment to extract paraffin from peat and the Garrabost brickworks were failures. In any case, the crofters' houses were built of stone and turf and not of brick, and at the time of the paraffin experiment, fish oil was used for lighting, so this loss should not be debited to the crofters.

Sir James did improve the means of communication with the mainland. In 1844, a sailing packet crossed twice weekly to Poolewe, weather permitting, and a steamer sailed once a week to Glasgow. (26) However, this was not frequent enough to please Sir James, so he offered a subsidy to any Glasgow shipowner who would run a service from Glasgow to Stornoway. No one accepted. He then began a service to the River Clyde, first with a vessel called *Falcon,* in which he had a share, and later with his own boat *Mary Jane.* As *Mary Jane* proved to be too small, she was replaced by *Marquis of Stafford,* which he owned in partnership with the Duke of Sutherland. Mr Ramsay of Kildalton then took over the run, followed by Messrs. David Hutchison and Sons, who in turn were succeeded by Mr David MacBrayne. (27)

In 1854, when Mr Munro Mackenzie resigned as factor, he was succeeded by a Donald Munro, who before very long, came to be nicknamed "the Shah". He ruled the Island with a rod of iron until his downfall twenty years later in 1874, as a result of his arrogant and inhuman treatment of the Bernera crofters. Sir James trusted him implicitly, for he was a loyal servant of the Estate. Much of the odium felt for Mr Munro came to be transferred to the Mathesons.

Mr Munro was a pluralist who held the following posts: Chairman of the Parochial and the School Boards of each of the four parishes; Vice-Chairman of the Harbour Trustees; Director of the Stornoway Gas Company; Director of the Stornoway Water Company; Deputy-Chairman of the Road Trust; Legal Adviser to each of the four Parochial Boards; Baron Baillie; Justice of the Peace; A Commissioner of Supply; a Commissioner under the Income Tax; a Notary Public; Commanding Officer of the Local Volunteer Force and Procurator Fiscal. (28)

Mr Munro insisted on the Rules and Regulations of the Estate being obeyed unquestioningly, and any transgressor was threatened with eviction. One man expressed his feelings of frustration thus "The Commandments of our Great Master are only ten in number, and a reward is offered if we keep them; but those of our well-meaning and easy insular tyrants are impossible of being observed; and all we can expect is to live as slaves and die as beggars".

The hatred felt for Mr Munro is manifest in the poem *"Spiorad a' Charthannais"*, "The Spirit of Charity" by John Smith, the Earshader bard, in which he says that even the Chamberlain of Lewis had to submit to a Higher Power who gave everyone his deserts and that when he died, he would only have, in spite of his wealth, a shirt and six feet of earth.

SPIORAD A' CHARTHANNAIS

An sin molaidh a' chnuidh shnàigeach thu,
Cho tairceach 's a bhios d'fheòil;
'N uair gheibh i air do charadh thu,
Gu sàmhach air a' bhòrd.
Their i' 'S e fear miath' tha 'n so,
Tha math do bhiasd nan còs,
Bho'n rinn e caol na ciadan
Gus e fein a bhiathadh dhomhs'. '' (29)

THE SPIRIT OF CHARITY

Then shall the crawling maggot praise
The bulkiness of your carcass
When it finds you stretched
Lifeless in the grave
It will say, "Here is a corpulent body
Whom the crevice creatures shall enjoy,
Since he beggared hundreds
To fatten himself for me."

Despotic as were the Articles of Set issued in 1849, those printed in Gaelic and English in 1879 made life even more intolerable for the crofters.

Every tenant who, before the term of Martinmas, 1881, shall execute in whole or in part, improvements upon his lands in terms of Article 1 here-of; and shall also erect a dwelling-house and offices on his lot, or make alterations on his present premises, in accordance with Article 2 here-of; and who shall further observe the Rules and Regulations hereinafter specified, shall, on the completion of such house and offices to the satisfaction of the proprietor or his factor, receive a lease of his present possession to endure until Martinmas, 1893, without any increase of rent. (30)
1. For wasteland, thoroughly improved by trenching and draining and brought into a proper state of cultivation, and for sufficient stone fences, enclosing a croft or lot, meliorations will be allowed the tenant at the end of the lease as follows: (31)
In order to fix the amount of the meliorations, a certificate will be granted by the factor at the end of each year, in a book to be retained by the tenant, of the nature of the improvements executed by him during the preceding year, shewing the date and the extent of the same, and the estimated value there-of at the time, and at the end of the lease, five per cent will be deducted from the amount for each year the tenant shall have possessed the lands after the dates of the outlays made by him. Should the tenant be removed from his occupancy before the end of the lease, on account of any contravention of these Articles, or from any other cause, he shall be allowed meliorations in the above proportion, at the date of his removal. (32)
2. The dwelling-houses to be erected by the tenants on their respective possessions, shall be built of stone and lime, or of stone and clay pinned and harled with lime, or with stone on the outside face, and turf or sod on the inside, and roofed with slates, tiles or straw, or heather with divots, which heather and divots the tenants shall have liberty to take for this purpose from such places only as shall be pointed out to them by the ground officer of the district; each house to have at least two apartments, with a glazed window in the wall of each, and a closet or small room, with chimneys in the

gables, or other opening for the smoke in the roof; the thatch or covering not to be stripped off or removed for manure; the byre to be built at the end or the back of the dwelling-house, as the site may admit, and to have a separate entrance. In the byre a gutter to be formed for the manure, which shall be regularly removed to a dungheap outside.

Any tenant, whether possessing a lease or not, who shall build such a house to the satisfaction of the proprietor or his factor, shall, in the event of his being removed, or otherwise quitting the croft, be allowed meliorations for the same by the proprietor or incoming tenant, at the value of parties mutually chosen. (33)

According to the other Articles, any tenant who allowed squatting on his croft would forfeit his lease; there was to be no over-stocking; village herds were to be appointed annually; sheep were to be sent to the hill pastures in April, in charge of herds; swine had to be kept in sties; rabbits were to be trapped, not shot; dogs were to be kept only with the factor's permission; peats were to be cut in certain prescribed places; no green sward or turf was to be carried away; muir-burning had to be controlled; heather was not to be pulled, nor rushes and bent cut, except on appointed days and in selected places; permission had to be requested for cutting seaweed; illicit distilling and shebeening were strictly prohibited; people had to stick to roads and pathways when going to kirk or market; tenants had to pay their share of the rates; township constables had to be appointed; land disputes were to be referred to the factor; game and fish belonged exclusively to the proprietor, who also had the right to enclose and plant land, build houses, shut up or alter roads and streams, and straighten marches. (34)

Any tenant who contravened any of the Rules and Regulations (of which only some have been mentioned), would have his lease terminated immediately, and on being informed in writing, would have to remove himself or be liable to a summary ejection. (35)

Apart from these written regulations, and a few unwritten ones, the tenants were free to do whatever they wished.

On the death of Sir James Matheson in 1878, his estates were left in life-rent to Lady Matheson (nee Perceval), and entailed on his nephew, Mr Donald Matheson, and all Estate expenditure was discontinued. (36)

About this time, the Mathesons were experiencing not only the consequences of their own short-comings, but also reaping the bitter harvest of the seeds of discord sown by the Seaforths who had cleared so many townships of their inhabitants to make way for sheep farms. So many defenceless victims were transferred to already over-crowded villages that their unwelcome arrival led to the sub-division of crofts and to increasing poverty.

The Highlands and Islands Commission (The Napier Commission) visited Lewis in 1883 to inquire into the distressing conditions then prevailing. A well-known doctor made the revealing statement that it was not surprising if acts of tyranny and misrule seemed incredible to those who knew the large outlays incurred by the late proprietor for a benevolent purpose. (37) Another witness, a lawyer, informed the Commission that the crofters had long been, and still were, insulted, trampled upon and terrorised over. Examples of this would just be to give the un-written history of Lewis. (38)

As a result of the findings of this commission, the Crofters (Scotland) Small Holdings Act of 1885 was passed, which gave the crofters, among other benefits, security of tenure and fair rents. From this time on, the

Government became responsible for much of the work formerly done by the proprietor. Lady Matheson's main problem was land agitation.

The scarcity of arable land was most acute in the parish of Lochs, and when the lease of Park Farm was about to expire in 1883, (39) several cottars from the parish wrote to Lady Matheson requesting possession of it. At first, Lady Matheson was inclined to accede to this request but was advised against doing so by the Estate officials.

When Park Farm became a deer forest in 1886, resentment ran high in the villages bordering Loch Erisort, and with the arrival of a new schoolmaster, a Mr Donald Macrae, in Balallan, this ill feeling was translated into action. Park was raided (the famous Deer Raid of November 1887), but it availed the raiders of nothing except a trip to Edinburgh.

This abortive raid was followed in quick succession by attacks on Aignish and Galson Farms, which finally forced the Authorities to send soldiers to restore law and order.

The McNeill Inquiry of 1888 spot-lighted the prevailing poverty, which led once again to unsuccessful farm raiding in Orinsay and Steimreway in Park, by descendants of crofters who had once lived there.

In 1880, 61 acres from Galson Farm were given to eight crofters from Mid-Borve, but further applications for the enlargement of holdings were unsuccessful. By 1894, there were 3,000 more crofts than there were in 1844, but the demand for more land was still clamant, for there were almost 1,000 squatters. (40)

The Crofters Commission provided much needed relief by fixing fair rents for 2,573 holdings, reducing them from a rental of £7,252/2/1 to £4,943/7/6. Of the £41,040/14/4 arrears outstanding, the Commission cancelled £30,186/15/7.

In 1892, the Deer Forest Commission which had been investigating conditions in the Island, scheduled the following lands for new holdings:

	Old Arable	Pasture
	(acres)	(acres)
PARISH OF LOCHS		
Stiomrabhagh Grazings	107	3,083
Eilean Chaluim Chille	17	203
Crobeag	29	126
Eilean Orasaidh and Eilean Rosaidh	—	90
PARISH OF UIG		
Mangersta Grazings	42	2,620
Carnish Grazings (part of)	30	628
Timsgarry	70	1,518
Reef	93	451
Linshader	152	10,977
PARISH OF BARVAS		
Dalbeag Grazings (part of)	78	1,795
Galson	692	5,248
PARISH OF STORNOWAY		
Arnish Deer Forest (part of)	42	163
Aignish Grazings	85	—
Gress Grazings	181	3,579
North Tolsta	—	3,035
	1,618	33,516

The Commission also scheduled the following areas for the extension of holdings:

PARISH OF UIG		
Morsgail Deer Forest (Formed 1850-51)	—	13,020
Scaliscro (Formed 1850-51)	60	1,825
PARISH OF LOCHS		
Aline Deer Forest (Formed 1850-51)	119	8,307
Park Deer Forest (Formed 1886)	165	40,135
PARISH OF STORNOWAY		
Aignish Grazings (part of)	82	57
Melbost Grazings (part of)	74	—
Goathill Grazings (part of)	49	29
Tong Grazings (part of Gearraidh Sgoir)	10	216
Coll Grazings (part of South Side)	106	620
Coll Grazings (part of North Side)	—	816
	665	65,025

(42)

During the period Lady Matheson was proprietrix in life rent (1878-96), hers was no easy task, for the land problem was becoming exceedingly acute. The increasing number of squatters wanted homes, either on their parents' crofts or on the common pasture, and although interdicts were served on the offenders to prevent the erection of dwelling houses, these were often ignored, and the building went ahead. This in turn, led to the ejection of the occupants and the demolition of the houses. (43)

The *Earraidean,* Sheriff Court officers, who had to perform the task of executing these duties were held in fear and contempt.

Lady Matheson's successors, Mr Donald Matheson and his son Major, later Lieut. Colonel Duncan Matheson to whom he handed over the property in 1899, were faced with the same task. In 1905, Aignish Farm was resettled by crofters, but this only satisfied a minute section of those demanding land.

In 1908, the congestion in Brenish, Uig, with its twenty-nine crofters and twenty-one squatters was such, that the place was described as being like an anthill, with people crawling on top of each other with nothing to do. For these unfortunates, the township of Mangersta which they had once despised (the inhabitants had been removed at their own request in 1872) looked like another *Tir a' Gheallaidh,* Promised Land.

The inevitable result was that the crofters sent the proprietor, Major Duncan Matheson, an ultimatum, that unless their demands were granted by 1 April 1909, they would appeal to "spade, pickaxe and shovel".

Major Matheson agreed to their request. (44)

Reef, also in Uig, was raided in 1914, but this effort failed and the raiders were punished.

In 1913, the Board of Agriculture for Scotland prepared extensive schemes for land settlement, in terms of the Small Landholders' (Scotland) Act of 1911. This was a futile attempt to satisfy the ever increasing demand as well as to try and improve the existing housing conditions.

It was decided that farms with a rental of £80. or more, or exceeding 150 acres, should be divided into crofts, and the following farms came into one of the two categories:

FARM	Acreage	Rent	New Holdings	Enlargements
Gress	3,967	£125	40	—
Galson	6,120	£235	54	—
Carnish/Ardroil	8,036	£150	20	17
Orinsay/Steimreway	3,993	£50	14	—

The outbreak of war in August 1914 caused the postponement of these plans, so the Matheson period of tenure ended with the land problem still unsettled.

Although the land question was proving to be intractable, much progress was being made in other directions with government aid which had been available since 1883. As a result of the Walpole Commission of 1890, the Western Highlands and Islands (Scotland) Works Act was passed, which authorised the granting of financial aid for the construction of new roads, the improvement of old ones, and the improvement of harbour facilities. (45)

The passing of the Congested Districts (Scotland) Act of 1897 led to the appointment of the Congested Districts Board, whose work affected the lives of all. Like its predecessor, the Highlands and Islands Works Act, it gave assistance to agriculture and fishing and encouraged the tweed industry. (46)

The improvement of the animal stock was given much needed attention. Well known and well bred stallions which were bigger and stockier than the Island ponies, noted for their hardiness and perfect symmetry were sent to service the mares. This introduction of an alien breed led, unfortunately, to the extirpation of the native breed, *"Iothagan beag an Taobh Siar."* "the small fillies of the West Side."

Highland and Ayrshire bulls were also introduced, and this resulted in the production of a larger type of cow which was too heavy for the boggy moors.

Rams, mostly of the blackface type, accelerated the extinction of the indigenous breed, a process which had been continuous from the introduction of sheep farming early in the century.

As the Island progressed during the Matheson administration, the provision of postal facilities became necessary, and an island which in 1831 had only one post office at Stornoway, had another ten by 1880. These were at Back, Garrabost, Crossbost, Balallan, Callanish, Carloway, Miavaig, Bernera, Barvas and Cross. By 1901, North Tolsta, Laxdale, Portnaguran, Keose, Laxay, Gravir, Islivig, Shawbost and Port of Ness also had their own post offices. By 1914, there was a post office in every village in Lewis.

At one time, telegrams were only received by the Stornoway Post Office, and were then forwarded to their destinations as letters. Before the end of the century, telegraph offices were opened at convenient district centres; Balallan (1886), Portnaguran, Back and Port of Ness (1888), Garrabost and Barvas (1889), Crossbost (1895), and Gravir and Keose (1901). (47)

Before granting telegraphic facilities, the Post Office required guarantees against loss. This was forthcoming from various interested parties; Balallan—Mr Platt of Eisken Lodge; Port of Ness—The Fishery Board and Lloyds; Portnaguran, Back, Garrabost and Barvas—The Fishery Board; Carloway, Miavaig and Crossbost—guaranteed through the Highlands and Islands Works Act. (48)

As the fishing industry caused business to increase and large numbers of Islanders were earning their living away from home, guarantees were abolished.

48

Between 1891 and 1901, the total expenditure on various Island projects was as follows:

Piers, harbours, boatslips, etc.	£36,501	16	9
Roads and footpaths.	£23,170	2	2
Telegraph and postal extensions.	£3,049	16	4
Miscellaneous—Agriculture, stock, home industries.	£2,140	0	0
	£64,861	15	3 (49)

The period from 1844 to 1918 saw the Island undergo tremendous changes and much credit should be given to the Mathesons for their efforts to improve conditions. The Government should also be remembered for its considerable support during this time.

THE PEOPLE

The Lewis tenantry, descendants of Picts, Scots, Norse, and probably many forgotten races, have over the centuries shown themselves capable of wresting a living from the infertile soil of their island and the treacherous seas around it.

A glance at any group of Lewismen, even family groups, soon makes one aware of their many different ethnic backgrounds. Even as late as the early nineteenth century, there was said to be a colony of Danish origin near the Butt of Lewis which seldom dealt with the other inhabitants and totally preserved its ancient character. (1)

The constant struggle with the elements on sea and shore, made these Islanders one of the most versatile races, a faculty which stood them in good stead when they became colonists. They had to be self-sufficient and self-reliant to perform the many varied operations connected with husbandry and fishing such as the making of agricultural implements of all kinds, often from the most basic materials, to build water-mills and boats, to sow and to harvest, build their own homes, handle stock, and anything else necessary for their comfort and livelihood. Many of these skills were acquired during childhood, quite unconsciously.

The people were on the whole, physically, mentally and morally well-equipped to face life. (2) They were also shrewd, industrious, hospitable, and capable of enduring much hardship, especially at sea, (3) and many of them lived to a great age.

In the eighteenth and nineteenth centuries, early marriages were very common, with the wife often older than the husband. Infertility was practically unknown among the women, and this led to a steady increase in the population. Large families were always desirable, as this made life easier for the parents in their middle age. Young children were especially useful for herding, helping at seed-time and harvest, for procuring bait, and for baiting the lines.

Other factors which allowed the population to increase, especially during the eighteenth and nineteenth centuries, were the end of the clan feuds, the introduction of vaccination against smallpox, and a gradual control of "Fifth Night's Sickness", once so prevalent and fatal among children. The introduction of the potato, a valuable new source of food, along with the money earned from the kelp industry were perhaps the main factors.

The following statistics for the four parishes illustrate how the population expanded.

Year	Barvas	Lochs	Stornoway	Uig	
1801	2,233	1,875	2,974	2,086	
1851	4,189	4,256	8,057	3,209	
1861	4,609	4,901	8,668	2,878	
1871	3,950	5,880	9,510	3,143	
1881	5,325	6,284	10,389	3,489	
1891	5,699	6,432	11,799	3,660	(4)

The people's needs were few, and as long as they had food and clothing and the wherewithal to pay their rents (thus avoiding eviction), they were fairly content. Their homes were often havens of happiness which belied their outward, un-prepossessing appearance (5) with a warmth and fellowship seldom found in the homes of the tacksmen. They were extremely diligent in the cultivation of their small run-rig plots of land but, being conservative by nature, and unwilling to appear different from their neighbours, they persevered with the primitive and inefficient methods of husbandry which had remained unchanged for centuries. (6)

Work started before dawn by the light of the fire, and often continued until after dusk. The women started their day at the querns preparing meal for the day's baking, while the men worked at various odd jobs until the dawn allowed them to work on their plots of land or set out to sea. (7) The benefit of an early start was proclaimed in the proverb *"Am fear a bhios fada gun eiridh, bidh e 'na leum fad an latha"*, "He who is late in rising will be in a hurry for the rest of the day".

During the long winter nights, the ceilidh houses (centres of hospitality and entertainment), of which each village had at least one, were packed. These places provided a valuable education, for it was here that stories were told (not only of days gone by, but also of topical events), of adventures on sea and land, on distant battle fields, in Arctic tundra and Polar seas. There was also music and dancing, practical instruction for the girls in sewing and knitting, and various kinds of handwork for the boys. Proverbial sayings were also passed on, and solving riddles formed a good part of the evening's entertainment. A visitor to Lewis in 1793 was surprised when entering such a house, to find people greeted each other courteously and blessed both the house and all its inmates. (8) The Great War of 1914-18, which claimed so many lives, more or less put an end to this long established and very valuable social institution.

Until the Poor Law Act was passed in 1844, the paupers in each village were dependent on the ungrudging charity of their neighbours, with occasional aid from the proprietor or the church. Each village cared for its own poor, and these unfortunates were treated with respect as they went begging from house to house. This asking for alms was called *foidh* and occasionally they extended their activities to other townships, especially if they could claim relationship, however distant, with anyone there. The gifts so freely given were usually potatoes, grain, eggs, butter, meal, wool and clothing. Rural beggars avoided Stornoway as there was not the same hospitality to be found there.

The people of Lewis enjoyed playing games, and the popular sports were quoits, putting the shot, jumping, vaulting with oars, and *camanachd,* shinty. Inter-village shinty matches, especially on New Year's Day, were common. There was no limit to the number of players who could take part, and both sexes participated, although the girls retired from the game early in their teens. The *camans,* shinty sticks, were made from any suitable piece of driftwood, or latterly, shortened golf clubs. The ball was either a knotty piece of wood or a cork from a fishing net.

Choosing sides for an ordinary village match, the two self-appointed captains followed a time-honoured ritual. One said *"Buaile nam port?"* (probably a corruption of *"Buaileam ort?"),* "May I choose?", to which the other replied, *"Leigeam leat"*, "I allow you".

The players were picked by each captain alternatively, the best players being chosen first and the weaker or younger ones left to the last.

When the teams were selected, the captain who had the second choice when selecting teams, said to his opponent, *"Co 's fhearr leat a' bhas na chas?"*, "Which do you prefer, the crook or the shaft?" to which the other replied, *"Is fhearr leam a' chas* or *a' bhas"*, "I prefer the shaft or the crook", whichever he fancied. A caman was then thrown into the air, and according to which way it fell, ends were chosen. To start the game, the ball was placed in a small hole in mid-field, then the captains took alternate swipes at it until one of them drove it out. As there were no goal posts, a *saoile,* hail, was scored (9) when the ball was driven over the end boundary of the pitch. The teams then changed ends. The game only ended when the players became too weary to continue.

The girls had their own forms of amusement such as a game called "chuckies" played with periwinkles, or *boinead bat,* where a cap was placed on top of a stick stuck in the ground, and attempts were made to dislodge the cap by throwing sticks at it.

These games were gradually abandoned, especially in Uig and Lochs. In Lochs, the games had gone out of fashion by 1833, although shinty was played in the parishes of Stornoway and Barvas until after the 1914-18 war.

In spite of the isolation of Lewis from the rest of Scotland in the nineteenth century, its lack of educational facilities, and the poverty of the people, the Rev. Robert Finlayson, a native of Caithness, could say with conviction in 1833, "It cannot be expected indeed, that a people shut out from intercourse with the civilised world, should be so polished as others who have better opportunities of improvement, but their general good behaviour is such as might put many of these more favoured individuals to the blush." (10)

It was not until money became more plentiful through the expansion of the kelp and fishing industries, that the Islanders began to import cloth. Previously, all their clothing was home-spun from the wool of their own small Hebridean sheep. In 1833, some unfortunate folk were forced to buy wool from their neighbours who had a surplus to their own requirements. (11)

The men usually wore blue kelt and flannel shirts, but for special occasions such as weddings, undyed woollen trousers which reached half way down their calves were worn. The durable Crimea shirt, as its name implies, became popular after the Crimean War (1854-56).

The women were fond of brightly coloured garments, and for everyday use, would wear a *polka,* long-sleeved blouse, with a *cota,* serge skirt, which hung a few inches below the knee. For special occasions, a hand knitted shawl might be worn over their best blouse and the skirt would be worn with one or two petticoats underneath. The earliest buttons were of bone or wood, and girdles and toggles were in common use. The snood was the symbol of maidenhood while the married women wore linen mutches fastened under their chins with ribbons or tape. The mutch was the symbol of marriage and was donned by a wife the day after her wedding.

As early as 1833, cotton shirts and print gowns were beginning to supersede the home-made garments, especially in the town. Gay colours appealed to the Lewis women, and as brightly coloured garments increased in popularity, the early evangelical Island preachers became extremely concerned. The Rev. Alexander Macleod of Uig thought that it showed unduly frivolous minds, which endangered immortal souls as well as spending money unnecessarily.

"The formation of the female habits," said another minister, "with their whole appearance, closely resembles that of the 'Wandering Bavarians' or Swiss 'buy a broom' singers, who itinerate through this country." (12)

For a long time, it was fashionable for Lewis ladies to dress on Sundays, in a large plaid with a well-starched mutch to hide their tresses. The minister's condemnation of bright clothing resulted in a long period when black was the common colour of the Islanders' attire. However, at the turn of the century, brighter colours again began to appear and the plaids and mutches were superseded by *cleoca agus boinead*, long fur-trimmed ankle-length cloaks and flowered bonnets, which in turn were replaced by costumes and hats.

For a great part of the last century, the women only wore shoes and stockings on a Sunday. The men, however, started to wear boots when they had to perform statute labour on the roads, and after 1830, when they went to the East Coast fishing.

Apart from the sale of their stock and fish, by the end of the eighteenth century, the tenants had very few opportunities to earn money. At certain well-defined seasons however, the people of Stornoway would employ them to cut, dry and transport their peats to their doors.

Although cutting peats is a dirty job, it has always been an occasion for mirth and hilarity. Eggs, butter, cheese and whisky were liberally provided by the employers and brought out to the peat banks, (13) where flocks of people from a radius of fifteen miles had assembled with almost as many women as men seeking work. Wages were from fourpence to sixpence a day.

Roadmaking, which started in 1791, although unpopular work, also provided some ready cash offering a wage of eightpence a day. The first group to labour on the roads was bare foot, and they were quite amazed when they discovered that boots were necessary for this kind of work. (14)

It is interesting to note that the total week's wages for forty-three men paid out on Saturday 4th June 1791, came to £7/18/8. The men did not have the expense of lodgings, since they built bothies for themselves to sleep in. (15)

In 1796, the wages paid in Stornoway were:

Male Labourers:	8d a day without meat or 6d a day with two meals and a dram.
Women Labourers:	6d a day without meat or 4d a day with two meals.
Carpenters and Masons:	1/6 a day with food.
Smiths:	2/- a day.
Tailors:	1/- a day without meat or 6d with meat.
Joiners:	1/6 a day.
Male Farm Servants:	from £2-£5 a year with two pairs of shoes at 7/- a pair.
Women Farm Servants:	from 10/- - £1. a year with two pairs of shoes at 6/- a pair.
Cattle Herds:	from 6/9 - 8/- and two pairs of shoes.
Domestic Servants:	Their wages were similar to those of other servants except that at one time they were allowed a wine-glass full of whisky every morning. (16)

The cost of living was not high in these days. Beef was sold in Stornoway from 1½d to 3d a lb.; mutton 5/- and 6/- per wedder; sheep 3/-, 4/- and 4/6 each; lambs 1/8 and 2/- each; butter 12/- and 14/- a stone; cheese 4/-

and 5/- a stone; calves at 2/6 each; pork 2d a lb.; a hen 6d and a cock 4d; ducks 6d and 8d; geese 1/6 and 2/-. (17)

As far as food was concerned, the people were always at the mercy of the weather. A cold wet summer or a late harvest could jeopardise their grain supply while stormy weather prohibited the boats from fishing. Two meals a day was the custom at one time, one before starting the day's work, and the other in the evening.

Well on into the nineteenth century, foreign produce such as tea, coffee and sugar was practically never used except by the Stornoway merchants. Tradition has it that a cargo of tea from a wrecked vessel washed ashore on the west coast of the Island, was spread on the fields as manure.

With the introduction of the potato around 1753, the food supply was greatly increased and before long it became the staple diet of the people relegating oatmeal to second place.

The women usually ground a day's supply of meal in their querns and baked before breakfast. Before the advent of the potato, breakfast chiefly consisted of oat and barley cakes, porridge, and, when available, fish and meat. Porridge was also eaten at supper.

Eventually, potatoes were eaten at every meal, either boiled in their jackets, mashed, or roasted in the hot ashes of the fire. As most families only possessed one pot, it was the custom to boil the potatoes with the fish placed on top, a flat stone or a piece of wood sufficing as a lid.

The contents of the cooking pot were emptied on to a wooden *clàr*, tray, between three and four feet long, about eighteen inches wide, with sides three inches high, sometimes hollowed out of a thick slab of wood. The *clàr* was lined with straw or grass, and after the meal, this juicy bedding was fed to the cows along with any other leftovers.

After the repeal of the Salt Tax in 1817, which enabled the crofters to salt herring, fish and meat for winter use, potatoes and herring became the principal articles of food. When, during periods of scarcity, there was nothing else to eat with potatoes, they were simply dipped into salt and eaten alone.

Barley cakes, because of their dark colour, were not as popular as oatcakes, but they had the double advantage of being extremely nourishing and easily carried without crumbling, qualities much appreciated by the fishermen who dipped them in the sea to moisten them. Dried or pot barley was used for the Sunday pot of broth and for the herds to eat on the moors. Both oatcakes and barley bannocks were placed on a hot girdle and toasted over the fire. When the bread was baked, it was buried in the meal kist to keep it fresh until it was required.

There were various types of bannocks. The *bonnach boise*, palm-bannock, was usually made from the meal left over from the ordinary every day baking. It was very thick and was toasted by the fire or between two layers of embers. The *bonnach-eitheir*, boat-bannock, was specially prepared for fishermen and was most nourishing, consisting as it did of oatmeal, butter, minced cod or ling livers, ground cod roe and eggs.

A *bonnach-grùthain*, fish liver bannock, was usually what was left over after a crappit head (stuffed haddock head) was made.

Herds were given a *bonnach-iomannach*, when a cow in their charge calved. This was an ordinary oaten bannock, with a mixture of eggs and butter spread on top (later improved with the addition of sugar or molasses). It was grilled by holding hot embers over it with the tongs.

Oatmeal was used for a great variety of purposes besides baking and making porridge. It was ideal for thickening fish soup and broth; a handful in a jug of water made a very cooling drink called *deoch-bhàn* on a hot day, while even the oat husks were made into sowens, a smooth pudding or gruel.

As cattle were the only commodity the crofters could sell to pay their rents, they were seldom slaughtered for food. They were far too important for that. It is therefore not surprising, that they were allowed to share their owners' houses.

The need to preserve cattle was probably the main reason why mutton was eaten rather than beef. In any case, until the end of the eighteenth century, there was no great demand for mutton on the export market, except by such ships as those of the Hudson Bay Company which called at Stornoway.

When a cow or sheep was killed, almost every part of it was put to use. The cow's hide could provide material for shoes, doors, chairs, ropes, and other articles; its horns could be shaped into spoons, its fat provided candles, and its intestines were used as casings for puddings made from oatmeal and suet. Sometimes the animal's blood was added to this mixture to make black puddings.

A sheep's carcass was treated similarly. When the skin was dried, it could be used as a mat, or, after soaking off the wool, the hide had many different uses. The intestines were again used for making *maragan,* puddings, black or white. A pudding made from the stomach, was called a *marag a' bhuachaille,* a shepherd's pudding.

The liver and the pancreas were fried or roasted shortly after the killing as a treat for the children, while the heart and the lungs made broth for the next day's dinner. It was a common sight to see the trachea hanging over the lip of the cooking pot with froth dribbling out of it. The head and trotters could also be used for making soup after they had been singed with a red-hot iron and thoroughly rubbed with the animal's brains to remove the taste of the singeing.

Braxy lamb often provided fresh meat outwith the meat-eating season (Lammas to Easter). Meat for this season was pickled in a tub for about three weeks then hung up to dry. This smoked and salted meat was known as *feoil-reist,* smoked meat. (18)

Hens were mainly used for kain (a payment of taxation), but all other birds, both of sea and land, were considered fair game, as were their eggs, until gamekeepers were appointed and *Bodaich nan Cearcan Fraoich,* War Pensioners, who patrolled the moors in summer to protect the moorland birds' eggs from the local herd children.

The gannets or gugas which the Ness men brought back from the Island of Suilisgeir, were salted in barrels for winter use.

Kail was grown until the potato became popular, and in times of scarcity, soup was made from nettles, but it was not until the twentieth century that vegetables such as turnips, cabbages and carrots came to be cultivated to any extent.

Trout were caught in the lochs and burns with a rod or with a pock-net, and when angling became popular as a sport, fly-fishing became common but trout were not considered to be a substantial meal. The illegal fly-fishing instrument, the otter-board (a weighted board with flies attached to a long cord), was worked on the same principle as the paravane which was used for mine-sweeping after the war.

Salmon were caught in season (and out of season) in the Grimersta, Barvas, Laxay, Creed, Laxdale and Gress rivers with rods or cruives (fish-traps). Fishing in these rivers was always free until the arrival of the Seaforths.

A great deal of food came from the sea; flounders, haddock, gurnards, dogfish, herring, mackerel, ling, cod, coalfish, skate, conger-eel, halibut and turbot. Herring and mackerel were salted in barrels, while cod roes were salted, dried, and often eaten raw.

The liver of the haddock, ling, cod and coalfish, formed the basis for the delicacy known as *cean cropaig,* crappit head. They had to be fresh and free from any blemish, and were first made into a creamy batter and the blood vessels removed. Oatmeal was added to make the mixture fairly solid and seasoning added. A well-cleaned fish head was then stuffed with this mixture, and boiled for about half an hour when it was then ready for serving.

Even more nutritious was the *marag eisg,* fish pudding, prepared by placing small pieces of liver into a cleaned fish gullet, adding pepper and salt and enough water to cover the contents. The mouth of the gullet was then firmly secured and placed in hot water to cook for half an hour. The vitamin-packed contents served hot, were delicious.

The tastiest puddings were made from ling liver placed in a cod's gullet, the liver of a ling being finer than that of a cod, but the cod's gullet was much stronger and not so liable to burst.

Fish livers were also added to the fish-pot, making an already rich soup even more nourishing. It was not surprising that men and women nourished on such a diet were capable of enduring great fatigue when conditions were unfavourable.

Autumn rockfishing supplied the people with cuddies, saithe and hake; some sandy beaches teemed with sand-eels at certain times and they were caught with a special kind of sickle, a *corran-shiol,* eel-sickle. Shellfish of all kinds were eaten, particularly lobster and crab. The ebb harvest, in times of scarcity, was often the only source of food for the poor. Clams, mussels, limpets and whelks were to be found on nearly every shore, and razor-fish and cockles abounded on the sands of Gress, Coll, Tong and Melbost. Once every seven years the shell-fish banks at Melbost were said to burst open when immense masses were thrown up by the tide and gathered by the local people. (19) They also enjoyed various types of seaweed, like dulse, which they plucked from the rocks and ate raw.

Whales and seals were to be had at one time, and seals were caught in great numbers in the Seal Cave at Gress. (20) Seal flesh was said to be as nourishing as beef or mutton while whale meat was very fattening. (21)

Apart from milk, home-brewed ale was a popular drink for most of the Islanders even at the end of the eighteenth century. Tea was still scarce and expensive, and in 1783, it cost 4/6 a pound in Stornoway, with sugar 1/- a pound.

It was quite legal at one time to distil whisky for one's own use, and the sale of this commodity helped to pay the rent. When national legislation made distilling illegal, the people continued to distil under cover as the rent still had to be paid one way or another.

At no time however, was the land produce more than barely sufficient to supply the necessities of life. Periodically, meal had to be imported from Caithness (22) and other parts of Britain to sustain the people in years of scarcity.

HOUSING

Successive invasions and internal squabbles, from pre-historic times to 1610, when the Mackenzies gained possession of the Island, were not conducive to the erection of permanent habitations. This caused the Lewis people, at various periods of their existence, to resort to caves, souterrains, crannogs, duns and brochs for protection.

Insecurity of tenure, from 1610 until 1884, also discouraged the building of substantial houses, so it is not surprising to find a writer in 1811, describing these as being such as would disgrace any Indian tribe, with few of their inmates having any knowledge of chimney, gable, glass-window, house flooring or hearthstone. (1)

In 1833, the houses of Stornoway were reported to be neat and slated, in contrast to those on the rest of the Island which were sordid and indescribably filthy (2) with the exception of course, of the tacksmen's homes, which were provided by the proprietor. The ordinary tenants had to build their houses from stones, turf and driftwood, which was not easy to acquire, since the proprietor, being the Admiral-Depute of the Western Isles, laid claim to everything washed ashore. Seaforth's officers marked the letter "S" in red paint on all moderately sized driftwood, and what little escaped their notice, was sure to be spotted by the Comptroller. On one occasion at least, this official made a tour of inspection of the Island to note all the pieces of driftwood in the people's possession. (3) Houses were searched, and any such timber, even if black with soot, was confiscated. (4) It certainly was not easy to provide oneself with a decent roof in these days.

Occasionally, timber was imported from the mainland and from North America, and it was on a return trip from the mainland about 1795, that a storm-driven boat from Mealista was grounded at Bàgh Ciarach in Park and her crew murdered for her cargo of wood.

The original Lewis houses were probably of two types; the stone-built corbelled type, *both,* some of which can still be seen in the parish of Uig; and the oval *airigh,* shieling type, once so common throughout the island.

As the housing of cattle became necessary, the houses were made rectangular, exactly like the *tighean-earraich,* spring dwellings, which began to displace the older type of shieling from about 1850 until about 1932.

The site for a house was never levelled, the building following the slope of the ground. This was necessary for drainage purposes, as the animals were stalled in the lower part of the dwelling. These old houses were not expensive to build, as neighbours were willing to lend a hand. Many were built and occupied in a day, as it was accepted by the factor that once a fire was lit in a new house, the building could not be interfered with for a year.

The term "black house" only came into use during the second half of the nineteenth century when *tighean geala,* white houses, houses of stone and lime, with felt or slated roofs, began to be erected.

Before 1849, when Sir James Matheson began to re-lot the Island, the one-roomed houses were to be found in clusters, some having their walls overlapping, but the new type of house (examples of which can still be seen in Arnol), were built into the dykes which separated the arable land from the common pasture. The front wall of the house was part of the protective dyke.

The typical black house was a long, rectangular building forty to fifty feet in length, with an interior width of ten to twelve feet. There was a *fosgalan,* porch, round the front door, with a small barn usually a third of the size of the house at the rear. As a rule, the walls were two drystone dykes, four to six feet apart, with the intervening space tightly packed with earth. In some cases, the outer walls were of turf or of alternate rows of turf and stones. The *fosgalan* provided the only entrance to the house, although there was, in the outer wall of the barn, a *toll-fhasgaidh,* a small rectangular hole which was opened when grain was being winnowed. There were no windows in the walls. Inside the *fosgalan,* a tunnel led to a small kiln for drying the grain, while on the other side was usually the stable door. The door of the *fosgalan* was about fifteen feet from the lower end of the house.

All the corners in the outside walls were rounded, and great care was taken to ensure that the outer walls, which were of undressed stone, had a slight slant, to allow the rain to drip off and not seep into the interior. There were also no gables on the house, the walls being from five to six feet in height all round, with projecting stones left in one wall to form a *staran,* type of ladder to provide access to the wide, turf-covered wall-tops for thatching purposes.

The couples for the roof were placed at wide intervals on the inner walls. A cross-piece was fixed near their apex, while a *gath droma,* ridge-pole, was laid along their tops. For the further strengthening of the roof, a *corra-thulchain,* strong piece of timber, was placed between the middle of each end wall and the apex of the adjacent couples. Two rows of side timbers or purlins, about three feet apart, were laid lengthwise on the couples. Occasionally, a stick was fixed to the tops of the corner couple, to which the ropes that bound the end thatch could be fixed. Smaller pieces of wood were laid between the ridge-pole and wall-tops to support the thatch, once wholly composed of overlapping slabs of turf. Later, rushes, fern, heather, straw or potato shaws were used as additional thatch. No nails were used for this roof structure, except latterly, for the couples. Straw or heather ropes and sometimes tangle fastened the various pieces together, until they were displaced by coir rope, locally called *siaman Thearlaich,* Charles' rope, after Stornoway merchant, Charles Morrison, who first introduced it into the Island. The thatching rope was looped round anchor stones, slightly above the wall-tops, below which there was another row of stones covering the bottom section of the thatch. When securing the thatch, the ball into which the rope had been coiled was thrown backwards and forwards across the roof and looped round the anchor stones.

Thatching required much skill, otherwise the owner might have to quote the proverb:

"Fuadach ort a' ghaoth an iar-dheas,
'S tu gheibh lorg air tigh gu shioman"

"Curse you, o south-west wind,
You always search out a ropeless house."

The houses were designed with their low, thick walls, rounded corners, low doors, low roofs, and lack of window spaces, to protect them from the full force of the winter storms. The doors, seldom more than five feet high, were made of wood or hide stretched over a wooden frame. At one time, these were made to open outwards, so that they could not be burst in by a gale, an event which might lead to the flimsy roof taking flight.

Wooden doors were made in two sections, the top portion being often left open to let out the smoke and let in the light, as the openings at the wall-top were inadequate for this purpose.

At first, there was no partition between the byre and the domestic sections of a house, but early in the last century barriers were erected to keep the "rational and irrational inmates" separate. (5) This form of apartheid the irrational inmates felt keenly.

The byre end was dug to a depth of three or four feet to hold the winter accumulation of manure, with the domestic quarters on a higher level except, perhaps, in the late Spring, when the dung (to which periodically creelfuls of *smùr,* dry, pulverised turf were added, to give the animals a firm footing) had reached such a height that it was no uncommon sight to see a cow's head sticking out through the thatch, which she had either eaten or destroyed with her horns.

To provide some kind of damp proofing, the floor of a house, when built, was packed with small stones placed on end, to allow any water seepage to move to a lower level, before being covered with a thick layer of clay which provided a level floor.

The peat fire was placed in the middle of the part called the *teine,* hearth, which was two inches above floor level and packed with stones, often enclosed by the iron rim of a cart wheel. The *farleus,* smoke outlet, was not directly over the hearth, but slightly in front of it, in the ceiling, to prevent any sooty raindrops from falling into the cooking pot or into the fire. The interior of the house was normally rather dark, as before the advent of glass panes, the window holes in the thatch had to be closed with straw during wet or windy weather. The height of the smoke base in a house depended on the kind of peat used, for black peat, from the bottom of a peat bank, gave the most heat and the least smoke. A newly lit fire caused the most reek since, as the old proverb asserts,

> "Blathaichidh an caoran dubh e fhein,
> ma's blathaich e duin' eile."

> "The black peat will warm itself
> before it warms anybody else."

From the ridge pole (or if convenient, a cross beam slung between two couples), hung the *slabhruidh,* a rope pot-hanger, and latterly, a chain with a pot-hook attached. The whole apparatus made an ideal swing for the children with the added attraction of risking the fire if the roof fastening gave way.

Night lighting was provided by the periodic turning of the burning peats and home-made tallow candles (whose holders were stuck into the unplastered walls), with rushes or strips of cloth placed in a clam shell of fish-oil to serve as wicks. Latterly, the crusie, a very primitive oil lamp was used.

An improvement on the crusie was the globeless tinkers' lamp, smoky and foul smelling though it was. It was eventually only used for lighting the byre and a paraffin lamp was used for the house. This was replaced by electric light.

After the cholera scare of 1832, the inside walls of the houses began to be plastered with clay and white-washed. Once the crofters were granted leases to their homes, they were encouraged to brighten them up, with recessed windows in the walls, and even wall paper on false ceilings in the bedroom and living-room.

When the Estate ordered that there should be two doors in each house, one for the humans and the other for the animals, some of the crofters complied but closed the byre door soon afterwards. The remaining door was then re-situated next to the partition separating the living quarters from the byre, as it enabled them to reach their firesides without walking through manure.

In 1833, of the three houses built of stone and clay in the Parish of Lochs, all occupied by farmers, only the Loch Shell Inn was slated. The other two houses, of stone and clay, were the manse at Keose and the farmhouse at Valamos. (6)

When the crofters first installed chimneys into their houses, they were situated in the end wall of the sleeping compartment, now partitioned off from the living quarters by a low erection of wood, turf or peat. Towards the close of the last century, chimneys were being erected to replace the original partition between the fireside and the byre. By 1914, most black houses could boast two chimneys, while white houses, with either tarred felt or slated roofs, were springing up in every village.

By the start of the Second World War in 1939, few black houses were to be found on the Island. Nowadays, the few of these old dwellings left standing, are regarded as museum pieces.

In the original type of black house, there was no privacy. Both sexes had to share the same room and made their beds on straw, fern or heather, in which ever part of the house they fancied, (7) tidying them away in the morning.

Later, to economise on floor space, beds called "crùbs" were built in the walls, similar to the fisherman's bunks in the old drifters, which one entered feet first. Some of these wall beds were still to be found in houses on the west side up until the close of the nineteenth century. An example can still be seen in Bragar.

An improvement on this was to make an open space in the thickened wall for a four foot wide bed. This was later modified by making the walls narrower, and instead of the bed recess being wholly in the wall, a two foot platform was built in front of it, with a low stone coping to keep the bedding, and the inmates, from tumbling out. There was no wood required for this bed, simply a layer of dry turf to separate the bedding from the stones underneath.

The enforced move to new houses, caused by Sir James Matheson's re-lotting, led to some innovations being made. One of these, was the replacement of the wall-beds by box-beds, and the separation of the sleeping and living quarters by a partition. At the top of this partition, at door height, was a small opening with a shelf in front of it where the lamp was placed to provide light for the two apartments.

The first box-beds were primitive in the extreme, being formed by binding together four wooden posts with side and end pieces of wood. The two posts nearest the wall were shorter than the front two, to allow for the slant of the roof, and so permit the structure to fit close against the back wall. The tops of the posts were also bound together by pieces of wood or rope, and on this was laid a flimsy, turf-covered roof as a protection against rain drips. The wooden bottom for the bedding rested on the side supports.

This type of bed was improved by having its three sides and roof made completely of wood, and the addition of curtains provided a great deal of privacy. These beds were like rooms within rooms.

As large families were common, it was not unusual for six people to sleep in a bed, three at each end. Extra beds were often placed in barns and also used to form one half of the partition between the living room and the byre, with its front to the fire, noted in song as *Leabaidh bheag an cul an teine,* a small bed behind the fire. Sometimes a small windowless cell-like room was built off the *cùlaisd,* bedroom. It was called a *tigh-fhuaraich,* and could hold one or two beds. A dresser was often placed to form the second portion of the partition behind the fire with the open space between it, and *leabaidh bheag an cùl an teine,* used as a door.

Kists for holding clothes or meal were ranged against the bedroom walls not occupied by beds. Each kist had a *seotal,* small, lidded compartment for keeping trinkets or anything of value.

All furnishings at one time were home-made and strictly utilitarian since, prior to security of tenure, only essential articles, easily transportable, were manufactured. Although much was lacking, an old proverb belies this saying *"Is aoibhneas gach tigh, teine mor is deagh bheann",* "The cause of joy in every house is a big fire and a capable wife." Most Lewis homes were blessed in this respect.

Tables and chairs were in common use by the eighteenth century, and some of the latter were made of straw, bent or hide, and were reserved for the senior members of the family, the rest having to be content with low three-legged stools, logs, large stones, or piles of peat. Later, benches with barred backs were placed alongside a wall or a partition. A long bench was called a *being,* and a short one a *séis.*

The cooking utensils were chiefly a black iron three legged pot with a detachable handle, hinged in its middle, which fitted many sizes of pots, and a griddle. These were among the few articles which had to be imported. The spoons were either of wood or horn, while knives were scarce and precious.

The *clàr,* wooden tray in which the prepared food was served and from which everyone helped themselves, was the centre-piece on the meal table. A baking-board, with its hen-feather brush, was almost in daily use. The meal to be baked was taken from the meal-barrel and kept in a *ciosan,* basket made from bent grass. Other familiar utensils were a porridge spurtle, an odd wooden cup, bowl or quaich, wooden cogs or cumans of various sizes for holding liquids, craggans, a churn, and in the porch, the quern.

The agricultural implements were creels, crooked and straight spades, wooden rakes, harrows, cromans, flails, peat-iron, harness, and cow and horse spancels.

Fishing gear included handlines, small and long lines, baskets, nets, sheepskin buoys, bunches of horse-hair for snoods, thigh-length seal-skin or leather boots, and a small low stool, specially designed for removing these sea-boots.

For making cloth, the distaff and spindle were very much in evidence until they were displaced, at the end of the eighteenth century, by the spinning wheel. Other essentials for this occupation were a loom, cards, a *mudag,* wool-basket, and the *crois-iarna* and *liaghra,* thread-winders.

Wash tubs were made by cutting barrels in two, and close by was always to be found a *slacan,* arm-length club for hammering out the dirt from clothing on a flat rock by a burn, or for cleaning or mashing potatoes.

It was the most important items in a household which were sequestered when a tenant fell into arrears with his rent, as the following list shows.

In 1822, Roderick Mackenzie of Eishken's sequestered goods were: 1 crooked spade, 1 even spade, 2 chests, 2 pairs of blankets, 1 bed covering, 1 spinning-wheel, 2 pots, 2 herring nets and 1 long-line.

Donald Macdonald, Skaladale, had to part with: 3 chests, 5 herring nets, 3 pots, 2 wash-tubs, while Angus Smith, Seaforth Head, lost: 2 even spades, 2 crooked spades, 2 rakes, 4 pairs of blankets, 3 bed coverings, 3 chests, 2 barrels, 2 wash-tubs, 5 pots, 3 herring nets, 1 press, 1 table and 1 chair.

Sir Arthur Mitchell, the writer, who visited the Island near the end of the nineteenth century remarked:

> People living in such houses would be expected to be in a state of great degradation. This would be incorrect, for the Lewis people as a whole are well-conditioned physically, mentally and morally, and there is certainly much more intelligence, culture, happiness and virtue in these black houses than in the comparatively well and skilfully built houses which go to make the closes of the Canongate and Cowgate in Edinburgh. The people living in these black houses are not the dregs of the community, they *are* the community.

These old houses were certainly primitive, and lacked much in material comforts according to present day standards, but that did not make those reared in them second-rate specimens of manhood or womanhood as has been proved in many a clime and in many walks of life.

Nowadays, most Lewis houses are well-designed, well-built, and amply furnished. Wells have closed, for practically all houses are now plumbed for water and wired for electricity.

HOUSEHOLD INDUSTRIES

Before manufactured goods became readily available, winter-time, when most out-door activities came to a standstill, was a season of intense activity in every home with a great deal of preparation for the following year.

The women, as in all such communities, had a heavier share of the work than the men, and they took a great pride in their ability to work hard. They were, indeed, the mainstay of each household, and felt ashamed if their menfolk had to perform any of the duties they considered to be essentially theirs.

Calanas, the careful preparation of wool for the manufacture of cloth, took up much of their time during the long winter evenings. It was first graded as rough and smooth, then washed, dried, teazed, oiled, carded, spun, dyed, woven, waulked and pressed, with a skill and knowledge passed down through the centuries, for even in the sixteenth century, part of the rents were paid with "quhyte plaiding". (1)

After the wool was washed, it had to be dried on a clean firm surface, and the teazing, oiling and carding had to be carefully performed before the long, soft rolls of wool came to be placed in a *mudag,* basket ready for spinning.

Originally, spinning was performed by means of the distaff and spindle, which, when compared with the spinning wheel, had the advantage of being easily transportable. It was no uncommon sight to see a woman carrying a huge creel of peats on her back with the wool-tipped distaff under her arm, her nimble fingers twirling the spindle as she walked. The spinning wheel was introduced towards the end of the eighteenth century by Mrs. (later Lady) Mackenzie of Seaforth who started the flax industry in Lewis. Through time, the distaff was discarded, but the spindle, although slightly altered from its original shape, still remains. It now has a wider bottom replacing the stone or clay whorls once fixed to it to give a fly-wheel effect. The discarded whorls were later called *clachan nathrach,* snake stones, and regarded as charms, (2) as their original use had been completely forgotten.

After spinning, the thread was thoroughly soaked in stale urine (specially collected for this purpose) which had the effect of stabilising the dye when it was applied.

The native dyes were made by boiling crotal, heather, dulse, the root of iris, soot, dandelion, tormentil, bracken roots and other vegetable sources. These were all eventually replaced by commercial dyes which were stocked by the local merchants.

After the dyeing, the thread was rinsed and washed in fresh water, and when it was completely dry, it was ready for the loom. At one time, there was a loom to be found in every cottage.

Weaving was once undertaken by both sexes, but later, it came to be performed by men, who, owing to some disability, were unfit for arduous outdoor work. Such men were ridiculed in the rhyme—

ILLUSTRATIONS

1. Map of Lewis and Harris (Reproduced by permission of John Bartholomew & Son Ltd., Edinburgh).
2. The Standing Stones of Callanish (Photo: B. C. Crichton).
3. Dun Carloway (Photo: Scottish Tourist Board).
4. Clach an Truiseil (Photo: T. B. MacAulay).
5. Operating the quern (Reproduced from: *Highlanders at Home* by R. R. McIan).
6. The church of St Columba at Eye, burial place of the Macleods of Lewis. The University Library, St Andrews).
7. Lazy-beds at Uig (National Museum of Antiquities of Scotland, Country Life Section).
8. Making a lazy-bed (National Museum of Antiquities of Scotland, Country Life Section).
9. The Hon. Mrs James Alexander Stewart Mackenzie, daughter of the last Earl of Seaforth, from a portrait in the Town Hall, Fortrose. (Reproduced by permission of Ross and Cromarty District Council).
10. A water mill at Bragar (National Museum of Antiquities of Scotland, Country Life Section).
11. The interior of the water mill at Bragar showing the funnel which directed the grain into the centre of the grinding stone. (National Museum of Antiquities of Scotland, Country Life Section).
12. A both in Uig (National Museum of Antiquities of Scotland, Country Life Section).
13. A plan of the interior of a both in Uig. (National Museum of Antiquities of Scotland, Country Life Section).
14. Sir James Matheson, proprietor of Lewis 1844-78. (Reproduced from: *Tales and Traditions of the Lews* by Dr D. Macdonald of Gisla).
15. Lewis members of the Naval Brigade at the defence of Antwerp in 1914. (Photo: The Amalgamated Press).
16. Winners of the Fleet rowing race 1916. (National Library of Scotland).
17. Lieutenant-Colonel David Macleod, D.S.O. from Arnol, 1917. (National Library of Scotland).
18. Lord Leverhulme, proprietor of Lewis 1918-23. (Reproduced from *The Book of the Lews* by W. C. Mackenzie).
19. Bringing home water form the well, 1937. (Photo: T. B. Macaulay).
20. Rafts of kelp at Keose, 1975. (D. Macdonald).
21. A Lewis blackhouse, 1951. (Photo: B. C. Crichton).
22. Interior plan of a blackhouse at Cuile Totair, Ness. (D. Macdonald).
23. The cas-chrom. (National Museum of Antiquities of Scotland, Country Life Section). The crann-nan-gad. (Dwelly).
24. A shieling at Tolsta, 1932. (D. Macdonald).
25. Murdo Gillies of Shawbost with one of the last of the Lewis ponies, 1946. (Photo: A. Gillies).
26. Market day at Stornoway, 1920. (Photo: T. B. Macaulay).

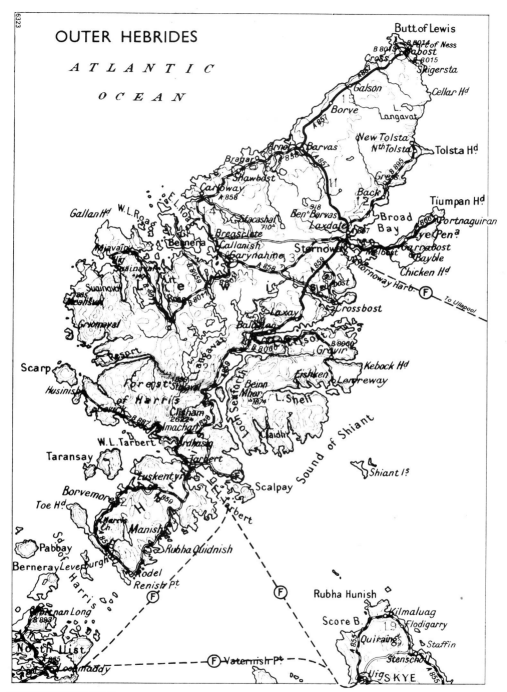

OUTER HEBRIDES

ATLANTIC

OCEAN

Butt of Lewis

Port of Ness
Habost
Cross
Rigersta
Galson
Cellar Hd
Borve
L.
Langavat
New Tolsta
Nth Tolsta
Tolsta Hd
Barvas
Brenish
Shawbost
Great
Carloway
Back
Tiumpan Hd
Gallan Hd
W.L.Road
Stacashal
Ben Barvas
Broad
Portnaguiran
Breasclete
Laxdale
Bay
Uye Pena
Miavaig
Bernera
Callanish
Stornoway
Garrabost
Garynahine
Melbost
Bayble
Chicken Hd
Suainaval
To Ullapool
Mealisbal
Laxay
Crossbost
Cromaral
Balallan
Scarp
Resort
Gravir
Kebock Hd
Husinish
Soay
Beinn
Eishken
Lemreway
Forest
Mhor
L. Shell
of Harris
Clisham
Scalpay
Amhachan
Cleidhr
Sound of Shiant
W.L.Tarbert
Ardhasig
Shiant Is
Tarbert
Taransay
Luskentyre
Scalpay
Borvemore
Toe Hd
Harris
Manish
Pabbay
Rubha Quidnish
Berneray Leverburgh
Rodel
Rubha Hunish
Renish Pt
Kilmaluag
Score B.
Flodigarry
Ath nan Long
Quiraing
Staffin
North Uist
Stenschol
Lochmaddy
Vaternish Pt
Uig SKYE

The Edinburgh Geographical Institute

1

2

3

7   8

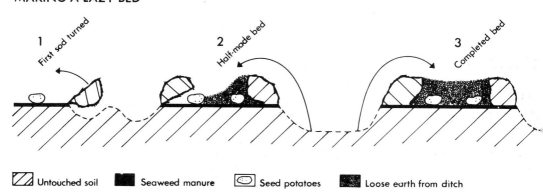

MAKING A LAZY BED

1 First sod turned
2 Half-made bed
3 Completed bed

Untouched soil   Seaweed manure   Seed potatoes   Loose earth from ditch

12   13

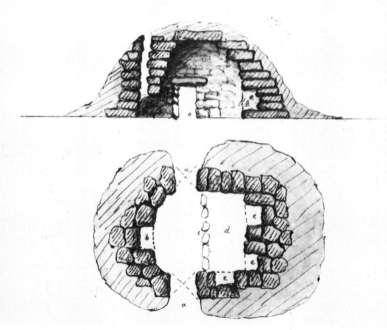

a   Doors, three feet high.   d   Bed on floor.
b   Fireplace, with a chimney above. (unusual)   e   Wall recesses.
c   Row of stones, front of bed.

15

16

17

19   20

21

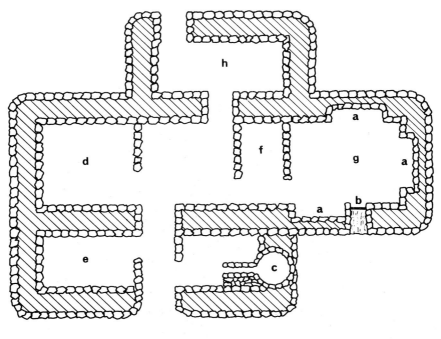

| a — bed | c — kiln | e — fosgalan | g — bedroom |
| b — window | d — byre | f — kitchen | h — barn |

22

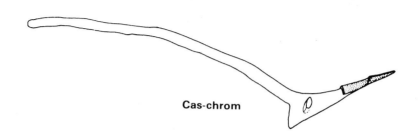

Cas-chrom

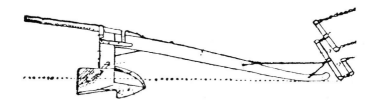

23

Crann-nan-gad

24

Fidhlear, is taillear, is cat;
Breabadair, is greusaiche, is muc;
Maighstir-sgoile is cearc.

A fiddler, a tailor, and a cat;
A weaver, a shoemaker, and a pig;
A schoolmaster and a hen.

After the cloth was woven, it was fulled or waulked, an arduous operation transformed by the women into a festive occasion. Not only were the participants in a merry mood, but also the many spectators attracted to the scene who added to the gaiety by joining in the rhythmic songs. Often these spectators were singled out as the butt of improvised verses, which caused the recipients some discomfort, but added to everybody else's enjoyment.

The process of waulking varied from district to district, but basically, the process was the same. Usually a rough surfaced barn door was placed on stools, allowing six or eight women and girls to sit with their legs underneath, and the wet cloth was placed on the table. Sometimes the waulking was done with the feet, the board being laid on the floor, with the performers sitting on a layer of straw. (3) The material was then moved 'deiseil' or sunwise round the board, each one lifting it from her right hand side where her companion had placed it, and dashing it down on her left hand side. The cloth was thus constantly moved round the table to the accompaniment of the songs, with one singer leading and the rest joining in the choruses. In this way, the cloth was shrunk one inch for every foot of length. The time taken to complete the work was measured in songs, and the shrinkage was checked by means of the length of the *cromadh,* middle finger. (4)

When shrunk to the required length, the cloth was laid out to dry and then firmly wound round a long slender stick, one half of the team winding, while the others held it firmly at the other end of the board to ensure that it was rolled tightly. As the roll grew thicker, some of the women clapped it with their hands to smooth it out while the singing continued unceasingly. The one special song for this occasion was called *Port nam Bas,* Song of the Palms. As the rolling of the cloth continued, impromptu verses were added in which every young girl in the troop had her name partnered with some eligible young man. (5)

When the cloth was completely rolled, the stick was withdrawn and the roll of waulked tweed stood on its end. It had to stand unaided to satisfy the women that the job had been completed satisfactorily. It was then turned three times sun-wise, and a blessing asked on whoever might wear it. (6)

Weaving has undergone many changes since these days. Stornoway mills now play an important part in the Island's economy, especially since the last war, farming out supplies of dyed yarn to the crofters and collecting the completed rolls of tweed. The clacking sound of pedal looms are to be heard coming from sheds all over the Island, and Harris tweed, mostly made in Lewis, has become world famous.

Although the women are no longer *a' sniomh 's a' càrdadh cloimh bhàn nan oisgean,* spinning or carding the sheep's white wool, or making garments for their families or knitting stockings and jerseys as much as they used to, they never lack for chores to keep them busy.

As early as 1764, plans had been set afoot for the introduction of flax-spinning, but the project met with little enthusiasm. The fact that the young women from the rural areas had to go to Stornoway to learn the trade was regarded as another instance of landlord oppression. (7) By the end of the century, a little flax was being grown in each of the four parishes, particularly in Uig and Stornoway, and the Society in Scotland for Propagating Christian Knowledge had established a spinning-school in the town of Stornoway, with a mistress in charge, at a salary of £10., of which the proprietor paid £6. Mrs Mackenzie, who took such an interest in the welfare of the Island girls, erected spinning-schools in each parish, two of which, in the rural part of the Parish of Stornoway, were closed by 1796, owing to a lack of pupils. (8) The proprietor and the S.S.P.C.K. shared equally in the salaries of the mistresses in Barvas, Lochs and Uig.

All the trainees at these schools were not only taught gratis, but were given ten pence for each spindle spun. As a further incentive, they could buy their wheels at a low price and some of the poorer girls were given them free of charge. Mrs Mackenzie also allowed each girl two pounds of coarse lint to begin with, and visited the schools regularly, organising competitions, and presenting prizes to the best spinners. (9)

Several Aberdeen merchants sent large quantities of flax to a salaried trustee in Stornoway employed by Mrs Mackenzie and the S.S.P.C.K., who arranged for its distribution throughout the Island. (10) By 1800 however, with the Seaforth finances at a low ebb, and with the Estate Trustees clamping down on any expenditure they considered unnecessary, Mrs Mackenzie was only allowed ten dozen spinning wheels and thirty reels for distribution. Her request for lint seed and a salaried instructor was refused. However, it was agreed that surveyors could visit the Island periodically to give hints on flax husbandry, ground preparation, and the weeding, watering, and management of flax. If this plan failed to materialise, it was suggested that a young Islander could be sent to Keith in Banffshire as an apprentice for two or three years to learn the trade and return as an instructor. He was to be given his keep, clothing and travelling expenses. (11)

When war broke out with France in 1804, foreign supplies of flax and yarn were interrupted, and the linen industry in the Highlands never recovered. Unfortunately, the growth of the cotton industry in the south of Scotland and Lancashire made recovery impossible. (12)

Perhaps if Seaforth had acted on the advice of a George Dempster of Dunnichen in Forfar, in 1794, things might have been different. Dempster recommended the introduction of spinning-jennies (machines which could spin a number of threads at once), as spun cotton shipped to Glasgow was guaranteed to sell extremely well.

In spite of these disappointments, Mrs Mackenzie had the satisfaction of knowing that she had improved the art of spinning in Lewis to the benefit of future generations.

In the nineteenth century, a certain amount of specialisation began to take place as some men developed particular skills. Self-taught carpenters, masons, net-makers and shoe-makers appeared, but the majority of the people still handled most of these tasks themselves.

The making of fishing gear was very much a personal affair. Net-making was a tedious task, for it took almost a whole year to make a hempen net. However, the introduction of ready made cotton nets soon put an end to this industry.

Before roadmaking started and protective footwear became necessary, *cuarans* were worn. These were brogues of untanned deer, horse or cow hide, fitted to the feet hairy side outwards while the skin was still soft and laced round the ankles. *Cuarans* must have been clumsy to wear, for an old proverb says *"Feumaidh fear nan cuaran eiridh uair roimh fhear nam brog"*, "The *cuaran* wearer must rise an hour earlier than the boot wearer".

The *cuaran* was succeeded by the *bròg*. The hair was soaked from the leather which was then tanned by means of the root of the tormentil. (13) After the shaped uppers were sewn to the soles with leather thongs, they were turned inside out, and were then ready to wear. (14)

When shoes with welts and thick, tacked soles came into use, the fortunate owner made a point of displaying such a sign of prosperity whenever possible. The loss of a tack was considered a calamity, so when one was found, the finder called out *"Co 'chaill tacaid?"*, "Who lost a tack?"

In Barvas in 1796, there was not a single trained shoemaker, although there were some in Stornoway. Balallan seems to have been the first township to support one, a Roderick Martin, who employed six men in his own village.

Mr Stewart Mackenzie introduced willow shoots from his native Galloway to encourage the making of creels and baskets, and the Hon. Mrs Stewart Mackenzie attempted, without much success, to popularise straw-plaiting by bringing instructors over from the mainland.

Murran, bent grass, which had been planted to preserve the sandy dunes from erosion, provided material for making horse collars, saddle-pads, meal-baskets, brooms, and even chair seats.

Rope was always in great demand in Lewis, and it was made from hide, hair, straw, bent and heather. The spinning of heather rope was extremely hard work, requiring strong, expert fingers, and a sharp knife. It was a common sight, until early this century, to see a man sitting inside a steadily mounting coil, and smell the scent of the crushed heather. The introduction of coir rope eventually replaced the other types.

Barvas and Ness were noted for blacksmiths, Morisons in the former, and descendants of the *Gobha Gorm,* Blue Blacksmith (a fugitive Murray from Dornoch), in the latter.

Clay vessels called *craggans,* primitive in appearance and shape, were made in all communities, although Barvas and Tolsta were noted as having the best clay for their manufacture. When making a *craggan,* the clay was kneaded until it was smooth and of the right consistency, then fashioned by hand without the use of a potter's wheel. The thick circular bottom was made first, and the rest built on to this, until the desired size and shape was achieved. The *craggan* was then left standing to dry for a couple of days before being placed in the centre of a fire and filled with glowing embers until it was sufficiently fired. Milk was then boiled in it to complete the operation.

AGRICULTURE

Even as late as the nineteenth century, Lewis, according to one authority, was the most backward of all the Western Isles, not only regarding the state of its inhabitants, but also agriculturally. (1)

The size of each township was limited by the area and the quality of the arable land, and the little fertile soil in the parishes of Uig and Lochs resulted from the hard labour of the people, as the numerous stone cairns testify. (2)

The small ridged plots, inappropriately called *feannagan taomaidh,* lazy-beds, varied greatly in size. They were formed by digging two parallel trenches, approximately six feet apart, and piling the soil in a heap between them. Where the soil was very shallow, the plots were the same width as the trenches which were also useful in providing a certain amount of drainage. (3)

These rigs were ideal in a community whose ideas on agriculture had hardly changed over the centuries, and whose agricultural implements, all home-made, were primitive in the extreme. Traces of these ridged plots are still to be seen in the vicinity of the deserted townships throughout the Island, especially by the shores of Loch Seaforth, in the Park district of Lochs, and down near the Butt of Lewis.

It was not until the nineteenth century that land measurement in acres came into use. Prior to this, land denomination was in davachs and penny-lands, with sub-divisions such as half-pennies, *clitigs,* half-farthings, and *cianags,* quarter-farthings. These terms were not based on any linear measurement, but on the number of cattle which each piece of ground could support. A davach was a tract of land which could support sixty cattle, and contained twenty pennylands. (4)

In the Island of Canna, in 1772, it cost £20 to stock a pennyland, which as well as maintaining seven cows and two horses, could also raise eight bales of small black oats and four of bere, the staple crops before the introduction of the potato. (5)

A reference to this old system of land measurement is found in a charter of 1590, by which, "Torquil Mcloyd of Lewis granted in life-rent to his wife Margaret Nyne Angus Makalexander, six davachs of land in the lord-ship of Lewis, including 20 penny-lands of Vallis (Valtos), 30 penny-lands of Lochis (Keose), 20 penny-lands of Uge (Uig), 20 penny-lands of Broagir (Bragar), 20 penny-lands of Gallis (Galson), and the ten penny-lands of Tolestaff (Tolsta)". (6)

These land valuations, founded as they were on what a certain piece of ground was expected to produce, were not constant. They varied in extent, as a penny-land on poor land was bound to be much more extensive than one on rich land. (7) Names like Five-penny in Ness and in Borve, and Penny Donald in Uig still commemorate this old system of land valuation.

Each township's moorland pasture was held in common, and the animals roamed freely, except at shieling time, when they were restricted to the land of their own township. The arable land, on the other hand, although held in run-rig, was also regarded as part of the common grazings, except between seed-time and harvest.

Under the run-rig system of land tenure, which was not confined to Lewis, no part of the arable land was held permanently by any individual, nor would the same person have two rigs or plots adjoining one another. Every third year, a third of this arable land was re-allocated in such a way that each person had his share of the best.

It was not until 1811 that the first lotting of run-rig land was undertaken to form individual crofts in Lewis, although this had been introduced in Argyll as early as 1776. It seems as if the term 'croft' is even older than this date, for there is a place called *'Croit an Righ'*, 'the King's croft', beside the Palace of Holyrood House, in Edinburgh.

This lotting of land was not universal throughout the Island, for in 1833, there were still lands in the parish of Lochs held in run-rig. (8)

The new system was anything but satisfactory, and led to much discontent among the people, and it was not until Sir James Matheson, who had recently bought the Island, engaged trained surveyors to undertake the proper lotting of the land in 1849-51, a task made easier by the disappearance of the tacksmen, that the crofts, as they are now, came into being.

Prior to the acquisition of Lewis by the Mackenzies of Kintail in 1610, rents were paid either in kind or in service. The men-folk seem to have been divided into two distinct groups, combatants and non-combatants. Of the former, there was estimated to be seven hundred in the period between 1577 and 1595, while the latter, the non-combatants, whose numbers were not specified, had to remain at home in time of war to work the land. (9)

Land tenure during the Mackenzie or Seaforth regime was as follows.

(a)   Tacksmen who held their lands direct from the proprietor, usually for a period of nineteen years. (10)
(b)   Small tenants, as distinct from the large tenants or tacksmen, who also held their lands direct from the proprietor, on a verbal lease of one year, terminable at Whitsunday. (11) These small tenants, tenants-at-will as they were called, were found in the conjoint townships on the infertile portions of the Barvas and Uig parishes.
(c)   Sub-tenants who held their lands from the tacksmen. This was the category that most people (the future crofters) were in.
(d)   The cottars or farm servants.
(e)   The *sgalag,* menial.

This system of land tenure caused much unhappiness. There were, perhaps, good tacksmen, or, at least some who were not as bad as others, but all had the reputation of being most despotic towards those who had the misfortune to be in their power. Obedience to their commands had to be prompt, or retribution was sure to follow. Some tacksmen were known to wait outside a church until the congregation was dispersing, to haul their sub-tenants away to perform some work these tyrants deemed urgent. Disobedience meant eviction. The usual threat for any sign of insubordination, or the neglect of any chore, was *"Cuiridh mi as an fhearann thu"*, "I shall evict you", no idle threat.

The relationship between the tacksmen and the rest of the community gave rise to the proverb, *"Aithne an Leodhasaich mhoir air an Leodhasaich bhig; aithne gun chuimhne"*, "The haughty Lewisman's recognition of the needy Lewisman; recognition without remembrance." (12)

Since they had little arable land and a wide expanse of pasture land, the people became more thirled to grazing than to tillage. The cultivation of crops, which required regular attention, was only of secondary importance, as there was seldom sufficient corn for their own needs, and often supplies of grain had to be imported, even in good years, from Caithness and Ireland. (14)

The people, conservative by nature, clung to the old methods of husbandry. The implements in use, and the mode of tillage and manuring, remained unaltered for centuries. They believed that what was good enough for their fathers was good enough for them. Seed selection was seldom practised, and often the poorest seed was kept for sowing. The first real change came when potato cultivation was introduced, with more land being allocated to this crop. This also led to a certain amount of crop rotation, chiefly because the grain and the potato crops needed different quantities of manure.

With the exception of the fields round the town of Stornoway, which had been reclaimed on improving leases, land cultivation, up until the beginning of the nineteenth century, was still in its infancy, (15) as there was no security of tenure, and the tenantry had no inducement to improve the land of which they were only in temporary possession. Stupid indeed would be the tenant who improved his holding, for, without security of tenure, this might lead to eviction or rack-renting. It was no wonder Lewis lagged far behind other parts of Scotland, in their improvement of the land.

During the period between the publication of the two Statistical Accounts, in 1796 and 1833, some slight progress was made, although the system of run-rig still persisted in some districts, and 'that notorious implement of Scottish Highland husbandry', the *cas-chrom,* crooked spade, was still very much in use.

In the Parish of Barvas, however, a parish not hitherto noted for its progressive outlook, the *cas-chrom* was beginning to lose its popularity for, in 1833, according to the minister of the parish, "A little refinement of taste, more than a sense of its disadvantages, has in some cases abolished the use of the crooked spade, a very indelicate instrument for females." (16) Probably the main reason for this was due, not so much to the minister's views on its use, as to the introduction of the common spade, which was much easier to handle, combined with the fact that the parish was fairly level, and the *crann-nan-gad,* one-handled plough could be used.

The people of the Parish of Stornoway were much better off as regards arable land, but the ladies there, evidently not so refined in their tastes, or possessing such a discerning minister, still continued to use the *cas-chrom.*

Uig Parish for a long time had very few ploughs although they could have easily been operated on the machairs.

Lochs, with its poor, thin soil, was less fortunate. It was practically impossible to use a plough on the run-rigs, and only about half of this parish could be regularly tilled.

No one would disagree with the statement that "The state of agriculture in every country may be estimated by the quality of the instruments generally used by the people", but many critics do not seem to realise that in a fairly primitive society, such implements have to be made from materials which are readily available. On a treeless island such as Lewis, wood, for making the simplest implements like the crooked spade and the one-handled plough, was not easily obtainable, and the inhabitants depended on driftwood and imported timber to supply their needs.

Open boats frequently crossed to the mainland for timber, trips that were often dangerous due to the elements, and also for other reasons, as the following tale will illustrate.

About the year 1785, a boat from the township of Mealista in Uig, sailed through the Sound of Harris to Wester Ross for a cargo of timber. Returning with their unwieldy cargo, they encountered tempestuous weather and were forced to seek shelter in *Bàgh Ciarach,* Gloomy Bay, in south-east Park, where two or three families lived. The unexpected arrival of so much timber on their doorsteps, and the exhausted state of the crew, was too much for their cupidity, and the defenceless men were murdered.

Back in Mealista, the boat was given up as lost at sea, and it was not until the following summer at the Stornoway Summer Tryst, that the foul deed came to light when blankets were offered for sale which were recognised by the pieces of Nicolson tartan which had been sewn into their corners as having belonged to the missing crew. A confession soon followed.

One of the murdered men later appeared to his wife in a dream and told her what had happened. When she wakened, she recited the following poem.

MORT NA PAIRCE

'S e nighean mo ghaoil an nighean donn òg;
Nam bithinn ri'taobh, cha bhithinn fo lèon.

Tha mo chuideachd am bliadhna 'g am shireadh 's 'gam iarraidh,
'S tha mis' am Bàgh Ciarach, an iochdar an lòin.

Tha fearaibh na Pairce air tomhadh na lamh-thuagh,
Ach 's e sinne bhi gun thamhachd dh'fhag iadsan gun lèon.

Bha Donnchadh 'gam fhaire, fear siubhal nam beannaibh;
Tha'n saoghal ro-charach, 's gur meallach an t-òr.

'S ann a' direadh na bruthaich, a chaill mi mi lùths'
'S fo leacan an Rudha, am fear buidhe 'ga lèon. (18)

THE PARK MURDER

The girl of my love, is the young brown-haired one;
If I were beside her I would not suffer harm.

My relatives are this year seeking and searching for me,
While I lie in Gloomy Bay, on the bottom of the pool.

The men of Park threatened us with their axes,
But our exhausted state left them un-wounded.

Duncan, the mountain wanderer, attended to me:
The world is deceitful, and gold beguils.

It was while climbing the hill-side, I lost my strength;
By the ledges of the headland was the yellow-haired lad murdered.

The *cas-chrom,* crooked spade, took pride of place among the early agricultural implements. It was simply constructed, consisting of a curved wooden shaft about six feet in length, to which was attached the head, a flat iron tipped piece of wood about two and a half feet long, thin and squarely shaped to penetrate the earth. The shaft was thick at its junction with the head, but like the handle of a peat iron, it became slender enough to handle. Just beneath the crook, or angle, a strong peg was fixed where the worker applied his right foot to drive it into the ground. A peculiar body-twist was then given, and the clod raised and turned out to the left. It could not be turned to the right because of the peg. (19)

It was estimated that an experienced labourer could dig as much ground in a day with a *cas-chrom* as four men with ordinary spades. It was also extremely useful on boggy land or rocky slopes, where neither a plough nor a *cas-dhireach,* straight spade could be used. The people also believed that ground dug with this clumsy looking implement was more productive than ground tilled any other way.

The *cas-dhireach* consisted of a straight piece of wood tipped with iron, with a driving pin or step on its right hand side, similar to a peat iron. (20) However, when roadmaking started, the labourers changed to the modern type of spade, and the *cas-dhireach,* and later the *cas-chrom,* went out of use.

The *crann-nan-gad,* one-handled plough, was the earliest type of plough used on Lewis crofts, and was not unlike the Chinese plough in appearance and construction. (21) It was made of a small crooked piece of wood with a stilt or handle fixed on top. The other end of the wood was iron tipped, and the coulter and sock were made of iron.

The plough could be drawn by one or two horses, but a writer describes how he saw this type of plough being pulled by four horses.

A man walking backward with his face towards four horses abreast, brandishing his cudgel in their noses and eyes, to make them advance to their enemy, followed by a ristle plough employing a horse and two men, the three commonly altogether superfluous, still followed by four horses dragging clumsy harrows fixed by hair ropes to their tails and almost bursting their spinal marrow at every tug and writhing of their tortured carcasses.

The ristle plough had only a sharpened share for paring the surface for the *crann-nan-gad,* while the harrows were light wooden affairs, with wooden teeth. When no horses were available, men, women and youngsters dragged these harrows. Where two or more people were harrowing, the strongest person led. Harrowing was not the most difficult part of croft work.

To break the sods, a *ràcan,* instrument with a long handle fitted into a block of wood was used. At one time, the *ràcan* had teeth, but later these were dispensed with.

After the introduction of the potato, four different types of hoes were in use. One was made in the local smiddy, and was quite heavy. The second was made from the blade of an old spade, and was the best, being light and sharp. The third was the narrow shop bought model, which was never really popular as it only penetrated the soil to half the depth of the other two. The last type, the *croman,* had a short handle, with a long narrow blade like the sole of a lady's shoe and was mainly used for lifting potatoes.

72

Changes were inevitable, and early in the twentieth century, iron Orkney ploughs were in general use. These ploughs, which required two horses to pull them, didn't have a wheel to ensure a uniform depth of furrow.

During the first World War, a one-horse plough, the Oliver plough, came into use owing to the scarcity of men and horses, but did not last for more than a decade.

Nowadays, horses rarely pull a plough, with tractors carrying out the little tillage required.

Before the introduction of the potato in 1756, the staple crops were barley, and small black oats. Towards the end of the eighteenth century, flax and hemp were grown for a while, but the increasing number of cotton spinning mills on the mainland lowered the demand for island spun material and these two crops were eventually abandoned.

Corca-dubh, black oats were preferred to the much taller and more prolific *corca-geal,* white oats, as they were able to withstand the autumnal gales which usually flattened the white oats.

Oats were always cut with the sickle, whereas barley was plucked up by the roots. Both hands were needed for this job, and three double handfuls were sufficient for one sheaf, while six sheaves made one stook. To form a sheaf band, about eight stalks were taken with their ears to the binder's left. This band was placed crosswise on the proposed sheaf, which was then raised off the ground and supported against the knee. Both ends of the band were entwined twice, and the root end was pushed down inside the band, leaving the ears sticking out. As the sheaves dried, they were built up into *torran,* little ricks.

Later, this corn was taken to the *iolann,* walled enclosure, where it was made into stacks. When required, the barley had its sheaves cut below the bands, and the lower portion used for thatching the cottages. Oat straw was used for cattle fodder during the winter months.

At first, the Islanders were no keener to cultivate the potato than were the people of Uist, when Macdonald of Clanranald introduced it from Ireland. His people told him that although he made them plant these worthless things, he could not make them eat them.

About 1870, Mr Munro, the minister of Uig, experienced the same difficulty. (23) He was almost obliged to give up the cultivation of potatoes for a while, as the people refused to eat them. However, his perseverance finally convinced them of their value, and when they realised how easily they could be cultivated, the potato took precedence over the other crops. However, the potato was much more popular in the other islands, where a boy, on being asked what constituted his three daily meals, gave the same answer each time, "mashed potatoes", and on being asked "what else", naively replied "a spoon". (24)

At one time there was no regular rotation of crops, although, when run-rig existed, it did happen, but usually accidentally. After the second lotting of Lewis during the years 1849-51, a certain amount of rotation took place. The potato plot was well manured with animal manure or seaweed. The *atharnach,* ground where potatoes had grown the previous year, was sown with barley as the second crop, which was followed by oats. The grain crops received little or no manure, so the returns were poor.

Where there was insufficient land to grow three crops, as in the case of many cottars and squatters, it was necessary to grow potatoes in the same place year after year, with diminishing returns. Insufficient attention was paid to the seed-corn and seed-potatoes. The corn was sown far too thickly as a rule, and rarely changed. As a general rule, the best seed was eaten, and the rest kept for sowing.

Sowing began in March, with the oats, which were followed by potato planting from mid-April, which was followed by the barley. Flax and hemp were sown about the same time as the potatoes, mid-April to mid-May. (25)

Very little corn was sown on the poor soil in Lochs, especially South Lochs, where the small ridges were chiefly devoted to potatoes. However, the inhabitants of this area relied mainly on fish for their subsistence. (26)

During the planting season, when food supplies were low, the root of *brisgean,* silverweed, was eaten. This could be eaten raw, slightly roasted, or boiled, but because of possible erosion on the machair lands, digging this weed was strictly forbidden by the proprietor. (27)

Before the potato became popular, it was quite common to grow kale, and although turnips were grown on all farms, it was a long time before they were grown on the crofts. The few people who did experiment, found that once the youths acquired a taste for them, they helped themselves during the winter.

For a long time, seaweed formed two-thirds of all manure used. Indeed, it wasn't until cattle-housing became common, that animal manure was used to any great extent.

Seaweed was ideal for mossy ground or ground newly cultivated, but it was believed that too much scourged the soil. (28) Seaweed was cut from the rocks or picked up on the shores, but only from the parts of the shore attached to the township, and only at such times, and in such quantities permitted by the factor or ground officer, and only when the village constables were present. (29) This regulation was strictly enforced when the kelp industry became profitable.

Cow-dung became very important after the introduction of the potato, which needed a lot of manure. The dung had a good admixture of peat, for, once a week, usually on Saturdays, creelfuls of peat dross were spread in the byre-end of the house to keep it dry and prevent a quagmire from forming. This manure was exceptionally good for machairs, providing the necessary humus. In this respect at least, the Lewis crofters were ahead of their time.

A *dùn smùir,* heap of peaty divots, was cut and taken to each home in late Autumn for winter cow-bedding, and it was this practice which led to the estate regulation that no tenant was to cut or carry away the surface of any pasture or muirground. (30)

A third type of manure was obtained by stripping the thatch from the house. (31) This operation usually took place towards the end of May, when the outer layer of thatch was removed and carefully laid on the wide *tobhta,* wall top. The inner layer of warm, brittle, soot-impregnated stubble, was even more carefully removed and scattered over the sprouting barley. Showery weather was considered a Divine favour during this operation, as it washed the soot down to the roots of the corn. Bread made from the corn thus treated, was reputed to cause jaundice. The Estate frowned upon this practice, feeling that the roofs should be left intact.

The thatch on the wall top was then replaced on the roof as the inner layer (to be removed the following year), and a new outer layer was placed over it. (32)

The people carried the manure to wherever it was required, either in creels on their backs, or in panniers slung on either side of their small, hardy, unshod island ponies. These panniers or creels hung on large wooden hooks on the crude, home-made pack saddle. The panniers were carefully unloaded simultaneously, but later, they were made to open at the bottom.

When carts came into use, the end wall of the house was left with an entrance wide enough for a cart to back into it during the annual clearing of the byre. This *toll innireach,* dunghole, was kept closed during the rest of the year, either by a wooden partition or by turf.

The long narrow cart which first came into use was called a *càrn.* Its main disadvantage was that the horse had to be unyoked each time it was emptied. It was replaced by the coup-cart.

The creels carried by the men and women had an *iris,* breast band made of hair, bent grass or rope. Sometimes, this band, which was about three inches wide, was beautifully woven, which made it much more comfortable, and it was regarded as being a much superior article.

To carry a creel, the women wore an old *cota,* loose kilted skirt, rolled up to form a *dronnag,* creel pad on the lower part of the back, where the creel could rest. Along with a well made breast band, this made it much easier for women to carry their burdens, and even made it possible for them to carry much heavier loads. The Lewismen of this period had no desire for women who were tall and slender. Strong, sturdy, broad-backed women who could also help to push the boats up the beaches were appreciated.

When carrying the wet, heavy seaweed, sheep skins were worn under the creels to keep the bearers dry. This work was sheer slave labour, hard on man and beast. When barrows came into use, this made life much easier.

Seaweed manure went out of fashion long ago, and hardly anyone keeps a cow nowadays. Today, the crofter usually buys artificial manure from a general store.

To a race of people who, before the introduction of the potato, had to depend on the uncertain produce of their small rigs for most of their food, the preparation of meal was of the utmost importance. When meal was needed urgently, an ancient method of producing meal called *gradanadh* was employed. (33) This old Celtic custom, as its name implies, was a quick way of converting grain into meal, and was still practised in Lewis well into the nineteenth century.

The process was recorded as follows:

> A woman sitting down takes a handful of corn holding it by the stalks in her left hand, and then sets fire to the ears, which are presently in a flame. She has a stick in her right hand which she manages very dexterously beating off the grain at the very instant when the husk is quite burnt: for if she miss of that, she must use the kiln, but experience has taught them this art to perfection. The corn may be so dressed, winnowed, ground and baked within an hour after reaping from the ground. (34)

The speed with which the corn was burnt in the woman's hand was controlled by the way she held it. To burn quickly, the ears were pointed downwards: to burn them slowly, they were held horizontally.

This *graddan* meal, although somewhat discoloured, was not unpleasant to taste, and was considered to be very nutritious. The bread made from it had a singed flavour, which was much appreciated at one time.

Small amounts of grain were also pot-dried, or, in some cases, dried on the hot, clean hearth, the fire being temporarily transferred elsewhere. The dried corn could then be ground in a quern or handmill.

To separate the grain from the stalks, several methods of threshing were employed. For oats, a *maide-frasaidh,* notched stick, about two feet in length was often used where only small quantities were required, but for larger amounts, the flail was the proper implement.

The flail consisted of two parts, a six foot wooden staff attached by a sheepskin thong to a four foot *buailtean,* swiple of wood, thick tarry cable, or dried tangle. The thong which tied the handle to the swiple, was held in place by being looped round the notched end of the staff and through a hole in the end of the wooden swiple, or round the end of the cable or tangle. (35)

The wooden swiple was generally reserved for the barley, although it could be used for the oats as well.

To thresh corn speedily and efficiently, equal numbers of sheaves were laid on the barn floor in such a way that the ears intermingled. A great deal of concentration was required on the part of the operator, as a moment's inattention, leading to a loss of rhythm, was promptly repaid by a sound whack on the back of the head from the swiple.

The most disliked method of separating the grain from the stalks was done by rubbing successive quantities of barley between one's feet. This *suathadh* was detested by the young folk who usually performed the task. The performer stood barefoot on the band of the barley sheaf (never oats), and having gingerly inserted a foot under some ears, rubbed these backwards and forwards over and under the arches of his feet, until all the grain was removed. The bare stalks were then bent backwards out of the way, and the same process was repeated until the whole sheaf had been cleared of its grain. By the time a dozen sheaves had received this treatment, the thresher's skin and temper were often the worse of wear. In some districts, the separation of the grain from the stalks was performed by burning the ears in tubs. (36)

About the turn of the century, the introduction of the hand-operated threshing-mill completed the job in a fraction of the time. It also provided a social occasion when many volunteers gathered to share the work.

Winnowing, the separation of the chaff from the grain, was often carried out in the open air. A dry day with a fair breeze was required to complete the job successfully.

Most houses had a barn at the back, with the intervening wall common to both buildings. The communicating door was usually opposite the front door of the house. A three foot square *toll-fhasgaidh,* winnowing hole, was made in the back wall of the barn, in direct line with the two doors, so that when all three were open, there was a through draught. Normally the winnowing hole was kept closed with turf.

On the chosen day, the grain to be cleaned was heaped on a piece of canvas, about a sackful at a time. If the wind was not blowing from the right direction, a door or something similar was placed on the leeward side of the hole, to funnel the breeze into the opening to provide the necessary through draught.

The *criathran,* sieves used, were made by forming a circle of thin wood and boring holes in the sides with a red-hot iron. A piece of sheep-skin was stretched across the bottom and attached by thongs to the holes in the sides. Fine holes were then burnt in the skin to allow impurities to filter through. These sieves were usually about two feet in diameter and four inches deep.

To winnow the grain, the sieve was half-filled, and shaken vigorously with a circular motion. Coarse impurities and chaff then came to the surface, and could be partly removed by hand. When the operator thought fit, the sieve was gently emptied on to the floor, and the wind carried the chaff away from the grain. The same method was used outside, where the operation was more effective.

One of the earliest methods of grinding corn was by means of a *brà,* quern. There were various types, like the saddle and trough querns. However, the most popular was the ordinary quern which consisted of two round flat stones of Lewisian gneiss, about two feet in diameter, laid horizontally on top of each other, the top stone being slightly smaller than the bottom one. In the centre of the top stone was a hole into which the grain was poured. A shallow hole was also bored near the edge of this stone where a *sgonnan,* wooden handle was inserted to rotate it. The upper stone could also be adjusted by means of an *aotroman,* wedge, to grind fine or coarse meal.

An early traveller to the Highlands described the operation of the quern as follows: "Two women sit down on the ground having the quern between them, the one feeds it, while the other turns it round, singing some Celtic song all the time."

In the home, the quern was kept in the porch, and was placed on a sheep-skin, to keep the meal clean when it emerged round the edges of the stones. The housewife ground a day's supply at a time, except on a Saturday, when a double amount was ground and baked for the Sabbath.

From as early as the reign of Alexander III, all those who held land and owned a mill, were against the use of querns, as this deprived them of a certain amount of revenue. An Act passed in 1248 stated:

> No man shall presume to grind quheit, maisloch or rye, with hand mylnes except he be compellit by storm, and be on lack of mylnes quhilk should grinde the samen, and in this case if a man grindes at hand mylnes, he shall give the thretieth measure as multur' and gif anyman contraveins this prohibition, he shall tyne his hand mylnes perpetually.

At one time, every village had its own *muilean-toin-ri làr,* a mill with a horizontal water-wheel. It was really an adaptation of the quern, with the basic principle of two horizontal stones, one rotating, being the same.

Place names like *Loch na Muilne,* Mill Loch, and *Allt na Muilne,* Mill Burn, commemorate these old mills, whose ruins can still be seen. Some of the streams operated as many as five mills, which were well-spaced out, except where there was a steep slope where the burn flowed rapidly, and in this case, the mills were fairly close together.

In 1833, the Rev. Robert Finlayson, the minister of Lochs, describing these mills in the New Statistical Account, wrote:

> The mills in Lewis are probably the greatest curiosity a stranger can meet with on the Island. There is scarcely a stream along the coast, on any part of the Island, on which a mill is not to be seen. These mills are of very small size, and of very simple construction. The water passes through their middle, where the wheel,—a solid piece of wood generally eighteen inches in diameter,—stands perpendicularly. A bar of iron runs through the centre of this wheel. This bar of iron or axle rests on a piece of steel, which is fixed on a plank, the one end of which is fixed in the mill wall, the other in the end of a piece of plank, which stands at right angles with the plank on which the wheel rests. The upper end of the axle fits into a cross-bar of iron, which is fitted into the upper millstone, the axle passing

through the centre of the lower millstone, which is rested upon wooden beams or long stones. There is a purchase upon the end of the said perpendicular beam or plank, by which the upper millstone can be raised or lowered. There are nine pieces of board, eight inches broad, and a foot and a half long, fixed in the wheel, parallel and at equal distances from each other, upon which the water is brought to bear; which, with a few sticks for roof, and some heather for thatch, constitutes a Lewis mill. (37)

However, there was more to it than that. The grain was suspended over the millstones in a bag, and was allowed to trickle through a hole in the corner into a wooden shoe. As the stone revolved, a projecting stick struck this shoe and tilted its contents into the hole in the upper mill-stone, the shoe being refilled on the next revolution of the stone. Like the quern, the meal emerged from the edges of the stones and could be ground to the desired grade. (38)

To cut these stones from Lewisian gneiss, a tremendous amount of work and skill was involved, a skill many Lewismen carried with them across the Atlantic, especially to the settlements around Sherbrooke and Lake Megantic in Quebec. (39)

District water-mills eventually replaced these old mills, although an example can still be seen in Shawbost, thanks to the efforts of the Headmaster, staff and pupils of the local school who have renovated the mill there.

These new district mills were opposed by the ordinary tenants, not only in Lewis, but elsewhere in the Highlands and Islands, who were quite content with their querns and small mills. Under a system of servitude called thirlage, the people were forced to grind their grain at one particular mill in their district, an unwanted and arbitrary privilege, which cost them mill dues or multures. If the tenant did not bring his grain to the mill he was thirled to, he had to pay 'dry' multure, in money or in kind. (40)

These large modern district mills were usually owned by tacksmen, and provided them with a fairly substantial revenue. Apart from multures, the tenants had to keep the mill, the mill lade, and the mill dam in order at their own expense.

The multures varied from mill to mill, from as much as a twelfth to a thirtieth of the grain milled. The measure for this purpose was a vessel called a *lipinn*, lippy, which could hold a quarter-peck.

In order to force the people to use their mills, the factor and the tacksmen attempted to destroy all the querns, but some managed to survive. The Laxay tacksman is said to have collected all the querns he could find on his tack and dumped them in Loch Erisort at a place still called *Poll nam Brà*, Quern Pool. (41)

The district mills were located at Stornoway, Aignish, Gress, Dell, Barvas and Callanish. Mrs Stewart Mackenzie, commenting on the erection of such a mill in Stornoway in 1816, on the site of one of the older type, stated that before that time, the Island mills were "wretched hovels, hardly above ground, and only capable of being worked when the burns were full in Autumn and Winter", (42) which was the time when the crofters needed them.

Each mill owner was naturally very jealous of his right of thirlage and looked with disfavour on anyone who interfered with this profitable privilege. Lewis Maciver, the arrogant Gress tacksman, was warned in

October 1820, that he must not interfere with the multure or thirlage of the Stornoway mill. (43)

In 1833, the Rev. William Macrae, the Barvas minister cum tacksman, complained of his thirlage being restricted to Upper and Lower Barvas. (44)

Thirlage caused the people much suffering and hardship, for many of the villages were miles, and roadless miles in most cases, from the prescribed mill.

The Tolsta tenants were thirled to the Gress mill, five miles over a roadless moor, and even longer if they went by sea. They had to pay the rapacious Lewis Maciver £6.10/- a year in dry multures as they preferred to grind their grain at their own mills.

The townships of Coll, Back and Vatisker were also thirled to Gress, and their inhabitants were charged every twelfth peck, besides mill services such as thatching the mill and repairing the dam and the lade. (45) The Stornoway Mill only claimed every sixteenth peck.

The Uig people suffered badly, having to take their grain to the Callanish Mill. Some had to travel twenty miles, or face the dangerous crossing of Loch Roag. This long and difficult journey entailed many days away from home, as well as much unnecessary discomfort. It was not surprising that many tenants preferred to pay the dry multures.

Improved transport and the use of money led to the purchase of imported oatmeal, barley meal and flour, so that by 1920, there were only two mills still in existence on the Island.

ANIMAL HUSBANDRY

Lewis, with its extensive moorland pastures, is ideal for rearing live-stock. It was natural therefore, that animals, especially cattle, should play a very important part in the economy of the Island and that the most important dates in the crofting calendar, *Bealltuinn,* Beltane, *Lunasdal,* the 1st of August and *Samhuin,* Martinmas, the 1st of November, should have a close connection with animals.

On *Bealltuinn,* or *La Buidhe Bealltuinn,* as it was usually called (13th of May according to our present calendar), all animals, except those tethered, had to be removed from the arable land and sent to their summer pastures beyond the *Garadh Dubh,* Black Dyke. It was said that at one time there were two of these, one on the east coast and one on the west. The former stretched from Dun Othail to Loch Erisort, and the latter from Ness to Garynahine. (1) This movement of stock was known as *Glanadh a' bhaile,* the Cleansing of the village.

Lunasdal was the day the animals were returned from their distant summer pastures to the village *cùl,* hinter-land, between the *Garadh Dubh* and the dykes protecting the arable land, and after the harvest was gathered in, they were allowed to roam at will over the crofts.

Samhuin, Martinmas, apart from being the time when the rents had to be paid, was also the time when young animals were given new names. An odd couplet says:

> *"La Samhna theirear gamhna ris na laoigh:*
> *La ' Illeain theirear aighean riu na dheidh."*

"At Hallowe'en, the calves are called stirks:
At St John's Day, the stirks are called queys." (2)

The *searrach,* foal, now became a *loth* or *lothag,* colt or filly; the *uan,* lamb, became an *othaisg,* wedder or ewe.

The Island stock were small in size, due to a variety of reasons, such as the rough pastures, the lack of winter feeding and, more particularly, the absence of selective breeding. In fact, far too many animals were reared, numbers being more important than quality.

In 1796, the stock in the four parishes was as follows:

Parish	Families	Cattle	Sheep	Horses	Goats
STORNOWAY					
(excluding town)	287	2361	2576	556	—
BARVAS	439	2670	3392	1050	—
LOCHS	366	2488	4000	348	—
UIG	387	2921	5044	682	304
	1479	10440	15012	2636	304

The average number of animals per family was:

	Cattle	Sheep	Horses	Goats	
STORNOWAY	8	9	2	—	
BARVAS	9	8	2	—	
LOCHS	7	11	1	—	
UIG	8	13	2	1	(3)

Each tenant was annually soumed or told by the village constable the number of animals he was allowed to send to the common pastures. If a person was short of one species of animal, he could if he wished, make up his soum with numbers from other species.

This equalising of stock was called *'colpachadh'*, and varied from island to island, but usually was balanced out as follows:

One horse was equivalent to 8 foals;
> or 4 one year old fillies;
> or 2 two year old fillies;
> or 1 three year old and 1 year old filly;
> or 2 cows;
> or 8 calves;
> or 4 stirks;
> or 2 year old queys;
> or 1 three year old quey and 1 year old stirk;
> or 8 sheep;
> or 12 hoggs;
> or 16 lambs.

Two sheep were equivalent to 3 year old hoggs;
> or 1 two year old hogg. (4)

At one time, the soum in Lewis was one milch cow and her calf till it was a year old, or ten sheep of the old breed, or five Cheviot, or seven black-faced sheep, or half a horse, for every £1 of rent. (5) Before the Island was purchased by Sir James Matheson, some tenants thought that their soum was one milch cow and her calf, and ten sheep, not *or* ten sheep.

Of all the stock kept, cattle were by far the most important, for it was from the proceeds of their sale that the rents were paid, and essential articles like shoes, salt, iron utensils, and, later on, clothing and groceries bought. They also provided a large part of the people's diet in milk, butter and cheese. (6)

These cattle were big-horned, long-haired, active and hardy, (7) weighing from two to four cwts., as opposed to the five or six cwts. of the mainland cattle.

The ideal cow for at least one Lewis woman was one that was small, light-footed on the moors, a good milker, and with the ability to run swiftly when chased by the farmer's dogs. (8)

In winter, when there was little shelter or food to be found, the milch cows and their calves were brought into the houses where they often shared their owners' food. The rest of the stock roamed outside, surviving as best they could on the scant herbage or the seaweed that was available at ebb-tide. It was estimated that the lack of winter fodder caused animal mortality to rise as high as one in every five.

Another result of this deprivation, was that milk became scarce in Winter and Spring and many cows only calved every second year, while heifers did not have their first calf until they were about five years old.

The milk produced on the summer pastures was very rich, small in quantity perhaps, but much superior in quality to that of clover-fed cows. The best Highland cows only gave six pints of milk a day in the early nineteenth century, but the milk was like cream. (9) Cows with the most slender tails were believed to be the best milkers.

The bulls were wintered separately from the cows in specially constructed bull-parks, or on off-shore islands as in Loch Roag. It would have been disastrous to have had Spring calving when cows were at their weakest, for even if they survived the calving, they might have had insufficient milk to feed their offspring.

The people knew the gestation period of their stock quite well, for even the children used to recite the following:

Tri miosan an cù;	Three months for a dog;
Tri miosan an cat;	Three months for a cat;
Tri raidhean a' bhó;	Thrice three months for a cow;
'S bliadhna mhór air an each;	And a whole year for a horse;

In the latter half of the nineteenth century, cattle-housing became common and fewer animals were kept. Besides sharing the families' warmth and comfort, there was now more food for them. The animals were fed on straw, boiled chaff (whose malty smell permeated everywhere), an occasional sheaf of unthreshed corn, potato peelings, herring bones and dried cod bones. Crabs were also greatly appreciated as was the water from boiled fish which all contributed to their nutrition.

Cattle, owing to their quarrelsome nature (especially if Ayrshire crosses, with their long, sharp horns), were tethered in the byre, either to upright posts, or to horizontal stones placed for this purpose in rectangular holes in the walls.

Cows which were restless at milking time, had their hind legs bound with a *buarach,* spancel, made of bent grass, straw, hair or rope, tied in a figure eight. If this was not a sufficient deterrent, a fore-leg was bent and fastened to their necks.

Each cow had its own name, such as *Màgan,* Mary, *Blàrach,* Dun one, *Sealbhach,* Fruitful one. Even the mythical sea-cows were given names.

In Spring, when the animals which had survived the winter emerged from the byres, they were usually in an emaciated condition, with manure-caked flanks, and many had to be lifted to their feet before they could stagger outside.

By the time the animals started to regain their strength on the inner pastures near the villages, the moors were drying and the time for clearing the arable land was drawing near. At this time, a *fear-coimhead,* watchman, was appointed by each township to protect the growing crops from hungry· animals. The watchman was paid partly in cash and partly in kind, and at one time was given the outermost rig in the township to ensure his diligence.

The annual migration of the animals to the moors at this time of the year was of vital importance to both man and beast. Not only did the cattle and sheep set out for the moors, but in Uig, Lochs and parts of Ness, where there was little depth of peat, the horses went also. (10)

The bothies which housed the *banachagan,* dairy-maids out in the wilds for six to twelve weeks were called shielings, and they were of three types. The oldest kind was conical in shape and built completely of stone covered with turf. Examples of these can still be seen on the Uig moors.

These beehive structures had two very low and narrow doors, the wind-ward one being always kept closed with turf. There were no windows, but there was a hole at the apex of the roof to allow the smoke out, and a little light in. The fireplace was between the two doors, and opposite it was a low bed on a shelf of stone or turf. In the older shielings, this was built into the wall. Rectangular recesses in the walls provided cupboard space.

The ordinary type of shieling was an adaptation of the beehive type. It was oval in shape and about ten feet in length with two low gables. Between the gables a ridge-pole was stretched with pieces of wood reaching the wall-tops to form a foundation for the turf-slabbed roof. The doors were almost wall high and fairly wide, and the interior was similar to the beehive type.

The most modern shieling was built like one of the old 'black' houses, and could shelter milch cows and calves on cold nights. This *tigh Earraich*, Spring dwelling, made it possible for stock to be sent to the moors earlier than usual, particularly when fodder was scarce after a bad winter. It was also much more comfortable than an ordinary shieling. It had only one wooden door, and there were windows on the wall-tops. The beds were sometimes built partly into the end walls which were thickened to admit them. The stone bed platform was raised about three feet from the clay floor and had a stone coping in front of it to keep the bedding from falling out. In the walls were large recesses 'milk-presses' where milk was stored. Good examples of these shielings can still be seen at Dibiodal near Cellar Head.

On the day of the journey to the shieling, the villagers rose earlier than usual. This was perhaps the happiest day of the year, a day of hope, a day of youthful memories.

Once released from their byres, the older cattle, sensing all the excitement, set off for their summer pastures without any coaxing, closely followed by the younger beasts. The herds and their helpers followed closely behind, loaded with all the necessities for the moorland sojourn. There was much laughter, and at one time, a hymn of some kind (now forgotten) used to be sung.

When the helpers returned to the village in the evening, only the milkmaids, the youngsters, and the old women remained behind.

Shieling days passed quickly, with cows to milk, milk to set, cheese and butter to be made, herding to be done, bogged animals to be dragged to safety, and for those who lived nearby, a daily trip home with craggans or pails filled with fresh milk. When shielings were a good distance from home, weekly visits were the rule, to collect provisions and see the family.

Oidhche na h-Iomraich, the Night of the Flitting, at the end of July, came all too quickly. Crowds came from the villages to help with the morning's transportation of goods and chattels back home, and there was little sleep for anyone that night, with feasting and ceilidhing.

After the morning's milking, everything was packed into loads, the turf roof removed to prevent it from damaging the timber during winter storms, and the grass and heather bedding carried outside and burnt. The old cows recognised this as the signal to start the homeward trek, and off they set as eagerly as they had set out in early May.

It was a day of sadness for the people as they trudged behind their stock, their backs to their summer homes which had been given such beautiful names as *Airigh na Gaoithe,* Windy Shieling, *Airigh Fad As,* Far-Away-Shieling, and *Airigh na h-Aon Oidhche,* The One Night Shieling. The Great War of 1914-18 practically destroyed this long established custom.

The first Cattle Show ever to be held in the Western Isles took place at Tarbert, Harris, in October 1820, and prizes were presented by the Highland Society of Scotland. The judges were James Alexander Stewart Mackenzie of

Seaforth; Major Forbes Mackenzie, Chamberlain of Lewis; Archibald Stewart, tacksman of Valamos; Lewis Maciver, tacksman of Gress; Donald Stewart, the Harris factor; Murdo MacLellan, tacksman of Scalpay, Harris, and various other Harris tacksmen. (11)

The first prize of ten guineas went to the factor of Harris, the second of seven guineas to the tacksman of Valamos, and the third of five guineas to Donald Macaulay, the tacksman of Crossbost. (12)

Although the tacksmen had introduced larger animals into the Island, up until about 1833, there was little or no improvement in the crofters' cattle. Large animals of the farm breeds were unsuitable for the boggy moors. In the same year it was suggested to Seaforth by his factor that ten bulls should be bought in Skye, at £7-£10 per head, and sold to the Uig crofters who could winter them on Isle Vacasay. The existing stock of bulls in Uig were a poor lot, those in Carloway were even worse, while those between Galson and the Butt were by far the worst of the lot. (13)

From the time the Congested Districts Board came into being in 1897, there was a marked improvement in the Lewis cattle. Ayrshire and Shorthorn bulls were imported and crossed with the Highland cows until finally, Highland cows were rarely to be seen at all, although they lingered on for some time in Uig.

The Annual Stornoway Tryst which attracted crowds of drovers from the mainland, was formerly held at Loch Airigh na Lic', but later the site was moved to *Beinn na Drobha*, Market Hill, where hundreds of cattle were sold for shipment to southern markets. On one occasion, nine drovers arrived with £4,000 between them to buy cattle at this July Trust. (14) Lord Seaforth and his tacksmen also engaged in this lucrative trade.

The cattle which Seaforth bought were called 'Lewisers' by the people at Brahan, and they were shipped to Poolewe before being driven to market at Beauly, Doune, Dumbarton or Falkirk. At one time, cattle were ferried in eight-oared boats from Loch Erisort to Poolewe, but this was eventually abandoned owing to the periodic foundering of some of the vessels.

The importance of the cattle trade to the crofters may be gauged from the money paid to them for cattle sent to Brahan:

1816	£704. 13. 6.
1818	£703. 15. 0.
1819	£1,239. 8. 6. (15)

Tryst Day was very important to crofter, tacksman and factor, as all were deeply concerned about the rents. As the number of stock each tenant possessed was well known to the ground officers, it was very difficult, indeed almost impossible for an animal to be sold privately. Therefore, when a crofter sold a beast, he had to hand over his rent money and arrears almost immediately, and often returned home without a penny to show.

The small Hebridean sheep, similar to the type once found in Shetland and Iceland, were of a species found all over Western Europe. These animals were extremely wild, and did not bunch as sheep normally do on the approach of man or dog. Lewis sheep still have this tendency, as they have demonstrated at cattle shows, much to the annoyance of visiting sheep-dog trialists and the amusement of the spectators.

At one time, each family kept a few sheep to supply wool for clothing, mutton, and occasionally cheese. (16)

In comparison with modern breeds, the old Hebridean sheep was a somewhat useless animal with white legs and face, a short tail, and wool which varied in colour from bluish grey to brown or deep russet. Sometimes all these colours were to be found in the fleece of the same animal. Sheep reared in favourable pastures had a fine, short wool with a softness comparable to that of Shetland sheep, while in other parts of the same island, the wool could be stunted and coarse. It was a puny animal with an average weight of 15 to 20 lb. and often had four to six horns, (17) with a long tuft of wool called a *sguman* which came down over its face. These sheep were free from the diseases later introduced by the *caoraich mhora,* big sheep, the black-faced and the cheviots. Their wool was plucked, not shorn, probably because shears were expensive to buy. This operation was not as painful as it might seem, as there was a new growth of wool under the fleece from which it could be easily separated.

After parting with its fleece, the sheep was given a spank on its flanks with the admonition, *"Falbh lom agus thig molach"*, "Go away bare and return woolly".

It was Seaforth and the tacksmen who introduced the black-faced or Linton breed of sheep into the Island. The Barvas minister had some as early as 1796, (18) and about 1802, the first sheep farm was established at Valamos in Park, by a party, one of whom was a Mr Mackinnon from Corry in Skye. It is probable that eviction in Park began about this time.

The introduction of the larger breeds eventually helped the crofters, as rams were encouraged to 'stray' at tupping time among the native flocks. By the end of the nineteenth century, the old breed was extinct, although an odd throwback, jocularly referred to as *"Sassenachs"* occasionally appeared. Through time, a distinctive type of sheep evolved with chiefly black-faced characteristics, but lighter in body-weight, with longer legs, ideal for boggy moorlands.

Both the black-faced and cheviot sheep were about three times as heavy and three times as valuable as the native breed. From the former, eight to ten fleeces were required to make the 24 pound stone, while twenty to thirty fleeces were required from the native breed to produce the same weight. (19)

Each tenant had his own special marks to distinguish his sheep, and lambs were earmarked soon after birth. These marks were once considered to be of such importance that no poor man dared boil a sheep's head until four or five days after it had been killed. This rule allowed anyone who had lost a sheep to try and trace it and perhaps pinpoint the guilty party if it had been stolen.

These earmarks also helped to trace sheep that had strayed to other township pastures.

The original *Na Naoidh Deargadh,* Nine Ear Marks for Lewis were:

1. Toll—a hole made in the centre of the ear.
2. Barr—the tip of the ear cut off.
3. Ribeadh or Sgoltadh—a downward slit from the tip of the ear.
4. Sulag—the tip cut off to form the letter 'V'.
5. Géugan—a triangular piece taken from the tip of the ear.
6. Béum—a semi-circular piece taken from the side of the ear.
7. Gearradh-Craucain—a slit taken diagonally upwards at the side of the ear.
8. Gearradh—a slit made at the side across the ear.
9. Slisinn—a slice taken from the side of the ear. (20)

By a combination of these earmarks, and the introduction of new ones, a great variety of marks were formed, making duplication almost impossible.

People closely related, tended to have similar marks. Sons, once they had established their own stock, only slightly altered their fathers marks, and it was considered a good omen for the future happiness of newly-weds if the earmarks on the sheep given to the bride for her dowry were similar to her husband's and could be easily altered to his.

Another method of distinguishing stock was by branding. Seaforth's animals had the letter 'S' branded on their noses. The tacksmen branded their initials on one horn and those of their tacks on the other, an idea later copied by the crofters, who had their initials branded on one horn and those of the village and their croft number on the other.

Before keel-marking was introduced (roughly marking with red dye), tar was used to mark sheep with the initials of the tack or owner. Some villages had their own special *tearr-baile,* tar marks, so that each township could segregate their sheep at fank-time (folding-time) (21).

Before the introduction of dipping, the sheep were smeared with a mixture of butter and tar before the tupping season began. 30 lbs. of butter and 12 Scots pints of tar being required to treat 100 sheep.

To apply the mixture to the animal, its wool was parted from head to tail and the mixture applied thinly on the bare skin. This operation was repeated over and over again until the whole body had been completely covered.

As the period of gestation for sheep is twenty-one weeks, tupping did not begin till around the 20th of November, to ensure that lambing did not start until mid-April, when there was a certain amount of growth.

Early in June, at the first shearing fank for hoggs and yeld ewes, the male lambs, other than those set aside to be tups, were castrated. This operation was administered by means of a sharp knife and one's teeth. A tobacco spit rubbed into the wound acted as an antiseptic. The other ewes were shorn early in July.

About the middle of August, the lambs were weaned and youngsters kept them closely herded in small groups on the *cùl,* hinterland. Several weeks later they were released among the flocks. During this period, a few lambs were tethered on crofts, singly, or in pairs.

In the winter, lambs were housed and hand-fed on small, unthreshed oats and potatoes. After individual crofts were fenced, they grazed there all day, but were put out to the *cùl* for the night.

Sheep farming caused untold misery in Lewis as it did elsewhere. In 1818, the proprietor, Mr Stewart Mackenzie, stated that if it became necessary for him to dispossess the overgrown population which was daily becoming more burdensome to pave the way for mutton in lieu of man, more than 5,000 souls might be spared from Lewis to render the change complete. (22) The numbers appalled him.

By this time, sheep farming had become a good source of income, and as the business took a firm hold in Uig and Lochs, a certain amount of stock was exported to the mainland. Sheep were also sold to local fishermen as well as the many vessels calling at Stornoway, including ships of the Hudson Bay Company.

Lewis horses were also exported to the mainland as well as to some of the other Hebridean islands such as the Uists, where the hardships of the kelp industry led to a wastage of animals.

Captain Burt, writing from Inverness between 1787 and 1790, remarked that the further north he went, horses and carts grew smaller in size. If he had gone to Lewis he would have found horses even smaller and no carts at all.

The Lewis horses were slightly bigger than Shetland ponies, predominantly chestnut in colour, and less stockily built. They were from eleven to twelve hands high, strong, sure-footed, hardy, mettlesome and beautifully symmetrical, exceptionally well-suited for carrying peats, seaweed, and for ploughing.

Mr Stewart Mackenzie was so proud of these horses, that he sent four to King George IV, as an example of the type found on the Island.

Lewis horses had to be strong to survive, for there were no stables provided for them until well on into the nineteenth century, and they had to fend for themselves all year round. In fact, many died of starvation in the Spring when grass was scarce, and it was a common sight to see them trooping down to the shore at ebb-tide in search of seaweed.

Due to this lack of nutrition, they were rough and ragged looking until mid-summer, never groomed and never shod. The crofters did not work their horses until they were about five years old, as they believed this would permanently weaken their backs.

The New Statistical Account of Scotland (Vol VII) states:

> No horse can surpass the native breed in hardy endurance: he will be fat where a larger horse will perish: he may be taken from the moor to trot ten or twelve miles an hour, and turned out to grass again, ungroomed. And he is fit for carrying twelve or thirteen cwts. along the Highland roads. Give him more size by better food, more beauty by attention to the breed, and for all the purposes of the Highland farmer, he will not be surpassed in usefulness by any horse in the world.

These remarks were equally applicable to the Lewis ponies. Unfortunately, the people of Lewis were not as far-sighted as the Shetlanders and allowed their mares to be served by mainland stallions supplied by the Congested Districts Board in an attempt to improve the breed, and as happened to the native sheep and cattle, they were bred out of existence. Few horses are now to be found in Lewis.

At one time, pig keeping was fairly common in Lewis, especially in districts within easy reach of the Gress, Dell and Garrabost mills, where there was always a plentiful supply of pig food. In 1890, a young pig could be bought for only ten shillings.

Goats were also kept at one time, and although *Rathad nan Gobhar,* Goat Track, is found as a place-name in various parts of the Island, goat-keeping seems to have been chiefly confined to Park, in Lochs, and Uig, both mountainous districts.

KELP

The kelp industry in Lewis greatly affected the lives of the Islanders during its short-lived existence from about 1760 until 1836. It gave them the opportunity to earn some money, and at the same time, it provided the proprietor with an unexpected source of revenue. (1)

Kelp-making (the conversion of seaweed into calcined ash for the production of soda and iodine), was introduced into North Uist as early as 1735 by Mr Hugh Macdonald of Baleshare, when he brought a Roderick Macdonald, *Ruairidh na Luathadh,* Roderick of the Ashes, over from Ireland. It was, however, some time after this before the Lewis proprietor realised the wealth that lay on his doorstep. (2)

Between 1764 and 1772, Lewis supplied only about 50 of the 2,000 tons of kelp produced annually in the Western Isles and part of the mainland, but by 1793, kelp manufacture had taken precedence over cattle and horses as the most important trade on the Island. (3)

During the period from 1776 until the end of the Napoleonic Wars, government policy protected the kelp industry from its major rivals barilla and potash. In 1809, kelp sold for as much as £18. 18/- per ton, but the price received for Lewis kelp never exceeded the £11. 11/- it fetched in 1819 and 1820. From about this time, prices started to decline, and the repeal of the Salt and other Acts ruined the industry and caused untold misery in the kelp-producing areas of the Western Isles, parts of the mainland, and the Orkneys.

Between 1812 and 1835, the proprietor of Lewis made an approximate profit of £37,000 from the sale of kelp. His best year, 1820, produced 627 tons and an income of £3,356. In 1829, he suffered a loss of £49.

During the profitable years, the factor was instructed to ensure that the tenants did not encroach on the seaboard reserved for the proprietor's kelp, nor exceed the quantities of seaweed allowed for manure. (4)

The manufacture of kelp was so profitable at this time, that the proprietor encouraged the population to increase, (5) as a larger work force would increase his profits, and they in turn, would earn more money to pay their rents. An indication of this is the fact that after one rent collection, the Lewis factor carried the sum of £10,986 across to the Earl of Seaforth at Brahan Castle. (6)

The people of Lewis did not take kindly to this new industry, so a certain amount of pressure had to be applied to make them undertake this arduous, unhealthy and far from congenial work.

The parish of Uig was the first important kelp-making area, and before long, the inhabitants developed such expertise, that they also kelped in Lochs, Harris, and even in Uist. They were probably forced to do this, as it is recorded that they went to Lochs in 1794, "but not until they were absolutely beat and forced by Mr Gillanders, the factor, who happened to be on his recruiting jaunt at the time." Evidently, they had to choose between kelping and the army.

Since the people of Uig were reluctant to go kelping in Lochs, the proprietor decided that the people of Lochs should manufacture their own kelp. As each family was only to be allocated a small portion of shore for kelping, he considered they would still have ample time to fish. No objections were to be sustained from the people of Lochs or from the people in the parishes of Stornoway and Barvas, where it was also proposed to improve the industry. (7)

The introduction of kelping into Barvas met with much resistance, as the people detested the work. The factor, however, was determined that their antipathy should be overcome, as to bring in kelpers from outside would reduce his profits. (8)

Even in 1821, Barvas was still backward in kelping and Mr Macgregor, the ground officer, felt that they would always remain so, since a West-side man would never do anything right without the threat of some punishment. No one could manage them unless they were kept in awe. (9) One of the reasons why little kelp was manufactured in Barvas was believed to be because the people did not finish their Spring-work until July.

Kelping was arduous work at all stages. It required forty creels of seaweed to make 1 cwt. of kelp, (10) and the labour involved in cutting, drying and burning the seaweed and watching the kiln day and night until the weed was converted into boiling lava was ruinous to the eyesight and quite repugnant. (11)

The cutting and gathering of the seaweed commenced about the 6th of June, and the burning ended about 17th of July, a period of approximately six weeks. During this time, everyone who could carry a creel or help to fill one, was engaged at different times, from the time the ware was cut, until the solid mass was shipped aboard a vessel and weighed. (12)

During the kelp season which occurred in the interval when the old crops were practically exhausted and the new season's supplies were not yet available, food was very scarce. The kelpers were therefore forced to live on shellfish most of the time.

> When the cuddies or other fish happen to be on the coast, these poor men make a kind of livelihood, but when they are not, their case is deplorable, one while at the kelp and immediately thereafter running to the shore for wilks and oysters, or anything else that can be eaten to quiet a hungry stomach. The meagre looks and feeble bodies of the belaboured creatures, without the necessary hours of sleep, and all over in dirty ragged clothes, would melt any but a tyrant into compassion, yet if any quantity of their set complement of kelp remained unfinished, the deficiency must be accumulated to their former debts to make up the pretended loss to the cruel men. (13)

The *min bhàn,* white meal, which was sold to them by their masters (as distinct from their own much darker *graddan* meal), was used sparingly, in case the cost of the meal exceeded the wage received for producing the kelp. If this happened, their earnings, instead of paying part of their rents, only forced them further into debt. (14) Rather than accept this meal, some of the kelpers who worked away from home, returned periodically to have their own grain mealed. (15)

The kelp ware grew in profusion on certain rocky shores, particularly in Uig and Lochs. However, as the demand for the manufactured article increased, large boulders were placed in sandy creeks and bays to encourage more seaweed to grow. (16) The ware was cut biennially or triennially with a sickle, as this encouraged growth. (17)

The ground officers acted as kelp superintendents, their chief concern being the quantity and quality of the manufactured commodity. Little thought was given to the condition of the workers, many of whom lived in rough bothies and on uninhabited islets.

At ebb-tide, the seaweed was cut as quickly as possible and thrown into a circular ring of heather rope around which tangle had been entwined. As the tide flowed, this *ràth,* raft, of seaweed floated and was eventually dragged ashore. (18)

Once landed, the weed was creeled by the people, or carried by horses to a *sgaoilteach,* green sward, where it was spread out to dry until it was ready for burning. (19)

Trenches called kilns were prepared for the burning, and these varied in length from ten to twenty-four feet, with a width of about two and a half feet and a depth of two feet. The sides of these kilns were formed of stones, while the bottom was lined with a layer of turf, peat or peat dust. In some sandy districts, iron plates were placed in the bottom to minimise the amount of impurities likely to mix with the molten kelp. (20)

From the moment the seaweed was set alight by means of burning straw or heather, the kiln needed constant attention, for it required gradual but consistent feeding. It was also important that the ware should not burn too quickly. (21)

When a sufficient quantity was burnt, the kelpers stirred the molten mass with a long wooden pole which was sheathed in iron at the bottom with a strong hook on the end until the matter had acquired the consistency of moist clay. It was then allowed to cool and covered with seaweed and clods of earth to protect it from the weather. (22) When it was cold, it was cut out in chunks ready for shipping.

Specially chartered vessels collected the kelp from the various manufacturing sites, and it was transported to Liverpool, London and various other seaports.

It was not always easy to load a cargo of kelp, especially from open beaches in bad weather. Sometimes boats had to wait several weeks to have their cargo loaded without endangering the lives of the boatmen or damaging the kelp.

According to Mr Macgregor, the Barvas ground officer, in connection with loading shipments from the West shore in 1821:

> Another obstacle, is the want of boats. As the poor people get no fish they cannot keep boats. There is not a merchant in Stornoway that would give them credit for a pint of tar since they got poor, and if I had not given them a piece of shore timber to repair their boats, I could never get the kelp shipped. . . . I was two days and two nights at Shawbost waiting for shipment of the kelp, and the people along with me, without going to a house, and as I didn't allow the people to go to the ebb as usual, for some shellfish or seaweeds, which is their daily subsistence, the last day they were not able to row their boats nor stand; only for some meal and bread the master of the vessel was giving them, I could not get anything done. What could be expected of people in such a state?

The kelp was weighed on board the vessels by the kelp officer, at twenty-two and a half cwts. to the ton, to allow for impurities such as sand and gravel.

The following attested statements seem to infer that these impurities were often deliberately put into the kelp:

We, the after-mentioned overseer and ground officers of Lewis, make oath and declare, that we shall respectively use all diligence in preserving the annual crop of kelp ware within our respective districts from being cut, destroyed or used for any purpose except for kelp, and that we shall, as far as lies in our power, cause the same to be made into kelp in a proper season of the year, in a fair and honest manner, and that we shall not ship any kelp which we may suspect to be adulterated, and lastly, that we shall annually furnish a list of defaulters, if any, to Lord Seaforth or his factor. Donald Macaulay, Overseer, Farquhar Smith, John Mackenzie, John Macleod, William Macdonald. (23)

Not to be outdone by the officers, the tenants also promised that when employed by Lord Seaforth, or those acting for him to manufacture his kelp, they would do so fairly and honestly, and would not knowingly, or intentionally, by themselves, wives, families, or others employed by them, mix or cause to be mixed, with any part of it, stones, sand, gravel, mud, or other impurities, with a view of increasing its weight. Nor would they connive at such improper practices in others. They also swore, that as far as lay in their power, they would carefully make into kelp, in a proper season of the year, the ware on such parts of the shore as might be pointed out to them, respectively, from year to year, by Lord Seaforth or those acting for him. (24)

A strict account of the quantity shipped by each individual was kept, and he was paid from thirty shillings to three guineas a ton, according to the difficulties of its manufacture and shipping.

It was the practice of the Lewis factors to pay the price received for manufacturing the kelp to the ground officers of each of the four parishes, who settled with the tacksmen and the tenants before the rents were due. (25)

From 1822, after the repeal of the Salt Tax, kelp was almost priced out of the market, as it was too bulky to store and other sources of alkali proved to be much cheaper. (26)

Although no longer used for the manufacture of soap, after 1822, kelp continued to be produced on a small scale for the production of iodine, with men receiving 1/6 per day and women and children much less. In 1833, Uig produced 226 tons, and Lochs about 100, for prices ranging from 30/- to 63/-a ton. (27) By 1836, the production of kelp may be said to have ceased in Lewis, although in the summer of 1850, necessity forced twenty-five families round little Loch Roag, Bernera, Callanish and Breasclete to manufacture 26 tons of kelp for which they received £2 per ton. (28)

FISHING

An old Hebridean proverb says *"Dh'iarr am muir a thadhal"*, "The sea wants to be visited", and over the centuries, the Lewis people have obliged, supplementing the meagre produce of the land with the riches of the sea and often paying with their lives for the privilege.

Fishing has always been attractive to the Lewis people for profit and for simple pleasure, and one method of catching fish which was once common was by building yares or stone dykes across a river estuary. The fish that swam in at high tide when the yare was submerged, were left stranded when the tide ebbed, and could be collected without much trouble. This method was popular in Lochs and Uig where the word *cairidh,* yare, is still to be found in place names.

Rock fishing for cuddies, saithe, mackerel and lythe, with rod and line, was very popular during Autumn and early Winter, and even flatfish, haddocks and herring were once caught this way.

In 1549, Dean Munro recorded "ane cove in this country quherin the sea fallis and is twa faddome deepe at the ebb-sea, and four faddome and maire at the full sea. Within this cove ther uses whytteins to be slain with huikes, verey many haddocks, and men with their wands sitting upon the craiges of that cove, and lades and women also." (1)

For a long time, the common implements of fishing were the rod and the *tabh*. The rod was Dean Munro's 'wand', while the *tàbh* was a large pock-net, like an oversized landing-net, minus its handle, bound round a large hoop about six feet in diameter, attached to a long pole. Two men were required to work this implement when fishing for cuddies, one to lower it into the sea, and raise it when necessary, and the other to throw the *scrùm,* bait, consisting of anything from mashed potatoes to parboiled whelks and limpets or pulped crabs.

Once a sufficient number of these small but nutritious fish had gathered above the net for the feast, it was gently raised to the surface and swung ashore, where the *scrùm* thrower was waiting to scoop out the wriggling mass into a sack before repeating the process until a sufficient catch had been made, or the shoal had vanished.

In the estuaries of the Laxdale and Blackwater Rivers on the Tong Sands, a string of blankets, tied end to end, was once used like a salmon net to drive the cuddies ashore. (2) The oil from their livers was used in the crusie lamps, and their sweet flavoured flesh, boiled in water, imparted its taste, providing a delicious meal and a pleasant hot drink.

As well as the rod and line, a *tàbh* or pock with a rectangular mouth, was also used to catch trout in streams at certain seasons of the year.

Salmon were also very plentiful at one time, and these could be slain in the shallows "with treis and bastonnis," as the inhabitants had "na uther craft nor ingyne to slay thame." (3) In the Barvas River alone in 1585, no fewer than 3,000 large salmon were taken. (4) The best salmon rivers were Morsgail,

Barvas, Laxay, Creed, Laxdale and Gress, and in 1765, forty-eight barrels of salmon were exported for £86. 8/-. (5)

For their own needs, the people engaged in small line inshore fishing all the year round, catching flounders, plaice, sole, haddocks, gurnards and dogfish.

The procuring of bait was very much a family concern, as even small children could dig up lugworms with a spade, use a *corran shiol,* eel sickle for sand eels, an *ord-maorach,* a small, broad-bladed chisel-like instrument to loosen a limpet's grip on the rock, or pick cockles, whelks and mussels, while their fathers were resting before returning to sea.

Some villagers, like the people round Loch Erisort, were blessed by having easy access to shell-fish beds, and it was possible to collect sack-loads of mussels at ebb-tide from the mud-flats between Balallan and Shildinish. Some fishermen even crossed the Minch to Lochcarron for mussels which were always a dangerous cargo as they quickly absorbed any water shipped, seriously adding to the weight of the boat. These mussels were stored in shallow creeks or rock-bound pools, easily accessible at any state of the tide. However, bait catching was not without its dangers, and some people had the experience of being cut off by the rising tide and spending almost twelve hours on a cold winter's night crouched on a narrow ledge, while others were never seen again.

Small lines consisted of four "strings", each about twenty-one fathoms long, with davins (foot-lengths of thinner cord, suspended from the latter, at one fathom intervals) to which horse-hair snoods, eighteen inches long were attached, white snoods being preferable where the sea-bottom was sandy. As horse hair was not always legitimately available, many a handsome colt was deprived of its flowing tail without its owner's permission. It is still remembered how some Luerbost youths tried to perform this operation by pulling a horse's tail through an opening at the top of a stable wall, but the animal, instead of co-operating, objected strenuously, and roused the neighbourhood. Each small line was baited into a *scùil,* a kind of oval-shaped basket made of woven willow, or strips of wood. The baited hooks were carefully placed in the narrow end in such a way that there was the minimum danger of them becoming entangled when the lines were being shot. The body of the line was coiled at the wider end, with a few inches of cord from the first string in the line left dangling over its rear-end, to which a string from another *scùil* could be easily attached when the lines were being shot.

The first and last lines were attached by a length of cable to a *cruaidh* or *clach bhàit,* anchor stones, which were marked by buoys made from the skins of dogs, sheep, and latterly, canvas, glass or metal. Very careful cross-bearings were taken of the position of the anchor stones. In former days when coracles were used, the one or two man crew used only one anchor stone, the other end of the fishing line being tied to a thwart.

Long lines, which were coiled in ordinary fish baskets, were made of heavier cord, and their davins were about five feet long and a fathom and a half apart. The boats used in long-line fishing were between eighteen and twenty-four foot keel. Anything longer than this would have been difficult to haul up the beaches. Bait for the long lines was procured by first shooting the small lines and using the haddocks, whitings, eels etc. caught, for bait.

Long lines were left out for forty-eight hours or more, though sometimes, if the weather was favourable and the fishing good, they might be shot twice or thrice before the boat returned to port.

The long-line fisherman had to dispense with the use of buoys when trawling became common, as lines were likely to be lost or stolen. This entailed even more careful cross-bearings for the anchor stones, so that the lines could be found again with a *sgrioban,* grapnel, towed on the end of a long cable.

For heating and cooking purposes, these larger boats carried huge three-legged iron pots in which a fire was kept alight. This fire-pot was placed on a thick layer of peats on the *sorla mhór,* floor-board in the stern, and a smaller pot placed on top of the large one, was used for cooking fish.

These fishermen who operated from open beaches required great strength and skill. Before being launched, a boat had to be pushed (usually stern first) over pieces of *lunnan,* wood, which lay like railway sleepers on the shore. When they reached the sea, the boat was laden with the necessary ballast (sometimes as much as a ton of sand or stones placed amidships) and moved further seawards until she was practically afloat. The four rowers sat themselves on their thwarts while *an gille toisich,* the bowman, held her firmly anchored to the land. On a signal from the skipper, the four oars dipped as one, and the bowman pushed hard until she was well under way. He then jumped over the gunwale as she rose and dipped, ploughing sea-wards to meet the incoming waves.

Beaching a boat was even more hazardous, especially on dark and stormy nights, and it was then, that the skipper, chosen by his crew for his skill and daring, had to show his mettle. The boat was hove-to just short of the breakers, and the sail and mast stowed in the bows. Lines and nets were placed where they would not hinder the crew, unnecessary ballast was dumped overboard, and the remainder moved towards the stern to keep the rudder in the sea.

When the skipper was satisfied everything was in order, he ordered the oarsmen to pull, and the boat's prow was directed towards the land. There she was held while he scanned the on-rushing waves. At the same time, the bowman, the youngest and most agile member of the crew, half-sat on her port gunwhale, one leg dangling over her side, with his right hand firmly gripping her painter as he too faced shorewards.

Gently, the boat was edged nearer the breakers, while the skipper scanned the sea for a *fàth,* calm period between a series of waves. At the appropriate moment, he gave the order to pull, just as the last comber before the fàth was level with the sheet hole. Immediately, the four oars flashed in unison, driving the boat on to the beach, a snatch of song sometimes helping to keep the rhythm. Perfect timing was an essential part of the operation.

This race to the land was always thrilling: one moment perched high on the crest of a wave, the next sliding down a watery slope, only to rise again amidst a welter of foam. Occasionally the order to "back water" was given, as an unusually huge wave was seen to threaten them, the race for the shore being resumed when this danger had passed. All the time, anxious eyes watched from the shore.

Whenever the boat's prow touched the beach, and not a moment sooner, the bowman jumped into the surf and waded ashore with the painter, where willing hands relieved him of his burden and started to haul the boat ashore. The bowman then turned back and joined the rest of the crew, all of whom, with the exception of the skipper, were now in the water, their backs to the boat, pushing her towards dry land, while the skipper with his boathook, kept his charge steady against the driving force of the sea.

Once clear of the most dangerous part of the surf, the men quickly unloaded their gear, while the women unloaded the catch. The bung was removed to drain off any water from the ship before she was hauled up to her resting place, well above high water mark.

The labour involved in this type of fishing took its toll of both boats and men. A boat only lasted about five years on these exposed beaches, and Donald Martin of Back once succinctly described the work entailed as "sufficient to make an old man of one while he is yet young" (6) and there were worse beaches on the Island than the ones at Back and Vatisker. It was no wonder so many men suffered from hernia and rheumatism.

Deep sea commercial fishing for cod and ling was started early in the eighteenth century by the Lewis factor and his tacksmen, many of whom were also merchants. They had the power to compel their tenants to fish for them and provided boats and tackle for the purpose. Any signs of objection led to the instant expulsion of the poor culprit and his family from his land, with little chance of being admitted to any other tack. When a boat was thus provided by these "philanthropists", it remained their property until it had earned its cost.

There was plenty of cod and ling to be caught about two miles off the east coast of Lewis, and Loch Roag was equally productive, so these fishermen had not far to travel.

Cod and ling were gutted before they were given to the curers, and the heads, livers, and the three-quarter section of back-bone extracted, were regarded as the fisherman's, along with any other fish such as skate and dog-fish which were not required for export. The fisherman's share of the catch was also noted, and a settlement was made after deducting the cost of any material which he had received from the fish curer's store or warehouse.

The cod and ling were pickled in large wooden vats before being laid out to dry, usually on a pebbly beach where the air could surround them. They were piled in stacks every night and laid out again daily. When they were completely dry, they were again stacked and covered ready for export in November, to southern markets like Greenock and Liverpool.

Among the listed exports from Lewis in 1765 were:

140 barrels of dog-fish oil, valued at £315. 0. 0.
17,000 barrels of dried ling valued at £637. 10. 0.
50 barrels of dried cod, no value given.
117 barrels of mud cod (barrelled salted cod) no value given.   (7)

At this time, Stornoway had no less than thirty boats, and rural Lewis had seventy, all engaged in the fishing industry. (8) In fact, during this period, Stornoway was the only fishing station in the Minch. (9)

In the Old Statistical Account of 1796, the ministers of the four parishes gave a detailed account of the state of the fishing industry in their respective parishes.

In Stornoway Parish, large quantities of ling and cod were caught with long lines, not only by the town fishermen, but more so by those in the Point and Back districts. The fish was well-cured, and sold for export to the Stornoway merchants at over £14 a ton, while fresh salmon was sold for a penny a pound. (10)

About this time, the factor of Lewis leased the Island from the proprietor and was reputed to be paying £13. a ton to the fishermen on the beach and re-selling to the merchants on the spot for £18.

The Barvas fishermen had not yet reached the stage of using long lines, being content to fish for cod, ling and haddock with a *dorgh,* handline with two large hooks on it. Large quantities of dog-fish were caught, and this was a favourite fish as the oil from its liver yielded an annual average of 2,944 imperial pints which sold to the Stornoway merchants at 6d to 8d a pint. The dog-fish were split open and salted for winter use. At this time, there were forty-two fishing boats from sixteen to eighteen foot keel in the Parish, some with six oars and some with eight. (11) There was no mention of sails during this period.

The Parish of Lochs had excellent fishing banks near at hand and a flourishing cod and ling industry. An average twenty-four tons were sold each year to the Stornoway merchants. Ling, when cured, fetched £15. 10. 0. a ton and cod £10. 0. 0. (12)

The people of Uig who were a good distance from Stornoway did not have the same facilities for disposing of their cured cod and ling, so each year, two or three boats made the long and hazardous journey to Glasgow with cargoes of dry salted fish and other commodities. Fresh cod sold in Uig for two-pence each. (13)

In 1796, the exports from Stornoway included over 549 tons of cod and ling, 4½ barrels of salmon, and 1,379 barrels of train oil manufactured from dog-fish. As a result of this large oil export, the other Hebrideans often referred to the people of Lewis as *Na Bioraich,* Dog-Fish.

Like many of his tacksmen and merchants, Lord Seaforth also advanced his fishermen money for boats, and he was largely responsible for the increased interest in the industry. In spite of all this encouragement however, the catching and curing of fish was comparatively primitive compared with the rest of Scotland, especially the Shetland Islands.

Among the most progressive of the tacksmen-curers at the end of the eighteenth century were John Morison of Shader, Point, Lewis Maciver of Gress, Robert Weir of Calbost and Roderick Nicolson of Stornoway.

Morison was quite determined that the Point fishery would improve, and not only equipped boats for his fishermen, but fished himself, and even engaged a man who had been to the Shetland fisheries (the most famous in Europe at the time) to teach his men the most modern methods of catching and curing fish. He also built curing stations and larger boats and, instead of sending crews to sea with only three sets of lines, having 80 hooks, three fathoms apart, he made them carry six lines apiece with 80 hooks at one and a half fathoms apart. He also suggested to Seaforth that Shetland fishermen should be invited to come and settle in Arnish so that the locals could learn something of their methods.

However, it was not until the duties on salt and barilla were repealed, ruining the kelp industry, that the Lewis people took to commercial fishing in earnest. In former years, their rents had come chiefly from kelp, now the main source of revenue was from fishing. Fish curers then began to engage crews to fish exclusively for them before the season started, with an arrangement to purchase all their fish at a stipulated price. (14) The crews were given a non-returnable cash advance as a bounty, in addition to the price stipulated for the fish. This sum usually ranged from £10-£20, varying from curer to curer. (15)

All the curers, including the proprietor, kept stores in which all kinds of goods were sold, not only for fishing purposes, but also for family use. Naturally, the curers expected the fishermen who were in debt to them, or those whom they had engaged to fish for them, to patronise their stores. This "truck system" was operated mainly by the curers of white fish as opposed to the herring curers who came later.

During the season, the fishermen bought what they required on credit from their employers' stores, where they were charged much higher prices for the credit facility. The prices charged depended on the curer's conscience, and curers' consciences, like their prices, differed greatly. (16)

As new fishing stations were established, new stores opened, and, according to a former Ground Officer, these were in the hands of greedy people who charged too much for their goods, and paid as little as possible for their fish. (17)

The curers were quite pleased to have the fishermen in their debt. As one of them replied when his wife remonstrated with him for having so many fishermen on his books, "If these people were not in my debt, you would not be as well-dressed or as comfortable as you are."

The fishermen themselves seemed ever-ready to get into debt. A favourite maxim of theirs was, *"Tha fear a' crathadh earbaill air an Tiumpan a phaigheas so"*, "There is one shaking his tail off the Tiumpan that will pay for this", forgetting that fishing is a precarious trade, a game of chance.

Mr Stewart Mackenzie of Seaforth, whose revenue from the kelp industry was sadly depleted, became very enthusiastic over the expansion of the fishing industry. He decided that his new policy of "improving" Lewis by evicting the inhabitants of Uig and Lochs to make way for sheep, should be adjusted, to accommodate his schemes for a greater exploitation of the cod and ling industry. With this end in view, he determined that every place suitable for a fishing station should be tenanted, and those evicted given fishing lots.

In 1823, James Adam, the factor, was ordered to lay out new lots for fishermen at Knockaird and Skigersta. (18) By 1827, some of the new houses erected at Cealagmhol, now renamed Port of Ness, were occupied, followed by the settlement of some dozen families at Skigersta. Sadly, seven of their menfolk were drowned shortly after.

There was also a suggestion that the Bernera tenants should be transferred to the Sound of Bernera, but on the factor's advice, this plan was dropped. So too, was the proposed settlement of new tenants on the arable land between Luerbost and Crossbost.

Even the Island of Rona, thirty-eight miles north-east of the Butt, was considered a suitable place to settle a fishing crew of six who were to pay an annual rent of £30, but it was the end of the century before fishermen were stationed there.

All this activity gave a boost to the boat-building industry on the Island. Mr Stewart Mackenzie toyed with the idea of prefabricating boats at Brahan, and shipping them to Lewis. The idea of a railroad for boats across the *Braighe,* Aignish Isthmus, was also considered as being a worth-while project at this time. (19)

Mr Stewart Mackenzie also realised that fishing could never be fully exploited until there were a sufficient number of safe landing places. Apart from Stornoway, and a small pier in Carloway, built by the British Fisheries Society, there was no other place of refuge for stormbound boats travelling between these two points. The Uig fishermen could always find shelter in Loch Roag.

Fog was another hazard the Minch fishermen had to face, and often their only means of determining their position was the fact that they knew heather grew right down to the cliff tops south of Loch Stornoway, while to the north it was grass.

In 1824, a list of places urgently requiring a pier was drafted. On the east coast was Sandwick, which already had a curing house, and a capacious two storey salt-cellar. The lower floor had a room for salt, and another for fish, while the upper floor was fitted out for dried fish. There was also a room for the sale of fishing materials. Sheshader, small as it was, had six fishing boats which had to be hauled up and down a rocky beach. Portnaguran was a busy fishing station, with a fish-curing house of stone and lime and a slated roof. On the west side, there were excellent cod banks, and it was from Loch Roag that the smacks sailed with live cod for the London market. Here again, the only really sheltered place was in the lee of Bernera Beag.

It was also agreed that piers were urgently required at Ness, Shawbost, (which had a natural harbour) and at Valtos in Uig, where there was already a fishing station and a salt cellar. (20)

The estimated cost to erect piers at these places was:—

Sandwick £250	Shader £250	Portnaguran £250	Ness £250
Shawbost £600	Bernera £500	Valtos £150	

A total of £2,250. (21)

However, nothing happened until 1828, when Cealagmhol and Carnish were surveyed along with Portnaguran, Upper Bayble, Calbost, Valtos and Gress, but it was not until 1835 that piers were built at Cealagmhol and Carnish. The Cealagmhol pier cost £1,645. (The Herring Fishery Board provided £1,096 13. 4. and the proprietor £548. 6. 8.). The pier at Carnish cost £1,810. (the Board paying £1,206. 13. 4 and the proprietor £603. 6. 8.). (22)

Although these two piers were small, they were of great benefit to the industry. The new Port of Ness, which previously had only five boats fishing out of it, soon after the completion of the pier had thirty, not all of which belonged to Ness. Perhaps another factor which added to the interest in fishing at this time was the fact that men now had more leisure time owing to the suppression of smuggling which had once been so prevalent. (23)

Although many improvements were later made to the Ness Pier, it was never really satisfactory due to continual silting. One of the safety measures suggested by the fishermen was to have a mooring buoy outside the harbour entrance, as it was felt this would prevent many of the accidents which occurred.

Small fishing stations began to spring up right along the coast wherever there was a pebbly beach where cod and ling could be sun-dried. At these stations, the fishermen lived in bothies, returning to their homes at the weekend.

Lobster fishing was chiefly confined to Loch Roag and the lochs of Park. In 1827, 60,000 lobsters were sent to the London market from Loch Roag alone. (24) The smacks, which took only a fortnight to reach London, were received with open arms.

In 1833, a Mr Robertson who fished for lobsters off Bernera, made a contract with the local fishermen to buy all their lobsters for seven years at 2½d each. He also supplied them with boats, which were to be repaid over three years. (25)

The men of Bernera are still noted lobster-fishers, but today, they have motor-boats, lobster ponds, and air transport to deliver their catch to the market.

Other shell fish were also gathered, and in 1864, a Donald Maciver of Callanish, had charge of the mussel, whelk and oyster beds in Loch Roag, from the Grimersta River to Strome, and between Callanish and Carloway. (26) By 1869, he was joined by Neil Mackay, also of Callanish, paying a rental of £15 for the Uig mussel and whelk beds, but they were forbidden to interfere with the oyster beds. (27) For each oyster found in their possession, they were fined a shilling, and at one time, two Luerbost children were even taken before the Fiscal in Stornoway for picking whelks without permission.

Sir James Matheson had very little interest in fishing, but believed it was the fish-curers who should spend money on harbours, as they benefited most from the industry. (28)

As the fishing industry expanded, and the men became more daring, drowning tragedies occurred almost every year. In 1798, a boat from the Parish of Barvas was noted as being lost with all hands, (29) and in 1835, a Skigersta boat was lost with her crew of seven, to be followed by similar tragedies shortly afterwards. In 1862, five boats from Port of Ness were lost, while in the same storm, two other boats were driven across the Minch and wrecked on the coast of Sutherland near Scourie. One young boy, a Murray, *Mac Iain Ruaidh,* son of red-haired John, from Swainbost, the only casualty, died from exposure and was buried at Scourie.

Between 1862 and 1889, no fewer than seventy fishermen from Ness were drowned, chiefly due to the lack of proper harbour facilities.

In the 1889 disaster, most of the Ness boats made the bay at Port in safety, but as the harbour had become blocked with silt, it was only accessible at half-flood-tide.

> The scene in the bay was something terrible to the anxious friends and relatives who crowded the outlying points and approaches to the harbour knowing full well the danger in which the boats were placed owing to the heavy seas and the cross seas caused by the violence of the gale and the action of the strong tideways which run along the coastline. Hour after hour the little fleet dodged under low sail, but as the tide made, the sea became heavier.
>
> About 5 pm the first boat ran the harbour entrance safely, but the *Look Sharp* with Donald Smith, North Dell, as skipper, was struck and capsized by a heavy sea, all aboard being drowned in full view of their relatives and friends.

Another boat, *The Diligence* from Lionel, with Donald Morrison as skipper, was lost the same afternoon. Three other boats made Stornoway safely, and one landed at Gress. (30)

Broad Bay has also experienced many disasters, especially the fishermen of the Back district, the worst event being in 1895, when nineteen men were drowned.

Point also suffered in February 1836, when two boats were caught in a sudden gale. After striving all afternoon to make their home port, by evening, they were forced to run for the Lochs coast at Cromore. In one of the boats, four young men all died of exposure, but the elderly crew in the other boat quickly recovered from their ordeal. (31)

In 1875, an oar from a Borve boat which had been lost at sea was found washed ashore at Bragar, and a Bernera boat was lost off the Flannans in 1877.

In 1883, the Lewis Chamberlain estimated that between 1849 and 1883, 293 fishermen lost their lives, while the Rev. Malcolm Macritchie of Knock stated that from Knock congregation alone, twenty men had been lost between 1869 and 1883.

The Hebridean herring grounds were exploited by the Spanish and the Dutch long before it dawned on the Scots that other nations were benefiting from their neglect. Hitherto, the Scots had been content to fish for their own subsistence, even though the lochs of the West coast were crammed with shoals of herring at certain well-defined seasons of the year.

It was possibly James V's visit to the Western Isles in search of unruly chiefs, not of fish, that made him realise the wealth that could be derived from the sea. This led James to encourage the Lowland burghs to build fishing vessels called busses, from 10 to 90 tons burden, which were to be crewed by some of the numerous vagabonds who plagued the towns.

The burghs were given the monopoly of the "land fishing" (fishing inside a twenty-mile limit in the Western Isles), but although it was known that the Dutch fished extensively on the West Coast, it was not until 1594, when James VI granted them permission to fish outside a twenty-eight mile limit, that anyone officially took notice of them.

The Islanders themselves, with the possible exception of the few who worked for the Lowland fishermen, took no part in this newly developed industry. They were content to fish for their own subsistence, as had been their wont for centuries. In any case, they had no experience of trading, and their boats and gear, all home-made, were only suitable for inshore fishing in favourable conditions.

Like the rest of the Hebridean chiefs, Macleod of Lewis charged the visiting fishermen exorbitant fees for anchorage and ground leave, and for every 120 barrels (last) of herring caught, as well as claiming Saturday's catch for himself. The ordinary people took their cue from their chiefs, and molested all visiting fishermen, Scots or Dutch, in every way possible.

The Privy Council Records of Scotland make many references to the ill-treatment which the Lowland fishermen had to endure, but make no reference to the Islanders who were driven from the best fishing grounds and maltreated on every possible occasion.

On 26th June 1576, Rory Macleod of Lewis and his son Torquil, had to appear before the Privy Council in Edinburgh, where they had to promise that they and their people would in future refrain from molesting His Majesty's subjects, while engaged in their lawful trade of fishing, "nor raise any towist, extortion or imposition," but to treat them civilly, and when necessary, provide them with food and other necessities at a reasonable price. (32)

This promise was no sooner made, than it was broken, and relations between outsiders and the Islanders steadily deteriorated. Even in 1600, the buss *Jonah* of Leith was pirated by two Skyemen while fishing in Loch Shell. (33)

The many complaints against the people of Lewis gave them a rather unsavoury reputation, especially in Edinburgh, where they were regarded as "professit and avowed enemies to all His Majesties guid subjects, and to all strangers quha aither in their lawful trade of fishing or be contrarious winds are set upon their coist swa that by reason of their barbaritie, the trade of fishing in these pairts is neglected and oursein." (34)

King James VI's decision to hand over Lewis to the Fife Adventurers, and settle the Island with law-abiding Lowlanders, was partly due to the Islanders' constant interference with the fishing industry, so depriving the nation, and especially His Majesty, of much needed revenue, as well as flouting the country's laws.

In the Commission of Justiciary granted to Kenneth Mackenzie, Lord Kintail, in 1610, for the subjugation of the Island (after the Fife Adventurers failed to colonise it), the Lewismen were referred to as "ane infamous byke of lawless and insolent lymmaris—miserable catives who not only quarrelled among themselves, but with any visitor to the Island, and making the herring fishing completely unprofitable.'' (35)

Even the Mackenzie conquest did not alter the Islanders' hostility to outsiders, all of whom were regarded as natural prey, to be abused and spoiled whenever possible, by stealing their food and interfering with their gear. Here again, it is unfortunate that nothing was made public to show how the Islanders were treated by those who were so ready to complain about them. Under the patronage of Charles I, several noblemen formed a company called the Association of the Fishing, to exploit the Hebridean resources, and Lewis was chosen as the centre for this operation.

This project did not please the Earl of Seaforth, the Island's proprietor, who had his own plans for the development of the Island's sea resources, and who had already invited Dutch fishermen to settle in Stornoway. Knowing that the free burghs would object to this breach of their monopoly of the fishing trade, he applied for King Charles's signature to erect the burgh and barony of Stornoway into a Royal Burgh.

This request received the royal assent, providing the royal burghs raised no objection. Needless to say, they did, most vehemently, and, after a considerable delay, Charles decided against granting the promised charter.

After this setback, the King decided to take matters into his own hands and manage the Island fishing himself, at the same time deciding to erect one or more free burghs there. (36) However, this plan had to be discarded owing to opposition from the royal burghs. Nevertheless, he was still determined to have the Island under his special protection and outwith the scope of the Association of the Fishing. For this purpose, he decided to buy the Island from Seaforth, but later discovered this to be unnecessary.

Seaforth was naturally displeased with His Majesty's schemes, and did his best to circumvent them as well as the Association's, a matter which attracted the full support of the Islanders, who had little liking for the Association's plans.

These new invaders were contemptuous of the Lewis people, for, not only did they want to colonise, they also wanted the Lewis children to be taught English or Scots, to be trained especially for fishing, and to be completely dissociated from the mainlanders with no intermarriages. (37) In other words, an island ghetto was to be created.

Retaliation followed. In 1635, three years after its formation, the Association complained that while loch-fishing, they were attacked by natives ''armed with swords, bows and arrows, and other warlike weapons.'' (38)

The people of Lewis, like other Hebrideans, were experienced wreckers, a legitimate and profitable source of income as far as they were concerned, and any vessel found in trouble on their shores, was regarded as a sign of divine favour, which, on occasion, was none the worse for a little help from themselves.

In 1634, the barque *Susanna* with a cargo of wine, was storm-driven to the coast of Lewis. On signalling for help, she was boarded by a crowd of men who agreed to pilot her to safety for a butt of sack or a barrel of raisins. Instead, however, they cut her cable, and when she was driven ashore, she was looted. Her crew were then threatened, that unless they sold their vessel to them for £8, they would be sent ''to the savages that dwell in the mayne.''

There was certainly no love lost between the English fishermen of the Association and the Scots fishermen, and when the *William and John* of Colchester was salvaged by Scots after being driven fully laden on to the rocks near Stornoway, serious rioting broke out.

The vessel's master, who had abandoned her when she went ashore, was furious at the seizure and collected about a hundred of his fellow countrymen to help him recover his ship. They took possession of Stornoway Castle, hoisted the St George's flag, and fired at the vessel without causing any damage. Other Englishmen went rampaging through the town waving guns and pistols, and threatening to kill all Scots there, unless the *William and John* was returned to them. Finally, for the sake of peace, the enraged master had his vessel returned to him. (39)

Meantime, King Charles, realising he would never get any co-operation from the people of Lewis until he made his peace with Seaforth, decided to give him a charter for the Island, reserving the town of Stornoway and its immediate neighbourhood for the use of the Association of the Fishing and erecting the town "in ane free burgh royall for reducing the inhabitants of the said Ile of Lewis to civilitie. And for increase of Policie within the same Ile", a charter which was later confirmed by the Scots Parliament on 17th November 1641.

The outbreak of the Civil War brought the Association's affairs to a standstill, and although later, in Charles II's reign, various attempts were made to establish a prosperous fishing industry in the Western Isles, they had little effect on Lewis, with the exception of the British Fisheries Society, which built a pier in Stornoway.

The Dutch fishermen, whom Seaforth had invited to settle in Stornoway, taught the people a lot about fishing and curing, so that they came to excel all their neighbours in the trade. (40)

By the end of the seventeenth century, the Islanders' former hostility to strangers had practically ceased, visitors were now offered hospitality, (41) and storehouses and fishing boats could be safely left at the end of the season with only one person on guard. (42)

After the Battle of Kilsyth in August 1645, when Montrose routed the Covenanters, so many people from the fishing towns bordering the Firth of Forth perished, that the herring fishing industry was eventually established in the West at places like Campbeltown, Rothesay, Greenock, Port Glasgow and other places in the vicinity of the Clyde. (43) This was to have a marked effect on Lewis, as these ports were nearer the Hebridean fishing grounds. With the Act of Union of 1707, supplies of cured herring and mackerel were sent to the British West Indies and America to feed the slaves. After the American War of Independence in 1776, this trade was limited to the West Indies, until the abolition of slavery in all British territories in 1833.

From 1707, the merchants of Stornoway became more and more ambitious. In 1720, Bailie John Stewart of Inverness bought a cargo of herring from Stornoway, where the factor, Zachary Macaulay (grand-uncle of Lord Macaulay), was his agent. (44) Stewart, however, did not have much trust in the Stornoway merchants. (45)

At one time, all the herring exported from Lewis was transported in hired vessels, but by the 1760's, this had changed, and cargoes were shipped in local vessels. Although the people of Lewis spent a great deal of time cultivating their plots and did not fully exploit the fishing, they were still considered more industrious than other Hebrideans. Indeed, they were regarded as being a "sencible, hardy and laborious race of people." (46)

An extract from the census of Lewis in 1763 reveals the following particulars.

Males		Females	
Men over 60 years	241	Women over 60	348
Men from 16 to 50	1331	Women from 16 to 60	1265
Boys from 7 to 16	1069	Girls from 9 to 16	1207
Boys under 7	714	Girls under 9	763
Total number of males	3355	Total number of females	3583

Of these numbers, 9 men and 12 women were over 80, and 2 women were aged 102 and 105. (47)

Of the males in the 16 to 50 age group, only 500 were employed in fishing for several months of the year, and most of these were from the Parish of Stornoway, which had fifty fishing boats, while the other three parishes combined, only had about the same number. Each boat crew had a minimum of five hands.

Lewis was ideal for the early summer fishing which began in May, concentrated in the lochs on the east coast, from Stornoway Loch to Loch Seaforth. Loch Roag, on the west, was the centre of the winter fishing.

Sometimes the shoals of herring were so dense in these lochs, that they swam ashore, when the people flocked in hordes to collect them. Indeed, it was not the lack of herring or lack of effort on the part of the inhabitants that prevented the expansion of the industry, but the injurious effect of the Salt Laws, which made it difficult to obtain casks and salt when required. It was not until 1764, that the first Stornoway buss sailed to Campbeltown, where herring busses were obliged by law to rendezvous by the 15th of September before proceeding to the winter fishing.

Fishing her way southwards, she had almost a complete cargo on board by the time she reached her destination. (48)

Until 1776, Stornoway was the only fishing station in the North Minch, but in that same year, some English merchants built houses on Isle Martin in Loch Broom and at Lochinver in Sutherlandshire, for smoking herring. Others followed their example, including Roderick Nicolson, a Stornoway tacksman-merchant, who, in partnership with some Londoners, built a fishing station on the Island of Tanera, near Ullapool. (49) He later extended his activities to Thurso and the Orkneys.

Overfishing was one of the reasons why the herring shoals deserted the lochs. They obviously did not like the constant splashing of oars, or perhaps the cutting of seaweed for the kelp industry. (50) Whatever the reason, Loch Roag was the first of the lochs to suffer. Before 1756, herring were abundant there, and sold for only a shilling a cran. (51) By the end of the eighteenth century, the other lochs were affected too, as the herring made for the open sea, where they were not so easily caught by the fishermen with their narrow home-made hempen nets.

The exports during the close of the eighteenth century illustrate this decline. The total number of barrels of cured herring exported in 1791 was 4,592½; 1792—6,163; 1793—10,945; 1794—6,739½; 1795—4,395½; 1796—1,753.

As the herring deserted the sea lochs, they seemed to move eastwards towards the coasts of Caithness where the herring industry started to prosper. From this time, the Dutch trade around the Scottish coasts started to decline, and finally ended with the Napoleonic wars.

At one time, European merchants would not consider herring from any other country if there were Dutch herring in the market for, "There is as much difference to the palate in eating a herring out of a barrell at Amsterdam, and one taken out of a barrell at Greenock, as is between the relish of a piece of pork, part of a swine fed at a meal-mill in Aberdeenshire, and a piece of the like creature fed among the sea wrack and shell-fish on the Coast of Ireland." (52)

Through time, the decline in the Lewis herring industry led to the Islanders following the fish to their new grounds on the East coast of Scotland, a seasonal migration, that gained impetus after the failure of the kelp industry. At first, it was only the menfolk who went, but by the 1860's, the women were also to be found in every fishing port between Peterhead and Lerwick. If this industry on the East Coast had not started at this time, the families of Lewis would have felt the effects of the famine years of 1846-50 far more severely than they did.

In 1860, an Act was passed which made it illegal to catch herring between Cape Wrath and Ardnamurchan Point between the 1st of January and the 20th of May, in order to preserve the fishing stocks there. This 'Close Time' only applied to the West Coast and not to the East. Whoever was responsible for the Act did not realise that during that period, the crofter-fishermen fished for their own subsistence, and the rest of the year, fished commercially. Great hardship and discontent resulted from this Act. A Point fisherman, nicknamed "Close Time" for his strong opposition to the Act, even went to the House of Commons in London to plead for its repeal. This eventually occured in 1865.

During this time, drifters came from all over Scotland, and new herring fishing stations were established at Gress, Portnaguran, Bayble, Holm and Cromore.

The summer fishing usually started about 20th May and lasted until mid-July, when the migration of fisher-folk and boats to Caithness began.

At the beginning of each season, the curers fixed their prices for the fish. In 1867, they were 21/- to 22/- a cran, plus bounty. During that summer season, 1,200 boats went to sea each night, and by June, 25,000 barrels were exported. (53)

From 1873-82, an average of 700 boats fished from the stations in Lewis, the average catch being 40,604 crans, averaging an income of £101,510. (54)

In 1876, the demand for fishing stations was so great owing to the increase in the number of curers, that the stations belonging to the Stornoway Pier and Harbour Commission were rouped. The two nearest the steamer wharf, which were let in 1875 for £6, were rouped for £28. 10/- and £30. The total sum realised from the roup of all the stations was £107, against the previous year's rental of £23, (55) and this year was the poorest in the ten year period mentioned, for in spite of 803 boats being engaged, only 7,434 crans were caught, at an estimated value of £18,585. (56)

In 1876, fishing was poor in Stornoway as well as on the east coast, and the 2,000 men who returned from there in September, had earned much less than in 1875. (57)

Lewis hands on east coast boats received a fixed wage of £7 to £10 for a six-week period, but were given an additional 6d or 1/- for every cran fished.

The fisher-girls' wages were also fixed before they left the Island. Before the start of the fishing, representatives from the various fishcurers either visited the villages themselves to engage crews, or else engaged a former employee to do it for them. Each girl engaged, received an *airleas,* arles as a pledge or engagement token. For a long time it was the ambition of every girl in rural Lewis to be old enough to accept this arles. Some girls did so when only sixteen, but most parents would not allow their daughters to go away until they were over seventeen.

104

There were three girls in each crew, the tallest being the packer, and the other two the gutters. During their first season they were referred to as "coilers", as were the young cooks on the fishing boats.

These fisher-girls worked under most unpleasant conditions. If they were travelling to Lerwick in Shetland, they were packed aboard a steamer to Kyle, crowded aboard a train to Aberdeen, and then crammed aboard a steamer to Lerwick. At some places like Bressay, they lived in huts, but in places like Peterhead, Yarmouth or Lowestoft, they lived in rooms, sleeping three to a bed. Their pay was poor, and even in 1914, they only received 1/- a barrel, with an additional 3d. an hour when barrels required replenishing as the contents became more compact. However, combined with their family's wages, it made a great difference to their standard of living, and helped the girls to stock their bottom drawers.

In 1884, herring began to be sold by auction. Under this system, the hired men were paid one twelfth of the proceeds of the season's catch, and so the take-home pay was not fixed as before, but was dependant on demand, the amount of fish caught, and the weather. The fishermen naturally suffered by this new system.

There was a fair amount of friction between the Gaelic-speaking fishermen of the north and west and the other fishermen when they met in their thousands at the east coast fishing ports, or at the Stornoway fishing, especially on Saturday nights.

On Saturday 27th August 1859, the riot which is still called *Sabaid Mhor Wick*, The Great Wick Fight, broke out. Trouble had been brewing for some time, and the weather being inclement, and the fishing poor, more men than usual were wandering about with little to do. A fight between a Lewis boy and a Wick lad, over an apple—always a fruit of discord—started the trouble. Police apprehended the Lewis youngster, and took him to gaol. On hearing of this, the boy's father, said to have been Alasdair Chaluim Alasdair, a skipper from Lochs, with the aid of his crew, used the mast of his boat to batter down the door of the gaol and release his son. The riots lasted a whole week, with hundreds engaged on each side. Several Highlanders were stabbed and many others hurt. (58)

One young skipper, Alasdair Ruadh, was thrown into Wick Harbour twice in the one day, but he had the satisfaction of taking an opponent with him each time.

Finally, the local authorities called in a detachment of the York Militia, a hundred strong, from Edinburgh, and with their arrival, and the help of the sailors from H.M.S. *Jackal,* and the revenue cutter *Princess Royal,* and perhaps even more so, with the efforts of the Rev. George Mackay of Tongue, Sutherlandshire, peace was restored, just as the fishing season ended. The Highlanders left for their homes believing that there was no justice for them in Wick, and vowing vengeance when they returned next season. (59)

Similar riots occurred in Fraserburgh in 1874 and 1881. In the first instance, the Police Station was wrecked when the police refused the request of some Lewismen to release their friend, a John Macdonald. The 1881 incident happened when a John Macleod, also from Lewis, was being taken into custody for a breach of the peace.

As a result of the Highlands and Islands Works Act in 1891, money was made available to help in the construction and improvement of small harbours, piers and boatslips all over the North of Scotland, and when the Congested Districts Board was established in 1897, the same principle was carried on.

Lewis received its share of the money the Treasury granted to the Fishery Board for the purpose of making loans to the crofting counties. Many new and second-hand boats were bought, and it was the latter that caused so many strange names such as *Tubal Cain, Ichthyology* (called Itchy), *Hephzibah, Notre Dame, Eubulus* and *Jerimiah* to appear in Stornoway. Some of the new ones carried Gaelic names like *Muirneag, Cabar Feidh, Cuidich an Righ,* and *Fionn*.

In 1898, 700 fishing boats, including one steam drifter, fished out of Stornoway during the summer season, and steamers took the herring and the kippers to England, Russia and Germany. The arrears of instalments for boats supplied under the Highlands and Islands Works Act were paid with less urgency than in former years. (60) The boats increased in number and in size, with decked vessels practically ousting the open boats, and some boats were now fitted with steam hauling gear for hauling nets and hoisting sails. (61)

In 1899, for the first time, Lewis fishermen sailed their own boats to Yarmouth and the Shetlands, five to the former, and two to the latter. On the return journey from Lowestoft, the *Morven,* skippered by Alexander Macleod of Knock, covered the five hundred miles to Stornoway in under forty-eight hours.

This unprecedented progress was curtailed when the Fishery Board decided not to make further advances to the fishermen, as so many were in arrears with their repayments.

In 1902, out of the 93 boats purchased with the financial help of the Board, 35 were paid up: 42 had been given up, and 16, though still in debt, were still in the fishermen's possession. In spite of this misfortune, the Lewis fishermen had repaid £82,470 of the amount advanced to them compared with the £59,970 repaid by fishermen from other crofting communities. (62)

Although many of the sailing boats were converted into motor-boats, and steam drifters became very common, as the twentieth century progressed, the herring and white fishing industries gradually declined, chiefly due to illegal trawling by fishermen from mainland ports such as Aberdeen and Fleetwood.

The 1914-18 war dealt a heavy blow to the industry, as many of the enlisted fishermen lost their lives. Continental markets were lost, unemployment and general disillusionment were rife, and people started to emigrate.

The former seasonal occupations had gone forever, mid-May to mid-July, the Stornoway fishing; mid-July to early September, East coast fishing and the Shetland fishing; October to November, East Anglian fishing, and on returning home, cod and ling fishing with the Ness-built *'sgoth',* with occasional incursions at herring fishing. Only a few crews continued to fish from Stornoway.

After the 1939-45 war, the Government once again came to the fishermen's aid through the agency of the White Fish Authority, the Herring Industry Board, and the Highlands and Islands Development Board. Modern boats were supplied by the Outer Isles Fisheries Training Scheme, of which eight of the twelve boats came to Stornoway.

Most catches are now landed at the mainland ports of Lochinver, Ullapool and Mallaig, for easy road transport to the towns and cities of the south. It is doubtful if Stornoway will ever regain its former importance as a fishing port, and education has diverted prospective fishermen to other professions. Perhaps the biggest enemy of the fishing industry in Lewis is Stornoway Castle Technical College, where the navigation course has trained the sons of fishermen to become the masters of some of the largest vessels afloat.

THE CHURCH

Today, it is impossible to ascertain what pre-Christian religion was practised in Lewis, although it is very likely that Druidism played a part at one time. Perhaps if the central pillar of the Callanish Stone Circle could speak (as its neighbour, Clach an Truiseil, is once reputed to have done) our knowledge might be improved. We might also find out why these stones came to be called *Na Fir Bhreige,* The Deceitful Men. Undoubtedly, they are memorials to a race and religion long since forgotten.

At the dawn of history, the people of Lewis would be mostly of Pictish origin, although there would be traces of other races, for the Minch was always a sea route for tribes migrating from the sunny south, and not all would choose to pass the Island by.

It would also be strange if some of the Scots who settled in Dalriada did not make their way north. After all, the southern tip of the Outer Hebrides is not far from Ulster in Ireland.

Although St Columba, who arrived in Iona in 563 A.D., is said to have visited Skye and established two centres, one at Snizort, and one on an island in Portree Bay, there is no evidence he ever crossed to Lewis. There are however, places throughout the Island named in his honour, where his zealous missionaries preached the Gospel.

The two men most closely connected with the introduction of Christianity into Lewis are St Ronan and St *Moluadh,* Mulvay. Ronan had two chapels dedicated to him, one in Eoropie, and the other on the Island of Rona where he is supposedly buried at a spot marked by a three holed stone.

St Mulvay, who died in 722 A.D., had his headquarters in Applecross, *A' Chomhraich,* Sanctuary. His successor, Failbe McGuarie, was unfortunately drowned, along with his twenty-one companions, while crossing the Minch in 737 A.D.

The length of Lewis was often expressed as being from *Tigh nan Cailleachan Dubha an Uig,* House of the Black-robed Women in Uig, to *Tigh Mhaoilruibhe ann a' Nis,* Mulvay's house in Ness. Its breadth could be equally well represented as being from *Pabbay,* Priest's Island in Loch Roag, to *Pabail,* Priest's village, Bayble, in Point. (1) Within this area, there were once thirty-six places of worship, which included those on Rona, Sulisgeir, the Flannans, and the Shiants. Some were probably built before the Norse invasion. Most of the chapels were very small, and those at Gress, Cliff and Gallon Head, were only eighteen feet in length. St Peter's chapel in Eoropie, was sixty-three feet, and St Columba's at the Braighe, was eighty-five feet in length.

The places of worship in Lewis were:

STORNOWAY PARISH: St Columba's at Eye (Braighe), St Columba's at Gearraidh Ghuirm (Upper Coll), St Aula's in Gress, St Michael's at Tolsta, and St Cowstan's at Garrabost.
BARVAS PARISH: St Ronan's in Rona, Tigh Beannachaidh in Sulisgeir,

St Ronan's in Eoropie, St Mulvay's in Eoropie, St Thomas' in Habost, St Peter's in Swainbost, St Clement's in Dell, Holy Cross Church at Galson, St Bridget's at Borve, St Peter's in Shader, St Mary's in Barvas, and St John the Baptist's in Bragar.

UIG PARISH: St Kiaran's in Liamshader, St Michael's in Kirivig, St Macrel's in Kirkibost, St Donnan's and St Michael's in Little Bernera, St Peter's in Pabbay, St Christopher's Chapel in Uig, (2) Tigh Beannachaidh at Gallon Head, a chapel in Valtos, one in Cliff, one in Mealista, Tigh nan Cailleachan Dubha also at Mealista, and St Flannan's on the Flannan Isles.

LOCHS PARISH: St Columba's on the island of that name in Loch Erisort, St Pharaer's in Kaerness, at Swordale on Loch Luerbost, (3) and St Mary's on the Shiant Isles.

All these places of worship were sanctuaries.

The account of King Magnus of Norway's expedition to the Isles in 1098, when fire is said to have burned fiercely over Lewis, gives a good idea of what happened to the old inhabitants and their chapels while under Norse domination. When Christianity was re-established, some time after 1098, the diocese of the Bishop of the Isles was made subordinate to the Archbishop of Trondheim in Norway, to which it was attached until 1380, when the Scots chose their own Bishop of the Isles. (4)

From this time, until Sir Donald Munro visited Lewis in 1549, we are largely ignorant of conditions on the Island.

Of the parish churches, the most important was St Columba's at Eye, near Stornoway, where many of the Macleod chiefs were buried. Among its rectors, were a John McCloid (who was to be succeeded by Sir John Polson, if for any reason he had to vacate office), Sir Magnus Vaus in 1534 and 1536, Sir Donald Monro in 1552, Sir John Finlay and Mr Lachlan McClane in 1559. By 1561, it belonged to the Bishop of the Isles. (5)

There is no record of the parish of Lochs before the Reformation. St Columba's Island contained a chapel and a cemetery, where the dead from distant Park were once taken. The first parish church seems to have been at Swordale, *Cathanais,* Kaerness, on Loch Luerbost, before a new one was built in 1831 at Keose.

The parish church for Uig was at Balnacille, where Ranald Anguson was parson in 1573. Ranald helped to draft a bond between the illiterate Rory Macleod of Lewis and John Campbell, the Bishop of the Isles, relating to a payment of tithes. (6)

St Mary's, at Barvas, was the fourth parish church, and is noted as having two rectors before 1560, Master Mertin McGilmertyne, followed by Master Roderic Farquhar Hectorissone, in 1536.

After the Reformation, Lewis was reduced to two parishes, or two parish churches, one in Stornoway and one in Barvas. The boundary between them ran from Fivig, near Shawbost, to the mouth of the Laxdale River, the northern portion being the Barvas Parish. This division existed until the Seaforth forfeiture of 1722, when the present parishes came into existence.

Sir Patrick McMaster Martin, who was in Barvas in 1566, and Ranald Anguson, of Uig, who was admitted before 1572, have the distinction of being the first post-Reformation preachers in Lewis. (7)

When James VI granted a charter to the Fife Adventurers in 1598, Robert Durie, the minister of Anstruther came with them in order to build a church.

After the colonisers' second unsuccessful attempt, Mr Durie decided to return home.

The next minister to come to the Island was Farquhar Macrae of Gairloch, who came across in 1610 with the Mackenzie conquerors. He was surprised at how backward the inhabitants were, which was not at all surprising after almost a century of feuding, the self-destructive actions of the Macleod chiefs, and mainland attacks. Few people under the age of forty had ever been baptised, nor had marriages been solemnised.

In 1626, there were two ministers at work, each on a stipend of 2,000 merks. (8) Between 1642 and the Disruption of 1843, the parish ministers were admitted on the following dates.

STORNOWAY:
Farquhar Clerk (1642), Donald Morison (before 1649), Kenneth Morison (1689), Daniel Morison (1724), John Clerk (1747), John Downie (1773), Colin Mackenzie (1789), Simon Fraser (1815), and John Cameron (1815)
BARVAS:
Murdoch Morison (1642), Donald Morison (1643), Donald Morison (1684), Alan Morison (1692), Murdoch Morison (1726), Alexander Mackay (1767), Donald Macdonald (1790), and William Macrae (1813). (9)
LOCHS:
Colin Mackenzie (1724), Alexander Mackay (1760), James Wilson (1728), John Fraser (1784), Alexander Simpson (1793), and Robert Finlayson (1831).
In the two quoad sacra parishes of Cross and Knock, the ministers were:
CROSS:
Finlay Cook (1829), John Macrae (1833), and John Finlayson (1840).
KNOCK:
Robert Finlayson (1829), and Duncan Matheson (1831). (10)

The Morison ministers in the above list were all descendants of the Brieve of Lewis, so it was not at all surprising that they were all gifted men, whose early congregations had no hesitation in exchanging Episcopalianism for Presbyterianism.

It was Donald Morison, the minister of Barvas, who gave the traveller Martin Martin much of his information when he visited Lewis.

In 1689, his brother Kenneth Morison, who was the minister of Stornoway, was for a long time at loggerheads with Mackenzie of Kildun, a Catholic, who lived in Aignish. The quarrel was so serious, that Kenneth always armed himself when he made his way across the Tong Sands from his manse in Tong to his church in Stornoway. He also took the precaution of having two men, with drawn swords, guard his church door every Sunday. (12)

Mackenzie once sent six strong men across to Tong to abduct Kenneth, who was so generous with liquid refreshment, that his would-be captors were rendered unconscious, and he was able to transport them, completely bound, across the water to Aignish, where he deposited them near the laird's door. When they were found in the morning, they were still stupefied, and had no recollection of how they came to be there.

Mackenzie congratulated them on their escape, saying that Black Kenneth must have been in a genial mood, as he might easily have left them below the low water mark. (13)

Daniel Morison, who succeeded Kenneth as the minister of Stornoway, was most unfortunate in his choice of wife. In 1743, matters became so bad, that the Presbytery held a special investigation into his mode of living, doctrine, conversation, and diligence in pastoral work. They came to the conclusion that his depressed condition was due to his wife's mismanagement of his temporal and spiritual affairs, and by his lenience to one who was a habitual drunkard. He was advised to find a distant place for her where she could not have access to spirits, and for himself to stop haunting taverns unseasonably. (14) Morison did not comply with this injunction, and on his case being considered by the Synod of Glenelg, of which Lewis formed a part, he was suspended from his ministerial duties. However, on appeal to the General Assembly, the decree was rescinded. (15)

Shortly afterwards, his wife grabbed the Bible he was reading, and threw it in the fire. Mr Morison, pulling in his chair and holding out his hands to the flames, remarked it was the best fire he had ever warmed himself at. His wife stood stunned, and then rushed from the room. She was a changed woman after that.

It is difficult to realise what the ministers had to contend with at this time, not only with their large parishes, and the difficulty of travelling in all weathers, but also in countering the superstitious practices of their scattered flock.

It was a common practice at one time to make a sacrifice to the sea-god Shony, about Hallowe'en, when a chosen man waded into the sea up to his waist, carrying a cup of ale. He then shouted "Shony, I give you this cup of ale, hoping that you will be so kind as to send us plenty of seaware for enriching the ground for the ensuing year". (16) Libation was also made to the *Gruagach,* a household goddess, and *Tamnadh* was the sacrifice of a sheep or a goat prior to the start of the fishing season.

Early on the first day of May, a man was sent across the Barvas River. If a woman crossed first, this was believed to prevent salmon from coming upstream.

There were also several springs and wells on the Island which were believed to possess wonderful properties. St Thomas' Well at Carloway, whose water never whitened linen, was also a healing well. St Cowstan's in Garrabost had the unfortunate quality of being unable to boil meat. St Andrew's Well in Shader was consulted to see if a sick person was likely to die. For this purpose, a wooden dish of water was brought to the patient, and then the dish was placed in the well. If it turned sunwise, the invalid would recover; if not, he died. (17) Water from under a bridge where the living and the dead crossed was exceptionally efficacious, but the best water of all was to be found in the vicinity of St Mulvay's Chapel in Eoropie, where lunatics were brought to be cured.

There was also an implicit belief in fairies, the evil eye, witchcraft, the efficacy of charms, clay bodies and leaden hearts.

It was not until after the great revival of 1822, that these superstitious beliefs were largely dispersed, although some still linger on today.

In 1791, the Presbytery became concerned that the Sacrament of the Lord's Supper had not been administered throughout the Island for some years, and recommended that in future, it should be administered in Uig and Lochs on alternate years.

Although catechists had been labouring in some mainland parishes since the end of the sixteenth century, it was not until 1737, that any came to Lewis. The first ones were John Maclennan of Keose, and James Thomson of Barvas, who were also schoolmasters, their salaries being shared by the S.S.P.C.K. and the Committee of the Church for managing the Royal Bounty. Later, the number of catechists increased until the whole Island was practically provided for.

These devoted men, who, for years, gave such faithful service to the church, trudging on foot in all weathers, summer and winter, in their chosen calling, are still fondly remembered. Among them are John Matheson, better known as *"Dall Ard-Tunga"*, The Blind Man of Tong, James Thomson and Murdo Macleod, *"Ceistear nan Loch"* the Lochs Catechist and bard.

Before the Annual Catechising Day in each village (a day eagerly awaited by a few, and dreaded by many), the catechist tried to ensure that all examinable persons, those over seven years of age, were well grounded in the Shorter Catechism. There were usually some amusing incidents during these sessions.

As the number of Gaelic speaking preachers increased, itinerant ministers were sent to the Island. Divinity students were also employed, and these men were a blessing to the community, especially where the parish minister was old and infirm.

Until the appointment of Sheriffs, Presbyteries had to deal with both civil and ecclesiastical offences. Moral lapses in particular, were harshly dealt with.

A couple from Stornoway Parish who admitted committing adultery, were excommunicated by the Presbytery. Later, the man showed signs of repentance, and the minister freed him from the sentence. However, he was ordered to appear on a Sunday, dressed in sackcloth, in the parishes of Lochs and Barvas to be rebuked in the presence of the congregation. The ceremony was then repeated in each place of worship in his native parish until the Presbytery thought fit to pardon him.

Two Stornoway women who stole peats were also ordered by the Presbytery to be reproved before the congregation with creels on their backs, while an over-zealous minister was rebuked by the Presbytery for man-handling one woman who had denied committing adultery. Although her case was not proven, the minister dragged her from her seat in the church and reproved her before the congregation.

Although Carswell's Liturgy of John Knox was translated into Gaelic as early as 1567, it was not until 1659, that the first fifty of the Psalms of David in metre were published by the Synod of Argyll. This was followed by a translation of the Confession of Faith by the same Synod, but there was still no Gaelic Bible, as the S.S.P.C.K., which did so much for education and religion in Scotland, believed that until Gaelic was rooted out, there would be no progress in the Highland area. It was therefore forbidden to teach the language in their schools. However, the Society later changed its policy and contributed towards the translation of the New Testament into Gaelic in 1767, and of the complete Bible in 1801.

Schools, established to teach the people to read the Scriptures in their own tongue, were opened in Lewis in 1811, by the Edinburgh Gaelic School Society, and had far-reaching effects. The people, young and old, flocked to these schools, and before long, Bibles began to appear where formerly there had been none. Among the most outstanding teachers at these schools were John Macleod, Angus Maciver, and John Macrae *(Macrath Mor)*.

Villages, some distance from the Parish Church, were spiritually backward. As recently as 1819, one of these townships in the Parish of Stornoway, was described thus:

> Having no roads and with several waters which are sometimes impassable, between them and the Parish Church, it is very seldom they can attend. Even in the summer season, it is only the stout and the strong, that can bear the fatigue of going such a distance. Old people and children

cannot attempt it. Some old people told me they had not heard a sermon for twenty years. It was most melancholy to see the people formerly on a Sabbath Day sauntering about, or collecting in groups together, talking idle stories, and knowing no better use to make of their time. They now all collect on the Sabbath in the schoolhouse, where the teacher reads to them a portion of the Scripture, and almost in every family now, they have someone of the family to read to them at home.

In the same village, a few years before, an old man of eighty, on hearing frequent mention of the Saviour, asked how long it had been since that man had lived.

The ability to read the Bible in their own language, brought a remarkable change in the mode of life of the people; prayer meetings, Sunday meetings and fellowship meetings became common, with family worship held in every home. They also became extremely critical of the few services they listened to. They were awakening, and were no longer content to accept the same sermon over and over again.

In 1822, a religious revival took place which strangely influenced some of the people. Some fell into a trance, while others became hysterical. The parishes of Uig and Barvas were chiefly affected, but the other two parishes had their frenzied moments too. One minister, was called "a murderer of souls" during a Communion service in his own church. The same minister, wrote to the Chamberlain of Lewis, describing what had happened during this period. One woman, he said, had committed suicide, another had died of despair, several were in a state of insanity, and the peace of many a household had been destroyed. All this was caused by two religious fanatics who had no qualification to preach. He suggested the Chamberlain stipulate that only ministers were allowed to preach, and that any transgressor would be dispossessed of his land. This, he thought, would have a salutary effect. (18)

It was impossible to stop the strong tide of religious fervour which swept through the Island during the succeeding years, encouraged as it was by the Hon. Mrs Stewart Mackenzie of Seaforth, who had the greatest sympathy for the new evangelical preaching. She was also responsible for bringing the first of these ministers into the Island, the noted Alexander Macleod, who was admitted to the church in Uig in 1824.

Mr Macleod found his parish in a very backward state spiritually, but he soon altered that. Before long, crowds made their way to Uig to listen to him, and he had to preach in the open air throughout the year, as the church was too small to hold them all. At Communion time, the congregation came by boat from places as far away as Ness and Harris.

The next evangelical preachers to arrive came to the Parliamentary Churches in Knock and Cross, both charges having become quoad sacra parishes in 1829. Mr Robert Finlayson was appointed to Knock, and Mr Finlay Cook to Cross. Mr Finlayson was translated to Lochs in 1831, and another evangelical minister, Mr Duncan Matheson, came to Knock in his place.

There were now four of the "religious clergy" or evangelical ministers in the Island, and two moderates in Barvas and Stornoway. The drift away from the moderates, which started as a result of the activities of the Gaelic School teachers, accelerated. The churches in Stornoway and Barvas began to be by-passed in favour of the other churches. Perhaps the parishioners did not benefit spiritually from these moderate ministers, but Mr Macrae of Barvas did much for the community in providing medicines and legal advice when required.

Mr Cameron of Stornoway had a difficult parish to labour in. Until the Parliamentary Church was built at Knock, he had to preach three Sundays in Stornoway, one Sunday in Knock, and another Sunday at Back. Mr Cameron was therefore frequently absent from his Stornoway pulpit. When the Hon. Mrs Mackenzie lodged a complaint, Mr Cameron gave her an account of some of the hardships he had to face due to the distance of his manse in Tong from the church in Stornoway. He explained how he often risked the lives of himself and his family by crossing the Tong Sands to Stornoway, but in future he would only do this when the tide was out and the sands dry. Many times he had gone to Stornoway on a winter's morning before dawn, and returned near midnight, having had to await the turn of the tide. Often the sea would be in the box of his cart, and if he preached too hurriedly, this was simply to finish his sermon in time to catch the tide. He also suggested that if her Ladyship had seen the many poor creatures, male and female, wading through the Laxdale and Tong Rivers, summer and winter, on their way to and from church, she would have made a road from Tong to Stornoway. (19)

Not only was there dissension in the Church on religious principles, but there was also controversy between the Church and the State. This dated from the Patronage Act of 1712, which conferred on a heritor the right of presenting his own nominee to a charge, even if the presentee was unacceptable to the congregation. In 1834, the Lewis Presbytery resolved to petition both Houses of Parliament for the abolition of lay patronage. The ministers of Barvas and Stornoway, Messrs. Macrae and Cameron, as one would expect, dissented, since they felt this was a matter for the General Assembly to deal with. (20)

The vexed question of patronage contributed to the separation of the Free Church from the Established Church in 1843, a severance which came to be known as the Disruption.

Among the signatories of the Act of Separation and Deed of Demission from the Church of Scotland, signed on 23rd May 1843, in Edinburgh, were Mr John Finlayson of Cross, Mr Duncan Matheson of Knock, and Mr Robert Finlayson of Lochs. (21) The following day, Mr Alexander Macleod of Uig signed the Supplementary Act of Separation and Deed of Demission. (22) These four ministers now became ministers of the Free Church of Scotland, and most of their parishioners followed them, including all the schoolmasters, with the exception of Mr Clerk of Stornoway.

The two Moderate ministers, Mr Cameron of Stornoway, and Mr Macrae of Barvas remained in the Established Church of Scotland, although they lost most of their congregations.

A period of confusion followed, for the ministers had to leave their churches and manses, and they had to preach in the open air. The loyal Mr Finlayson of Lochs, although he and his family had to live in Stornoway, continued to preach in the open air until a Free Church was erected at Crossbost. (23)

The other three ministers who came out did not show the same devotion to their people, for by December of that year, Mr Finlayson of Cross and Mr Macleod of Uig had left their congregations and departed from the Island. The following year, Mr Matheson of Knock went to Gairloch.

There was some criticism of these men who had taken their people out of the Established Church into the Free Church and then left them. The people felt they had been ill-used. In the end, only Mr Finlayson of Lochs remained. (24)

A mainland minister later taunted Mr Finlayson during the General Assembly, saying that all the Lewis ministers had left their people to take care of themselves, to which the latter replied "Yes, but we have left the Gospel there." (25)

This was perfectly true, for there were men there, in addition to the schoolmasters, who were more than capable of preaching and expounding the Scriptures. The acrimony which developed between the two churches was considerable.

When the Rev. Roderick Reid, who had been presented to the Established Church at Keose by Queen Victoria, went to preach there, none of the parishioners appeared, and the only ones who listened to his sermon were those who had accompanied him from Stornoway. When he was preaching, the locals barricaded the church doors from the outside to prevent him from leaving.

Mr David Watson, who was recommended to be parish minister in Uig, also met with opposition before he was appointed. When it was impossible to find a crew for the ferry from Callanish to Uig, the Presbytery met in the Callanish Schoolhouse, where the call to Mr Watson was signed by Mr Scobie, the factor, and a Mr Murdo Macaulay, a tacksman, who were the only witnesses along with the Presbytery. Mr Watson was ordained in Stornoway as minister of the parish of Uig. (26)

The Free Church was then faced with the formidable task of finding ministers for the new charges, as well as finding churches and manses. It was estimated in October 1843, that there were 150 vacant congregations in the Gaelic speaking districts, and only about 31 preachers available. (27)

Twelve of the most outstanding ministers of the day were given six months' leave of absence from their own congregations to visit the remote parts of the Island, and a vessel was specially built to transport them from place to place. The boat was named the *Breadalbane,* and she is noted as landing Mr Colin Mackenzie of Arrochar, and Mr Mackenzie of Beauly, in Stornoway in 1846. (28)

Eight new congregations were formed in Lewis, and these were:

BACK.
This included the villages of Tong, Coll, and North Tolsta. A catechist was stationed there immediately and a charge sanctioned in 1845. However, the first minister to settle there, Mr Macmaster, did not arrive until 1859. Until then, both the minister and the catechist were shared with Barvas.

BARVAS.
This district was sanctioned as a charge in 1845, but did not get its own minister until Mr Macarthur arrived in 1857. Until then, it shared with Back.

CARLOWAY AND CALLANISH.
These villages were sanctioned as a charge in 1844. Its first minister, Mr Maclean, came in 1858. (29)

CROSS.
Mr John Finlayson left four months after the Disruption, but a new minister came the following year, the genial Mr Donald Macrae, but the congregation had to worship in the open air until 1846, when the Marquis of Breadalbane bought driftwood to help build a church at South Dell.

KNOCK.
Like Cross, the other Parliamentary Church, Knock lost its minister only a year after the Disruption. The arrival of Mr Donald Murray in 1845, was of great benefit to the whole Island. He was a nephew of *Dall Ard-Tunga,* John Matheson, the famous catechist.

LOCHS.

This parish was fortunate, as its minister did not leave them when he took them out of the Church of Scotland.

STORNOWAY.

The town was without a minister for a long time, but the congregation was fortunate in having an eminent elder to lead them. The Rev. Duncan Macgregor was appointed in 1849.

UIG.

So long regarded as the most fortunate congregation in the Island through having Mr Alexander Macleod as minister they seceded with him almost to a body, but he left them after six months. His successor in 1846, was Mr John Campbell. (30)

Later, other Free Church charges came into existence in Stornoway, Park, Kinloch, Shawbost, and North Tolsta. (31)

St Peter's Episcopal Church was built shortly before Sir James Matheson bought Lewis, and he gave it his full support.

The year 1892 saw the beginning of a second Disruption in the Highlands when the Rev. Donald Macfarlane of Raasay and the Rev. Donald Macdonald of Shieldaig, protesting over a Declaratory Act, seceded from the Free Church and formed the Free Presbyterian Church. Congregations were formed in Stornoway, Breasclete, Skigersta, North Tolsta and Achmore.

In 1900, the majority of congregations in the Free Church of Scotland joined with the United Presbyterian Church, to form the United Free Church of Scotland, but most of the Lewis people were against this union, and remained in the Free Church.

Unfortunately, a great deal of bitterness ensued. Families, friends and boat crews were divided in their allegiance to the respective branches of the Church, and the community spirit was adversely affected.

In 1902, the minister of the United Free Church in Ness was even prevented from entering his church, as the doors had been barricaded from the inside. It took the threat of invasion by about fifty policemen to restore order. (32) In 1929, the United Free Church merged with the Church of Scotland.

The three main denominations in Lewis today are the Free Church, the Church of Scotland, and the Free Presbyterian Church. There is also a small Episcopalian Church in Stornoway, and Roman Catholic and Moslem communities are also to be found on the Island.

The religious communities in Lewis are extremely devout. In addition to the two, two-hour services held on Sundays, there are mid-week prayer meetings. There are also special meetings for communicants, and every year, two Communion services are held by each congregation, one in the Spring, and one in the Autumn.

The oral traditions, so carefully fostered by previous generations, were at one time actively discouraged by the Church, and most of them have been lost. Anything that savoured of the past was once frowned upon, and contemptuously referred to as *goraich*, foolishness. In this way, much of the Island's heritage of songs, stories, customs and beliefs, came to be abandoned. Even the fiddle and the bagpipe had to give way to the *triomb*, Jew's harp.

THE ARMED SERVICES

In the same way as they fought for the Macleod chiefs, so the men of Lewis fought for their Mackenzie overlords. They also fought in the battle of Auldearn in 1645, where the Lewis contingent perished almost to a man, Sheriffmuir in 1715, and Glenshiel in 1719. However, the Island escaped involvement in the Forty-five uprising, as Lord Fortrose, the proprietor, was a staunch supporter of the Hanoverian regime.

At the outbreak of the Seven Years' War, 1756-63, one hundred and forty men from Lewis were on active service in America with the 77th Regiment of Montgomerie's Highlanders, one of the newly raised Highland regiments. Only thirty-four of these men returned home, eighteen of whom were Chelsea Pensioners. Most of the others died of disease or were killed in action. (1) One Islander, Lewis Macleod, who had fought at Killiecrankie and Sheriffmuir, sent six sons to this war. Only one of his sons returned, and he was a Chelsea Pensioner. (2)

From 1778, the fortunes of Lewis soldiers have been closely connected with the Seaforth Highlanders. In that year, Kenneth Mackenzie, Coinneach Og, in gratitude for being raised to the Peerage of Ireland, raised the 78th Regiment of Highlanders, 1,130 strong. Five hundred of these men came from his own estates, which included about two hundred from Lewis. (3)

While this regiment was at Leith, waiting to embark for India, the men, annoyed at what they considered to be an infringement of their engagements, and non-payment of arrears of pay, refused to embark. Instead, they marched out of the barracks up to Arthur's Seat in Edinburgh, where they remained for several days, enjoying the hospitality of the citizens. Once their grievances had been settled, the men cheerfully marched down the hill again with the Earl of Seaforth at their head, back to their barracks. As there were so many Macraes involved in this incident, it came to be known as "The Affair of the Wild Macraes." (4)

The voyage to India was most unfortunate for the regiment, as the Earl of Seaforth died before they reached St Helena. By the time they reached Madras in 1782, two hundred and forty-seven men had died of scurvy.

Seaforth was succeeded in the command of the 78th by his cousin, Colonel Frederick Mackenzie Humberstone, who had purchased the Seaforth Estates from the late Earl. The Colonel had previously held commissions in the Dragoon Guards and the 100th Regiment of Foot, which he seems to have raised himself. (5)

In 1781, the 100th Regiment formed part of a joint naval and army expedition sent to capture the Cape of Good Hope. A squadron of Dutch East Indiamen was encountered in Saldanah Bay, north-west of the Cape. In the ensuing action, one vessel was burnt by its crew, two were later lost in a gale in the English Channel, while being taken back to Britain as prizes, while the other two returned safely. (6) There were twenty-four Lewismen in this engagement with the 100th Foot. (7)

Not long after taking over the command of the 78th, the Colonel died in

Geriah, India, of wounds received in a sea battle with a Mahratta fleet in 1783.

Seaforth's Highlanders, who had enlisted for a period of three years or for the duration of the war, now had the choice of remaining in India or returning home. Many accepted their discharge, but their loss was not felt too keenly, as many of the 100th Foot transferred to the 78th. This regiment became the 72nd in 1786, and later in 1881, the 1st Battalion, the Seaforth Highlanders.

This regiment was, at various times, on active service in India, Ceylon, Mauritius, Cape of Good Hope, Afghanistan, The West Indies and the Crimea. It was named "Saviours of India", for its heroism during the Indian Mutiny. It also took part in the famous march from Kabul to Kandahar, in Afghanistan, and the decisive battle of Tel-el-Kebir, in Egypt. Among the dozen or so Sergeant Instructors chosen to convert the Egyptian fellahin into soldiers were two Lewismen, one of them being the future Lieut. Colonel David Macleod of Arnol, who died on active service in 1916.

Colonel Mackenzie Humberston's heir was his younger brother Francis Humberstone Mackenzie, known as *Mac Coinneach Bodhar*, Deaf Mackenzie. Mackenzie was keen on soldiering, and at one time offered to raise a regiment of 1,000 men, an offer he later withdrew in favour of raising a Fencible Regiment of 500 men for home defence. This notion came to nothing, but he did recruit soldiers for other Highland regiments. In 1791, Alexander Gillanders, the factor, was paid £46. 14. 4½ for expenses incurred during a recruiting campaign by a Lieutenant Douglas, (8) while Donald Macaulay, the tacksman of Linshader, was paid 5/- for drams he had given to a party of Uig men who were going to Stornoway for recruiting purposes. (9)

Mr Dundas, the Secretary for Scotland, was delighted with Seaforth's martial ardour, and proposed that he should raise a regiment of 600 men, to be numbered the 78th, of which Seaforth himself was to be the Lieutenant Colonel Commandant. Major Mackenzie of Belmaduthy was to be his second in command, and would succeed him when he got tired of playing at soldiering. (10)

Later, Mr Pitt, the Prime Minister, and Mr Dundas, decided that Seaforth's Highlanders should consist of 1,000 men. A Letter of Service for raising this battalion was granted to Seaforth in March 1793.

Many of the tenants on Seaforth's estate had no desire to embark on a military career, even though the Letter of Service gave the assurance that the men were on no account to be drafted into other regiments, and would be discharged in their own country at the end of the war. The over-riding factor in their opposition to recruitment was their reluctance to leave their parents to the mercy of others, especially the factors, tacksmen and ground officers. Apart from that, they had no guarantee that they would be given land on their return. (11)

When Seaforth arrived in Lewis on his recruiting campaign, the men of Uig took to the hills, and set up a camp near Uig Lodge. A boat, manned by women, was sent to Callanish to ferry Seaforth across. He was far from pleased at this unexpected reception, but the parish minister of Uig, Mr Munro, managed to cool his temper, and assured him the people would soon tire of the cold hill-tops. (12)

The next day, Seaforth and the minister set off for *Cnoc a' Champ*, Camp Hill, where the latter remonstrated with his suspicious flock for their unpatriotic conduct. After a good deal of discussion, an assurance was given that wherever a man had only one son, that son would not be taken, but where there was a large family, two might be taken.

It was felt in some quarters that the formation of the camp at Uig would prove beneficial to recruiting in the long run, as the men would have to submit, and, as a peace offering, a good number of recruits would be secured. (13)

Before long, 100 men were recruited, and shortly after, were followed by some more who were ferried across to Ullapool, where they were met by an armed escort.

Seaforth was quite surprised at the difficulties he encountered in his recruiting campaign, and as atonement for not having his regiment of 600 complete in the stipulated period of three months, he agreed to increase the number to 1,000 men. (14)

The need to recruit more men was probably what caused Seaforth to send a press-gang to the Island. (15) When the factor heard what was being planned, he wrote to Seaforth, asserting that such an action would be fatal, as not a soul in either the town or the country would remain at home.

This news was most unwelcome, as the country people had already given more than their complement of men, especially in the Point area, where there was likely to be land left untilled, as the wives of the enlisted men refused to work it.

It was probably at this time that a press-gang came to the village of Knockaird in Ness. All the fit males between sixteen and thirty were marched away in spite of the repeated attempts by their women-folk to free them, attempts which were foiled by bayonets held at their breasts.

These "volunteers" were marched across the moors by Muirneag to Stornoway, from where they were immediately shipped to the mainland. Years later, the sole survivor of these *Balaich a' Chnuic Aird,* Lads of Knockaird, John Macdonald, Iain Buidhe, returned, to find that his old father had been evicted to the bogs of Habost, and that he himself could get no land from the ground officer. He had to go and live on Cuile Totair, south of Cellar Head, miles from any other habitation.

Seaforth's forceful recruiting was so successful, that within four months of the granting of the Letter of Service, the new regiment paraded on 10th July 1793, at Fort George, up to its full strength of 1,000 men. This battalion later became the 1st Battalion of the 78th Seaforth Highlanders, and was always known in Lewis as *Saighdearan Mhic Coinnich Bhodhair,* Deaf Mackenzie's Soldiers, and sometimes as *Saighdearan Cnoc a' Champ,* The Soldiers of Camp Hill.

A second battalion was raised in 1794, which was also referred to as *Saighdearan Mhic Coinnich Bhodhair.*

No recruit for these battalions was to be over thirty years of age, or under five feet four inches in height, although well-made lads, between sixteen and eighteen might be enlisted. This regulation was later altered to five feet three inches because of the 'low stature' of the men from the Isles.

The first battalion took part in the disastrous campaign in Holland in the terrible winter of 1794-95, where, at Nimeguen, they first came under fire. In spite of appalling conditions and poor leadership, they did credit to their country. In 1796, the battalion was sent to Cape Town where it was amalgamated with the second battalion.

In the 1st battalion, there were 300 men from Lewis. Several years elapsed before any of these men were charged with a crime deserving severe punishment. In 1799, a man was tried and punished, and this so shocked his comrades, that he was ostracised as a degraded man, who had brought shame on his kindred. The unfortunate outcast felt his own degradation so much, that he became unhappy and desperate, and

Colonel Mackenzie, to save him from destruction, applied and got him sent to England, where his disgrace would be unknown and unnoticed. It happened, as Colonel Mackenzie expected, for he quite recovered his character. (17)

A further tribute to the character of the men from the same source reported: "Their sobriety was such that it was necessary to restrict them from selling or giving away the usual allowance of spirits to the other soldiers." (18)

From the Cape, the battalion sailed to India, where it took part in many engagements under the command of Sir Arthur Wellesley, the future Duke of Wellington. The most important of these was the Battle of Assaye in 1803.

Meanwhile, a lone Lewisman was steadily making a reputation for himself in India. He was Colin Mackenzie, the son of Murdo 'Carn' Mackenzie, Stornoway's first postmaster.

Early in life, Colin Mackenzie had become interested in the history of India, and when, in 1782, through Lord Seaforth's influence, he was appointed a Cadet of Engineers in the service of the East India Company, he took full advantage of the opportunities this afforded him to pursue his studies of native culture.

As an engineer, he was not only concerned with surveying, but also in military operations. He took part in many actions, the major one being the siege and attack on Seringapatam, in 1791, where the 72nd were also involved. By 1798, he was Lieutenant-Colonel, and later, was promoted to the post of India's first Surveyor-General. However, Colin Mackenzie is best remembered, not for his professional service, but for the mass of material he collected during his thirty-eight consecutive years in the East, dealing with the history, religion and literature of India.

Back home, in 1804, a Letter of Service was granted to Major-General Alexander Mackenzie Fraser (the Fraser part being a comparatively recent addition) to raise a second battalion for his own regiment, the 78th. (19) Although Seaforth was abroad in Barbados, he permitted Fraser to enlist 200 young men from Lewis. (20) Among them, was Ensign John Munro, the son of the Uig minister, Mr Hugh Munro. Owing to this, the regiment was known in Lewis as *Saighdearan Mac a' Mhinisteir,* the Soldiers of the Minister's Son, the fourth Seaforth battalion to be raised in 30 years. (21)

Sir John Stuart, the commander of the British forces fighting against Napoleon in southern Italy, is said to have been extremely disappointed when the new battalion arrived there in 1806. He had been expecting the experienced 42nd. (The Black Watch) instead of which, he was sent from Gibraltar, a "corps of boys" (22) However, Sir John soon changed his tune when, at the Battle of Maida, they played an important part in the defeat of Napoleon's veterans. (23)

The battalion also took part in the ill-fated expedition to Egypt in 1807, known to the older generation as *Cogadh na Tuirc,* the Turkish War, as the Turks were at this time, the masters of Egypt. During an attempt to capture Rosetta, some of the British, including three companies of the 78th, were surrounded at El Hamet, and fought until only a couple of officers and twenty-two men were left alive. Eleven of these were from the 78th. (24) The commander of the expedition, General Fraser, agreed to evacuate if all the prisoners in the hands of the Turks were returned, but one Uig pensioner claimed that he was kept a prisoner for seven years. (25)

Many of the soldiers became blind through ophthalmia, and Lewis had its share of these blind pensioners. One of these was ex-Corporal Norman

Morrison of Kneep in Uig, who died in 1875, aged ninety-five. Of those who fought at Maida, he was believed to be the oldest survivor on the Island. (26)

From 1811-16, the first battalion of the 78th was on active service in Java. Casualties were numerous (more from disease than enemy action), and only 400 of the 1,027 men who left India in 1811, returned there. One of those who did not return was Lieutenant John Munro, the Uig minister's son, who had been drafted from the second battalion. He was killed at Weltevreeden, near Batavia, on 10th August, 1811. (27)

Returning to India, the transport carrying six companies of the first battalion struck a reef in the Bay of Bengal. Although the vessel was in imminent danger of sinking, there was no panic. The women, the children and the sick, with all accessible provisons, were ferried to a nearby island, and some of the soldiers were rafted to a partly covered reef, where they tied themselves to the rocks, in order to avoid being washed away at high tide. They remained there for four days with very little food or sleep until all their comrades left on board were ferried to the island. The men on the reef were the first to be rescued, as a storm prevented the rescue of the others, who had to spend a month, half-starved, on the island. (28)

From about 1810, the second battalion, much reduced in strength through supplying men for the first battalion in India, spent the next six years on garrison duty, and so missed the Waterloo campaign. The second battalion became part of the first battalion in 1817.

During the Napoleonic Wars, the loss of manpower to Lewis was incalculable, especially during the years 1795-96. In less than two years, 500 men were claimed by the Army, and 80 by the Navy, (29) in addition to those press-ganged.

A succession of recruits was always required to replace casualties, and Seaforth's Commissioner in Lewis was especially active in this field. When some stragglers were pointed out to him in 1796, he was not certain they could be made to volunteer, so strong arm measures were taken. He did not consider it advisable to send the "recruited" men to the Regulating Officer at Dingwall or Inverness, as they might desert on the way. Instead, he suggested that they should be taken by H.M. cutter to the Regulating Officer at Greenock. (30)

Manpower on the Island was further reduced when it was decided to start a militia force, and Seaforth was given command of the 2nd Battalion of the North British Militia. Men were raised for these regiments by ballot. Lewis was to supply 146 men, fourteen from the Parish of Stornoway, thirty-six from Lochs, forty from Barvas, and fifty from Uig. (31)

The Militia was no more popular than the regular army at first, and Seaforth was annoyed at the difficulty he encountered in raising men. He attributed this to ignorance, obstinacy and indifference. (32)

Some of those balloted paid others to act as their substitutes, but they had to be fit for service, unmarried, and over five feet five inches in height. Deserters from the ballot fled to Harris for refuge, but, in spite of this, the Militia provided a good recruiting ground for the regular battalions, 400 men being drafted in 1800 alone.

Men were unwilling to enlist due to the fact that they had seen so many leave never to return, and of those who did come back many were pensioners of Chelsea or Chatham.

Many Islanders served with the Seaforths in the Crimea, and were later engaged in the suppression of the Indian Mutiny. Here the Seaforths earned national acclaim for their conduct, especially during the struggle to relieve Lucknow.

The South African War also took a heavy toll of Island lives, particularly at the battles of the Modder River and Magersfontein.

By 1900, the Militia had become more popular through the retaining fee which was paid. This provided the youths with much needed additional capital. The Seaforth Militia volunteered for garrison duty in Egypt during the South African War to release the regular soldiers stationed there for active service.

During the eighteenth and nineteenth centuries, the Navy held little appeal for the young men of the Island. What they knew of the *balaich-ghorma,* the boys in blue, due to the press-gang system, abolished in 1812, they regarded with horror. Very few were prepared to enlist in a service where criminals abounded, conditions were harsh, food meagre, and floggings frequent. However, one of the tacksmen class, Lieutenant John Morison of Aignish, made the Navy his career and fought at Trafalgar.

Fishermen, regarded by law as sea-faring men, were consequently liable to be impressed for the Navy. In 1807, the Admiralty decided to exempt those on the west coast of Scotland on condition that one man out of every six enlisted for the service. (33)

It was not until 1859, that the Royal Navy decided to follow the example of the Army by having a reserve of men who could be called upon in an emergency. This resulted in the passing of the Royal Navy Reserve (Volunteer) Act. (34)

Because of the retainer involved, this service soon attracted many seamen, and also because it only involved short periods away from home and did not interfere too much with their livelihood. When their period of service in the Militia was over, most of the Islanders joined the Royal Naval Reserve. Indeed, some were so keen to join, that they did so while still in the Militia, and found themselves jailed for a month. (35)

For a long time, the Reservists trained on H.M.S. *Black Prince,* at Greenock, until 1876, when, amid great excitement, H.M.S. *Flirt* arrived in Stornoway from Greenock with stores for the new reserve battery there. (36) The fishermen were eager to enrol as second class Royal Naval Reservists. Those who had experience of deep-sea sailing, were allowed to enrol in the first class group.

Those who lived far away from Stornoway, in Uig for example, were discouraged from joining, as they were likely to incur heavy travelling expenses. Only those who did not need such expenses, were allowed to enrol. At one time, men travelling from Portnaguran to Stornoway, were allowed one shilling each way for expenses, a practice later discontinued.

For a few weeks in November, December and January, from 250 to 650 men came to drill at Stornoway, some from as far as Wester Ross, but from February to May and from the end of August to November, most of the men were engaged in fishing for cod, ling or herring.

By 1900, the Admiralty felt that the Lewis Reservists were too divorced from the prevailing conditions in the Navy and invited them to volunteer for the manoeuvres planned for that year. No one responded.

Later, H.M.S. *Camperdown* was sent to Lewis, and many Reservists completed a month's training in the Minch.

This closer liaison with the Navy made it much easier for the Islanders to adapt themselves to the new conditions. When the Stornoway base was closed, training became centred on places like Chatham and Portsmouth. Many young lads, completing their training in the south, proceeded to London where they began a career in the Merchant Navy.

While the R.N.R. and the Militia of the Seaforths, Camerons and Gordons provided the fishermen with experience of the services, the town of Stornoway had its own battery from about the middle of the nineteenth century. This was the 1st Company of the Ross-shire Artillery Volunteers of the Royal Garrison Artillery. This was disbanded in 1908, and replaced by the Ross Battery. (37)

That fateful Sunday of 4th August 1914, when the postman delivered the buff-coloured envelopes to the Militia and Naval Reservists, will long be remembered, and how readily the men answered the mobilisation call. They made for Stornoway on foot or by gig or cart, and from Ness by boat. They were then quickly ferried across the Minch to Kyle of Lochalsh before travelling on to Inverness. The Militia men were directed to their respective regimental depots, with the Naval Reservists heading for the Channel bases. Some lads fishing on the East Coast reported direct for duty without taking the time to return home.

Lewismen from all over the world volunteered. They came from Australia and New Zealand, from Canada and South Africa, and from places as far apart as Alaska and Punta Arenas. A good number also came from the U.S.A.

Being trained soldiers, the Militia men were soon sent to France, and before long, the postmen were delivering their grim messages of death. First to fall, were the regular soldiers fighting at Mons, the Marne and the Aisne, followed all too quickly, by the young Militia lads, some under eighteen years of age. French names like Loos, Cambrai, Ypres, Hill 60, and Passchendale became familiar, all associated with the death of the young Islanders.

As the Germans drove all before them in their advance through Belgium, many Lewis reservists were drafted into a newly formed Royal Naval Division. This was chiefly because the Admiralty knew that most, if not all of them, had been at one time in the Militia. They were sent to Antwerp, but only managed to hold the town for a few days, before being forced to retreat to Ostend. The Germans managed to cut off the retreat of one Brigade numbering almost 1,000 men, while another 1,500, rather than be captured, crossed into Holland, to be interned in a camp at Groningen for the duration of the War. Many Lewismen were in this last group, and some of them made good use of their enforced leisure by studying navigation and other subjects, and at least one man studied for the ministry.

Lewis soldiers fought in France, Italy, Russia, Egypt, Mesopotamia, the Dardanelles, Palestine, Greece and Bulgaria. The Ross Battery, which included many youngsters who had gone straight from the Nicolson Institute, distinguished itself at the landing in Gallipoli.

Naval losses were also mounting up. Islanders were with Admiral Sturdee at the Battle of the Falklands, and many did not survive the Battle of Jutland, where H.M.S. *Invincible* was sunk taking many with her. The Dover Patrol and other sea routes also claimed their share of lives. Lewis was paying dearly.

Perhaps the most cruel blow was struck on 1st January 1919, when hundreds of servicemen were coming home.

The previous day, Kyle of Lochalsh had presented an animated scene as many friends and relatives were reunited, some for the first time in four years. The war was over, and Lewis and their loved ones only forty miles away.

The usual mailboat, the small, sturdy *Sheila,* could not carry them all, so H.M. Yacht *Iolaire* was called upon to transport the sailors, while the *Sheila* carried the soldiers and civilians.

Early on New Year's Day, the *Iolaire* missed the entrance to Stornoway Harbour and was wrecked on the Beasts of Holm, within a few yards of the shore. There were some attempts to lower boats, but no boat could survive in the tempestuous seas. Many a strong swimmer tried for the land, but the huge waves that came sweeping shorewards and the strong under-tow took their toll.

Some survivors did not know how they reached the shore, but most of them owed their lives to the strength of the daring John F. Macleod from Port of Ness. Macleod jumped from the boat with a heaving line, and after an almighty effort, found himself among the boulders on the beach. He wedged himself there, and then hauled a hawser ashore, and it was along this hawser that most of the survivors struggled.

Some of those coming ashore were flung off the hawser as the retreating waves surged back, engulfing them in the angry surf. Altogether, seventy-five men were saved, but more than 200 lost their lives. Luerbost and North Tolsta each lost eleven men. In some cases, two members of a family perished. A night of sorrow was followed by years of mourning.

Many decorations for gallantry were won by both services. The Seaforth Highlanders won over thirty Military Medals, twenty-four Distinguished Conduct Medals, five Military Crosses, four Distinguished Service Orders, and other decorations. Two sergeants, the Macleod brothers from Borrowston, were outstanding. Donald was awarded the D.C.M. and the M.M., and recommended for the Victoria Cross, while Angus was also awarded the D.C.M. and the M.M. (38)

John Macleod, of *Iolaire* fame, was awarded the Distinguished Service Medal. The casualties were heaviest among the Militia lads, and most of those who returned were pensioners.

The Second World War, 1939-45, saw Lewismen once again on active service, accompanied this time by their women folk. It has been estimated that almost 4,000 men and girls out of a population of approximately 25,000 were in the Forces, with more than 500 in the Merchant Navy. In addition to these, many Lewismen living in other parts of Britain and overseas answered their country's call. Few had to be conscripted.

Unlike the 1914-18 War, when most of the men served in Scots infantry regiments or in the Navy, this time they were to be found in every branch of the Services.

The loss of the Armed Cruiser, H.M.S. *Rawalpindi,* early in 1939, brought sorrow to many homes, and, as the war progressed, the death-roll at sea mounted steadily. The Murmansk convoys, bringing much needed supplies to the hard-pressed and unsociable Russians, cost the Island dearly, as did all the convoys that brought food and munitions of war to Britain's beleaguered shores, or to Malta and other theatres of war. Many Islesmen were decorated for their skill and daring in the handling of life-boats from torpedoed vessels, under most adverse conditions. One of these was young Malcolm Morrison from Lochs, one of the crew of the *Arlington Court.*

The short Norwegian campaign of 1940, and the retreat across France to the Channel ports brought death and misery into many homes. The Highland Division, which included the Seaforths and the Ross Battery, were forced to surrender, which led to five years in captivity. Lewis sailors were among the personnel who helped to evacuate the troops at Dunkirk and elsewhere along the French coast.

History has recorded the land, sea, and air battles, in and around the Mediterranean Sea, especially at El Alamein, where General Montgomery defeated the Germans. At the conclusion of the British drive along the North African coast at Tunis, it was said that a Lewis Pipe-Major played as the Highland Division entered the town.

Islanders took part in the landings in Sicily, Italy, and on the Normandy beaches, on and after D. Day, and also with the Air-borne Division at Arnhem, as well as in the far East.

The Island girls also rendered great service in many spheres for the war effort. Nursing sisters served wheresoever duty called. Others served with the W.R.N.S., the A.T.S., the W.A.A.F., the N.A.A.F.I., the Land Army and in munition factories.

During the First World War, relatively few men attained commissioned rank, but the reverse was the case in the last war, when Islanders held high positions in all the services.

A former proprietor once complained that the men of Lewis were not Highlanders, but merely a starving people, who added to the landlord's poverty, and not to his military means. He claimed that no one ever left the Island, and never would, unless compelled to do so. (39)

Two World Wars have proved this assertion false, and the men and women of Lewis have every reason to be proud of the contribution they made in the defence of their country.

PERIODS OF SCARCITY

As in all primitive communities, dependent on their own labour for their subsistence, periods of plenty alternated with periods of scarcity, both depending on the vagaries of the weather. Unseasonable conditions, at seed-time or harvest time, made all the difference between sufficiency and want. (1)

As early as 1695, the Island was noted as being fruitful in corn. In succeeding years, however, food became scarce owing to poor weather. In 1718, Zachary Macaulay, the factor, in his report to the Forfeited Estates Commissioners, stated that "the hag, Poverty was always present".

In 1782, there was widespread destitution throughout the Highlands, which caused the Government to come to the aid of the people, supplying them with pease meal. (2)

Deprivation in the nineteenth century was due to the population exceeding the natural food resources. Owing to the failure of the 1816 grain crops, the inhabitants faced famine in 1817. It had been an exceptionally bad Autumn, with early frost damaging the potatoes, the main source of food. (3) When Mrs Stewart Mackenzie sought Government assistance, it was speedily granted, although not in the form requested. (4) Instead of the meal required, a surplus of grain was poured into the Island, so that every available storage space in Stornoway was filled to capacity, and some of the grain even had to be ferried across for storage at Seaforth Lodge.

The proprietrix had requested meal, seed oats, and seed potatoes, but instead of sending the 4,000 bolls of meal which one vessel could have easily carried, nine ships were required to transport the grain, which the London authorities, in their wisdom, thought the natives should grind to suit themselves.

Mrs Stewart Mackenzie later informed her London agents that, if a modern up-to-date mill had not been erected in Stornoway in 1816, not a single grain of oats could have been milled, as the older mills were wretched hovels, which could only function when there was enough water in the burns. The grain however, did save many souls from starvation. (5)

The crofters were debited with the price of this grain, for which they paid by labour, with cash, or in kind. Money was still fairly plentiful at this time, for the kelp industry was still flourishing, and, in addition, the Chelsea pensioners brought in £2,000 annually. (6)

After 1823, the steady decline of the kelp industry resulted in the loss of a valuable source of income, and this, combined with Mr Stewart Mackenzie's eviction policies, led to much misery.

As they found it difficult to pay their rents, many tenants began to engage in illicit distilling as an additional source of income. Some villages became noted for the regularity with which they paid their rents due to their income from the sale of their whisky. (7)

In 1828, there was a scarcity of provisions in Uig, while the tenants of Enaclete (Newton) were so wretchedly poor, that they could not be evicted as they were unable to build houses for themselves elsewhere. (8)

125

The situation deteriorated. The Spring of 1835 was cold and wet, so planting and sowing were carried on under very unfavourable conditions. The practice of allowing the township stock to wander freely over the arable land till mid-May damaged the sprouting crops, and incessant autumn gales and diseased potatoes produced a poor harvest.

In 1836, the Rev. Mr Macrae of Barvas wrote:

> This year is one of alarming and unprecedented scarcity of provisions—indeed of absolute famine and general mortality among cattle, and if a merciful God prevent not, among men also.
>
> During the latter part of Winter, and the whole of Spring, the weather has been unusually severe, and continues so till this moment, the ground being covered with snow. The cattle, after consuming all the provender long since, are dying in scores, and although the poor people wasted a very great proportion of their grain and meal in endeavouring to keep their bestial from perishing, it is not likely that a tithe of them will survive. This has already occasioned a greater dearth of food than has been known here in the memory of the oldest person living. The prospect is truly appaling. The extreme severity of the weather continues unabated, more resembling the middle of Winter than the approach of Summer—the labour of Spring hardly commenced—a general scarcity of corn seed, and the little store of meal almost exhausted—no money—no employment, and no means of procuring subsistence. (9)

Dysentry was rife. A Destitution Fund for the relief of the poor in the Highlands and Islands was set up in the major towns like Edinburgh and Glasgow, and subscriptions came pouring in from all quarters, warding off, temporarily, imminent starvation.

The year 1837 was no better than the two years before, with the potato crop a complete failure. At ebb-tide, the people gleaned the shores for shell-fish.

In 1837, the Rev. John Cameron of Stornoway estimated that out of his parish of 5,491 people, 2,000 were destitute. Their position was critical, with little or no food, and, as in 1836, in some cases, the whole of the potato crop had failed. Bad weather had also stopped the oats from filling and ripening, while the incessant Autumn rains and an early snowstorm had damaged what had been cut. The grain malted and heated in the cornyards, causing dysentry. The herring industry had also failed, so immediate relief in potatoes and oats was necessary for food and planting.

In 1835, the people had sacrificed their crops of oats, barley, potatoes and even their bread, to keep their cattle alive. In many instances, they lost everything. In 1836, the late wet harvest, and the October snow, frosted, rotted, and ruined their crops, and this led to many previously honest people stealing from those who had been fortunate enough to save their potatoes for pitting in the fields. (10)

Mr Cameron felt the Government should provide aid for a moral, peacable race of beings, who were not given to agitation, incendiarism, turbulence, or revolutionary schemes. They deprecated such measures, and abhorred such conduct, but Poverty and Famine, stared them in the face. With starvation entering their homes, and hunger gnawing at their vitals, and the wailing of their children, a terror to them, a reaction might be produced. Hunger was the enemy of morality and religion: hunger would break through stone walls, as well as through earthen pits, to obtain potatoes and sustenance.

The Uig tenantry were in a similar plight, and would be in need until a new crop was ready. They were already in debt for the meal supplied to them the previous year, and as well as having to face the prospect of famine, the threat of eviction hovered over them. They did not want to go to the new fishing lots in Ness, where there was no promise of land or stock to support their families. They implored Seaforth to ask the Government to help them to emigrate to any part of the British Colonies where they could have land to live in comfort. (11)

Conditions were similar in Barvas and Uig. In Lochs, 400 families were expected to be in need until mid-August, besides 150 aged and infirm people, who were wholly dependent on their poor neighbours for their very existence.

In 1837, the Rev. John Macrae of Cross reported that two years before, the Hon. Mrs Stewart Mackenzie had given a donation of blankets for distribution among the destitute of the Island. As a result, he examined the sleeping places (he could not call them beds) more carefully than he would normally have done. He found cases of a most distressing nature. In one instance, two plats of dried turf thrown over a man's body, formed the only shelter from a cold winter's night, while his wife and three children covered themselves the best they could with a half-pair of blankets. (12)

Mr Stewart Mackenzie thought that the best way to help the 16,000 inhabitants was to place the parishes of Uig and Lochs under sheep, and to transfer their tenantry to other parts of the Island where there was plenty of fuel and good soil waiting to be reclaimed. (13)

The estimated requirements of meal to relieve distress for the Spring and Summer of 1837 were: Stornoway, 700 bolls; Knock 150; Lochs 800; Uig 1,000; Barvas 1,050; Cross 700; making a total of 4,400 bolls. This allowed each adult 1½ stones of meal per month.

In 1837, the supplies of meal and seed corn provided by the Edinburgh and Glasgow Relief Committees enabled the people to support themselves and to avert the threatened famine, so that from 1838-40, the rents were promptly paid.

Until the Poor Law Act of 1845, each village looked after its own poor, the Church door collections and voluntary subscriptions being totally inadequate for their support. (14) The poor people usually lived in a small bothy of their own, and sometimes had a young relation living with them who kept them supplied with peats and water. These bothies were not much worse off than the crofters' houses, except that the latter were better thatched. In Widows' Park in Stornoway, there were thirteen bits of ground which Mrs Stewart Mackenzie had given to widows. (15)

These paupers made periodic excursions throughout the Island begging for corn, wool, and anything else which was easily transportable. Not many of the country poor came to Stornoway, but many of the Stornoway poor travelled into the country districts. (16) Generally, these people were badly off for bedclothes, but usually had adequate body clothing. They lived on the same food as the crofters, only not quite an adequate supply. Towards the latter end of the Summer and the beginning of the Autumn, the poor lived on mussels, cockles, limpets and whelks. (17)

In 1845, the failure of the potato crop brought considerable distress to all parts of the Highlands and Islands. It was called *A' Bhliadhnaa thainig an Cnàmh dh'an Bhuntat'*, The Year in which Disease came into the Potatoes, and it came to be used as a year from which other events were dated.

There had been signs over the preceding years that all was not well with the potato, but when the black disease came unexpectedly, it caused consternation, for the potato had become the staple crop in the north. The

ILLUSTRATIONS

27. Carrying home peats. (Photo: R. Smith & Sons).
28. Filling a peat cart in North Tolsta, 1928. (Photo: D. Macdonald).
29. Splitting boulders by heat for house-building and road-making, 1938. (National Museum of Antiquities of Scotland, Country Life Section).
30. A fisherman with his *poca-chudaig,* pock-net, 1930. (Photo: T. B. Macaulay).
31. Launching *The Brother's Delight* from Tolsta beach, 1928. (Photo: Catriona Murray).
32. Arnish lighthouse at the entrance to Stornoway harbour, 1904. (The University Library, St Andrews).
33. Sunday morning gossip at Stornoway harbour, 1920. (T. B. Macaulay).
34. The old fish mart at Stornoway Pier, 1920s. (The University Library, St Andrews).
35. Herring gutters at Stornoway, 1906. (The University Library, St Andrews).
36. Barrels of herring on Stornoway Pier ready for export, 1951. (Photo: B. C. Crichton).
37. Cromwell St., Stornoway, in the early 1900s. (The University Library, St Andrews).
38. South Beach St., Stornoway, in the early 1900s. (The University Library, St Andrews).
39. Gugas nesting on the cliff face of Suilisgeir, 1960. (Photo: J. MacGeoch).
40. At midnight, after a forty mile trip to Suilisgeir, the Nessmen put ashore their water kegs, peats and food supplies and then manually haul their twenty-three foot open boat out of the sea and up the sixty foot cliff for safety. During their three week stay on the island, the gales will cause heavy seas to sweep the shore and everything must be made secure, 1960. (Photo: J. MacGeoch).
41. Snaring a guga, 1960 (Photo: J. MacGeoch).
42. A group of guga hunters on their return to Ness, 1960. (Photo: J. MacGeoch).
43. The women of Ness plucking gugas, 1960. (Photo: J. MacGeoch).
44. A group of women waulking tweed, 1936. (Photo: A. M. Macdonald).
45. A tweed weaver at his loom (Photo: N. Mackenzie).
46. Passengers disembarking from the ferry boat *Suilven* at Stornoway, 1978. (Photo: N. Mackenzie).
47. Calum Graham, Manager, (left) and John Murray, Director of Acair, the first bilingual educational publishing company in the Western Isles, established in Stornoway in December 1977 to meet the needs of Gaelic school children. (Photo: G. Wright).
48. Rev. Donald Macaulay, first convener of Comhairle nan Eilean, 1975. (Photo: Horst).
49. Alexander Matheson, the last Provost of Stornoway May 1971-75. (Photo: Dorchester Studios Ltd.).
50. Angus Macleod, Comhairle nan Eilean's first Director of Education, 1978. (Photo: Angus Smith).
51. Rt. Hon. Donald Stewart, Scottish National Party M.P. for the Western Isles, 1978. (Photo: G. Wright).
52. The cliffs near Mangersta, Uig, 1945. (Photo: A. M. Macdonald).
53. Garry Sands, Tolsta, 1977. (Photo: Scottish Tourist Board).
54. The Lewis mainland from Bernera Mor, 1950. (Photo: A. M. Macdonald).
55. Carloway, 1977. (Photo: Scottish Tourist Board).
56. Stornoway Harbour, 1965. (Photo: Scottish Tourist Board).

28

29

33

34

37

38

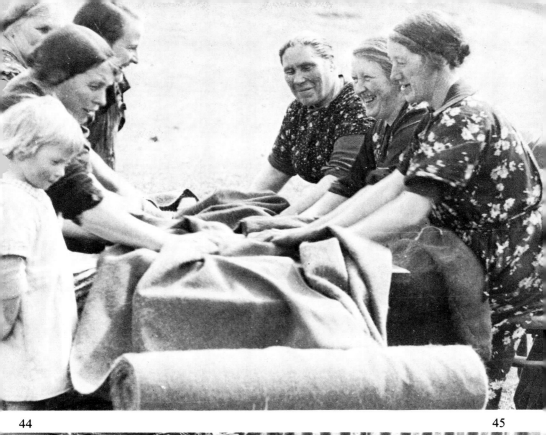

48

49

50

51

53

54

55

56

smell from the fields of rotting potatoes made people sick, and when the potato pits were opened, the smell was dreadful. 1846, the second year of the disease was even worse, and left the people facing starvation once again. (18)

Lewis fared better than many other parts of the Highlands owing to the success of the fisheries and the work provided on the land by the proprietor, Mr Matheson.

As the Matheson resources became severely depleted, the Highland Relief Society was approached for aid, but even with its help, there was still widespread evidence of poverty. The people were forced to part gradually with their stock, and as prices were low in the south, no drovers came to the Stornoway market. The estate officials were therefore in a position to buy cattle at their own valuation, making the payment of the rents even more difficult.

During the nineteenth century, the population, as described in the following figures, trebled, and this led to the sub-division of crofts and to squatting.

YEAR	POPULATION	
1801	9,168	
1821	12,231	
1841	17,037	
1861	21,056	
1881	25,487	
1901	28,948	(19)

The Winter of 1882-83 was one of the worst ever experienced by the people of Lewis, and once again, poverty was rampant. In the Autumn of 1882, the fishing had been a complete failure, and much of the potato crop was diseased. As if this was not enough, on the 1st October, a severe gale scattered the stooked corn. Like the year 1845, 1882, *A' Bhliadhna a Sgapadh an t-Arbhar,* The Year in which the Corn was Scattered, was used to date events. In some districts, 50 to 75% of the grain crop was lost, leaving many of the people destitute, especially the landless squatters.

In December 1882, a public meeting was held in Stornoway to raise funds. The response proved to be extremely good, and by the following March, £3,858 had been subscribed, the Matheson Trustees contributing £1,000 and Lady Matheson £500. (20)

It was this period of destitution, and the squatters agitation for more land, that led to the Commission of Inquiry of 1883, and the passing of the Crofters' Holdings Act of 1886, which conferred security of tenure on the crofters.

SMUGGLING

The fifth of the Statutes of Icolmcill (Iona) (1609) affirmed that one of the chief causes of poverty in the Isles, and of the inhuman barbarities practised in the feuds there, was due to the Gaels' inordinate love of strong wines and aqua vitae, which were purchased from locals and mainland merchants. Any Islander who bought liquor from a mainland trader was to incur a penalty of £40 for the first offence, £100 for the second, and on the third occasion, all his movable goods were to be forfeited. It was, however, lawful for an individual to brew as much aqua vitae as he required for himself and his family.

The provisions of this Statute seem to have been largely ignored, for Acts were passed by the Privy Council in 1616 and in 1622 against drinking in the Isles.

During his visit to Lewis around 1695, Martin Martin reported:

> Their plenty of corn was such, as disposed the natives to brew several sorts of liquors, as common usquebaugh, another called trestarig, id est, aqua-vitae, three times distilled, which is strong and hot: a third sort is four times distilled, and this by the natives is called usquebaugh-baul, id est, usquebaugh, which at first taste affects all the members of the body; two spoonfuls of this last liquor is a sufficient dose; and if any man exceed this, it would presently stop his breath, and endanger his life. The trestarig and usquebaugh-baul, are both made of oats. (1)

The Rev. J. L. Buchanan, who visited Lewis a century later, observed that the men were extremely fond of "spiritous liquors" and also that the whisky was made from oats and not from barley. The Island was also well supplied with rum, brandy, gin and wines, all of which had been smuggled in. (2) The ordinary people drank ale.

During the eighteenth and the first three decades of the nineteenth century, illicit distillation was common everywhere in Lewis as it was throughout the Highlands, chiefly as a result of the duty imposed on each gallon of whisky produced. In 1814, the Government, in an attempt to stop smuggling and to make it easier to collect the Excise duty, prohibited the use of stills north of the Highland line with a capacity of less than 500 gallons.

There was such an outcry at this imposition, that the restriction had to be lifted, and stills with a capacity of not less than 40 gallons were allowed. (1)

There does not seem to have been as much lawlessness connected with smuggling in Lewis as on the mainland. Until the introduction of gaugers into the Island, distillation was practised quite openly. Even when this occupation came to be considered illegal, the people felt they were quite justified in converting their own grain into whisky, as they had done for years, to pay part of their rents.

Illicit distillation, or smuggling, as it came to be commonly called, was not confined to any one section of the community; the Church, the tacksmen, the merchants, as well as the tenantry, were all involved. It was the law that was wrong, not the distillers, for at one time, distillation had proprietorial sanction, probably because the latter may have received a share of the proceeds. (3)

In conjunction with the illicit distillation of whisky, smuggling in its proper sense had been practised for centuries.

The writer of an anonymous letter in 1786, complained that there were some black hearts in the Island who were giving away secrets which might affect the Stornoway merchants. He suspected that *Sliochd a' Bhreitheimh,* the Brieve's Clan, the Morisons, were responsible. (4)

The information revealed was to suggest that smuggling had been carried on for years under the cover of fishing. The merchants were accused of having supplied themselves and their neighbours, from Cape Wrath to Ardnamurchan Point, with local and imported spirits and liquors, as well as tobacco, tea and coffee.

Even the factor was suspected of being involved at this time, although there was no actual proof of this. However, there was no doubt about his son, whose position gave him an absolute advantage over the poor defenceless Islanders, thus enabling him to secure a handsome profit.

As a result of these illegal activities, it was proposed that two revenue cutters, based on Stornoway, should patrol from Cape Wrath to the Sound of Mull, supported by an armed boat which would search creeks and bays which the cutter could not enter. Two excise officers or gaugers were to be appointed to prevent distilling; one of these, stationed at Borve, to supervise the district from Ness to Carloway, while the other, stationed at Stornoway, was responsible for that parish. In addition to his anti-smuggling duties, this man was also an Assessor of the Window Light Tax, the House Tax, the Shop Tax, the Commutation Tax, and of any other tax which Parliament might impose. (5)

The Earl of Seaforth was solicited to help quell smuggling, and his opposition to this traffic was embodied in one of the Estate Regulations, any infringement of which was to lead to immediate eviction. However, distilling continued, for it was not easy to give up such a long established habit. The *tighean staile,* smuggling bothies, with their black pots, were common to all townships, until the constant hounding and harassment by the gaugers caused them to be hidden in lonely moorland glens, caves like *Geodha Beuc,* Noisy Cave, at the Butt (now closed by a landslide) and the *Geodha Thogallaich,* Brewing Cave in Tolsta, which is only accessible at ebb-tide, or by climbing down a two hundred foot slippery watercourse.

It seems as if Angus Mackay, the Stornoway gauger in 1796, was somewhat remiss in carrying out his duties, as a town resident asserted:

Sir,
You are put here as gager or excise man and as you are not doing your duty you must be spoken to about it, the law of the land is against distilling in all England and Scotland. But it seems the law is not against distilling on the poor country as you are allowing the people of this country to distil as they please when we and our families are starving and cannot get a peck of meal to buy for our money. You have allowed the parson of Barvas to be bruing with his still this month (January) past and all the other stills on the west side and a still at Nether Coll that was bought from George Gillanders (the factor's son), as you promised him you would not take it till he would be paid. We all know that you will not take the still from the parson at Barvas because he is your own friend and

if you do not take all the stills in the country and all the malt and deliver the whole to your superiors if my Lord Seaforth himself was along with you—you are a gager going about the streets as Gentleman and get presents from the country people and our families starving, and if you do not in a few days take all the stills in the country you will see what will become of you. (6)

It had been hoped that the appointment of gaugers and the enforcement of the excise laws would lead to the speedy termination of this illicit trade, but such was not the case. Rents had to be paid, and the factor received these either in whisky or in money acquired from its sale.

The year 1796 was a poor year for the payment of rents, especially in Carloway and Barvas. It was felt that if the tenants were allowed to distil, they could raise sufficient money to pay their rents. (7)

The gaugers and the revenue cutters were regarded as public enemies, bent on the destruction of the people by depriving them of an important means of subsistence, and there is no doubt that when Sir John Reid's cutter was driven ashore in Stornoway Harbour, it was regarded as judgment from on high for his constant interference with the work of decent people.

John Morison, a former tacksman (and so likely to have first hand knowledge of the smuggling trade), in a letter to the proprietor in 1819, expressed his feeling of discontent at the continual harassment of the poor whisky distillers by the Excise and Revenue officers. The former, he said, levied their contributions at their thresholds, while the latter waylaid them, to make an unmerciful grasp at the returns of their year's labours, which rendered them not only unable to pay their rents, but depressed their spirits so much that it was with difficulty they would arouse themselves to persevere again. (8) Distillation was not considered to be a crime, for Morison thought this "gourmandising" was the more unpardonable in that duty did not call for such shabby vigilance. (9)

Morison's outburst was probably connected with some of the gaugers' recent successes in catching smugglers, five of whom came from Back and Coll, five from Barvas, and one each from Habost, Lochs, South Lochs, Shawbost and South Bragar. (10)

The decline of the kelp trade, the low prices received for cattle, and the consequent lack of money, gave an added impetus to illegal distilling in the 1820s. However, the tenants seemed to become increasingly reckless, or the gaugers increasingly skilful, for fines, imprisonment and evictions became common.

In 1824, Mr Stewart Mackenzie of Seaforth requested permission from the Treasury to establish a distillery in Stornoway, in order to end what he termed:

the wicked and disastrous system of vexation and fines, and all the frauds and oppression caused by the excise system, which the ignorance and prejudice of the poor wretched tenantry would never view in any other way, recollecting or acting upon the knowledge that until a very short period, their landlord, by a very small pecuniary compromise with the Government, purchased for them a special immunity for carrying on illicit distillation, by farming the excise. (11)

His wife, the Hon. Mrs Stewart Mackenzie, felt equally vexed at the fines imposed which absorbed more of her tenants' limited resources than she received from them in rent. As fines increased, so did the arrears of rent. It was considered that the laws on distilling should be simplified, as at present they could cause the imprisonment and beggary of eighty-six tenants at one court sitting.

Mr Stewart Mackenzie's request was eventually granted, and a distillery was opened in Stornoway in 1825. By 1831, there was also a distillery in Ness. Eventually, illicit distillation practically ceased.

There was only a limited sale of legal spirits at first. Even in 1827, the Ness tenants informed the factor that they had a considerable quantity of fair barley for sale, and, if they could escape detection, they could produce two years' rent that season. Quite a tempting offer to a factor trying to collect arrears of rent for a proprietor in financial difficulties.

For distilling purposes, the best barley came from Aignish and Holm, which gave 52 lb. to the bushel; Coll and Garrabost came next at 50 lb. to the bushel, while other areas gave as low as 35 lb.; prices ranged from 1/8 to 2/6 a bushel.

The success of the distilleries at Stornoway and Ness led to a demand for the erection of others. Lewis Maciver, the ambitious Gress tacksman, wanted to build one on his tack, but his request was refused, as it might have affected the output of the Stornoway Distillery, which belonged to the Estate.

A promising proposition came from a group of Shawbost crofters who decided to club together to build a small distillery on the North Shawbost River to distil the surplus grain of the neighbourhood. They felt they were too far from the other two distilleries to transport their grain there. Obviously, the best plan was to convert it on the spot. Unfortunately, the plan did not materialise, (12) as the people concerned had neither the necessary cash nor the credit.

Stornoway whisky seems to have been of superior quality, for in April 1833, at 11 o.p. it fetched 8/6 a gallon in the Glasgow market. However, in a competition in Liverpool with Islay and other Highland whiskies, Ness won the prize. (13)

The suppression of illicit distillation however, had some unexpected benefits, as the new distilleries bought the crofters' surplus grain for cash. Before long, a bad harvest came to be dreaded, as the tenantry now depended on this source of income to pay their rents. In 1833, the tenants of Ness received £499. 13/- in cash for their grain. More time could also now be devoted to fishing and the cultivation of land for growing more barley, time once devoted to distilling.

There were other side effects from the decline of illicit distilling. In 1833, Stornoway had eighteen licensed premises, consisting of four inns, seven shops, and seven petty public houses, "the pest of the morals of the people", according to the local minister. (14) Uig had one inn, as had Lochs, at Loch Shell, which was mostly frequented by sailors, as the Park district had practically been cleared of its inhabitants by this time. In 1836, Barvas had neither inn nor alehouse.

In 1827, a Highland newspaper stated that there was not a drop of illicit whisky to be got from the Butt of Lewis to Barra Head, owing to the vigilance of Captain Oliver of the revenue cutter *Prince of Wales*. (15) Yet, in 1834, Factor Knox reported to the proprietor that the tenants along the north shore of Broad Bay were better off than those in other districts owing to their distillation of whisky.

The village of Borve is said to have been the last township to give up distilling. At first, neither fines nor imprisonment could compel them to abandon it. Distilling came to an end when the potato crop failed in 1846, as they required all their grain for their own sustenance. However, it is Geodha Beuc in Ness, that has the doubtful honour of being the last stronghold of distillation in Lewis.

LAW AND ORDER

During the Norse occupation of the Island, law, as we know it today, did not exist. In the society of that time, might was right. "Land was the only wealth, its ownership the sole foundation of power, privilege or dignity. As no man could win or hold possession without the strong arm to defend it, every landowner was a warrior, and every warrior a husbandsman." (1)

When the Norse left Lewis and the Lordship of the Isles was established, there was possibly a *Breitheamh,* or Brieve in every island who acted as a judge and settled disputes. He was granted land by the Macdonalds, and was allowed an eleventh part of any fine he imposed. However, an appeal could be made against a Brieve's decision to the Council of the Isles in Islay.

The office of Brieve in Lewis was hereditary, and was held by successive Morison chiefs, who had their seat in the *Tigh Mor,* Big House, in Habost in Ness. From there, like his counterpart in the Isle of Man, the Brieve was expected to administer justice between man and man as evenly as the backbone divides the two sides of a herring. (2)

Of the Brieves of Lewis, only the last two, Hucheon Morison and his son John, achieved prominence.

There was never much love between the Macleods and the Morisons, and the little there was, vanished, when Hucheon committed adultery with Janet Mackenzie, the wife of the chief, Rory MacLeod, and the mother of the ill-fated Torquil Conanach. This led to the downfall of the MacLeods, the Siol Torquil.

The Mackenzies felt that only Rory's son, Torquil Dubh, stood between them and possession of Lewis, so it was decided to dispose of him. On the promise of a substantial reward, John Morison, the Brieve, agreed to help, and soon afterwards, he captured Torquil Dubh by treachery, and took him across to Ullapool, where Kenneth Mackenzie had him executed, in July 1597.

This led to many skirmishes between the MacLeods, aided by the Macaulays,and the Morisons, who were forced to take refuge in Dun Eistein, in Knockaird in Ness, and later among their kinsfolk round Durness, in Sutherland. It was here the Brieve paid for his misdeeds when he met by chance, in Inverkirkaig, Little John Mac Donald Mac Hucheon, of Isle Handa, a MacLeod, who killed him. The Brieve's friends in Lewis retrieved his body, but due to contrary winds, became storm-bound on an island near Edderachyllis, where they disembowelled the corpse and buried the intestines, before re-crossing the Minch. Since then, this island has been named *Eilean a' Bhreitheimh,* the Brieve's Island.

Little John MacLeod later captured Malcolm, the late Brieve's eldest son, and had him taken across to Stornoway, where he was beheaded. The Brieve's remaining sons, including the famous Allan, were pursued across the Minch by Neil Odhar MacLeod, and killed in a sea-fight near Dun Othail, between Tolsta and Ness.

Life was cheap at this time in Lewis, as elsewhere. There was a Gallows Hill at Kneep in Uig, Bragar in Barvas, and across the bay from Stornoway, where the last victim was a man who was said to have stolen a hen. Where gallows were not readily available, a ship's mast was equally effective, or a plank across a crevice.

It is said that the notorious Donald Cam Macaulay, the Uig chieftain, was stopped from executing a blacksmith, who had thrust a red-hot iron bar into his eye, because he was the only smith in the community, and too useful. However, there were two tailors on whom he could exact revenge, so the superfluous tailor paid the penalty.

When the Mackenzies gained possession of Lewis, the ruthless Tutor of Kintail introduced his own particular brand of justice. Successive factors, ground officers and tacksmen closely followed his example, keeping the Islanders in subjection.

From 1789, the early Sheriffs and Sheriff-substitutes were not exactly noted for leniency. Neither of them lived on the Island at this time, and up to the passing of the Crofters' Act in 1884, the law seemed to be very much on the side of the proprietor. Removing summonses were so common at this time, that one exasperated Nessman was heard to say that when the Law came to Lewis, Justice sailed out by Goat Island in Stornoway Harbour.

The most common crimes during the eighteenth and nineteenth centuries were theft, chiefly sheep-stealing, assault, illegal distilling, and attempts at prison-breaking to release friends. Drunkenness is a comparatively recent innovation due to closer contact with civilisation. Murder or attempted murder was very rare. Over a century ago, Bayble was the scene of a ghastly murder, when a schoolmaster killed his wife. A body found in a peat bog near the end of the Grimshader Road, some years back, was judged to have lain there for close on two hundred years. The story of this accidental fatality was well known. (3) Other people were said to have been murdered long ago near Callanish, and between Barvas and Shader.

In 1816, the master of the brig *Fly* was accused of ill-treating and murdering one of his crew by running a sword or cutlass through him. Another man, *Mac an t-Srònaich*, Stronach, who belonged to Garve in Ross-shire, is believed to have killed a few Islanders, and attempted to murder more, during the years 1831-38, when he roamed the moors of Lewis. One of his victims was said to be a young boy from Ness whom he drowned in a pool near Muirneag, a murder which lay on his conscience for the rest of his life. He is reputed to have made the following statement:

> *An t-sùil a thug an leanabh orm anns a' bhotan bhùirn,*
> *Gum b'fhearr leam na na chunna' mi, gu robh e air mo ghlùin.*

The look the child gave me from the deep pool;
I would rather than anything that he were on my knee.

On the scaffold he is reported to have said:

> *Seachd bliadhna ghleidh thu tearuint' mi,*
> *A mhointich, riabhaich, Leodhais:*
> *Agus fhad's a ghleidh mis' thus'*
> *Ghleidh thusa mis'.*

Seven years you kept me safely,
O brown moors of Lewis,
And as long as I kept to you,
You preserved me.

136

Cases of stealing were always dealt with severely. In a case of sheep-stealing heard before Sheriff-Substitute Munro in 1789, one of the three men accused was acquitted, the second found guilty, while the third "by a plurality of voices", was found proven a "habit reputed thief." Both were ordered to be carried "from the Bar to the Tolbooth of this village (Stornoway)," from where they were taken out after a period of detention with a rope round their necks, and with placards on their breasts, bearing the words "SHEEP STEALING". Thereafter, the executioner led them through the streets of Stornoway, Goathill and Bayhead, and between noon and 4 pm, they received ten lashes on their backs at each of the following places: Point Street, near the Old Custom House; on the South Shore, near Morison's house; in the middle of Goathill Street, opposite the Bayhead houses; and finally, on Cromwell Street. They were both then set free, and banished from the Island for five years, and warned that if they returned within that period, they would be publicly flogged once again and banished for a further five years. (5)

Imprisonment, neck-roping, breast-placarding, public flogging, pillorying and banishment were the usual forms of punishment. Pillorying was restricted to Market Days and Sundays.

A young woman caught stealing bread from a baker's shop who did not want to stand trial, petitioned the sheriff to banish her for whatever term he liked. He took her at her word, and banished her for seven years.

Another young woman from the country was caught shop-lifting in Stornoway, and after being imprisoned for three days in the Tolbooth, was led out with a rope round her neck and a placard on her breast bearing the words "HABIT AND REPUTE A THIEF". She was then pilloried for two hours and banished for seven years, with the usual threat of a similar punishment if she returned within the stipulated period. She returned in less than a year, was again imprisoned, pilloried, and banished for a further seven years. Nothing more was heard of her. No doubt she would have a difficult life having no English to help her earn her living. (6)

A native of the parish of Barvas, during a period of imprisonment in 1819 for stealing seed from a neighbour's barn, discovered that the post of executioner was vacant. He applied to the sheriff for the post, at the same time stipulating that reasonable provision should be made for his family. His application was successful, and he was released to take up the position which entitled him to certain fees and perquisites connected with the job. (7)

Assaults were also fairly common, and were not confined to men. A lady from Bayhead, with an apron full of stones, ambushed a mainlander with whom she was in dispute. Unlike most women, she was an excellent shot.

The crime statistics for Stornoway for 1842-49 were:

YEAR	ASSAULT	CONCEALMENT OF PREGNANCY	THEFT	SWINDLING	MALICIOUS MISCHIEF
1842	2	—	3	—	—
1843	5	—	1	—	—
1844	8	—	10	—	2
1845	11	—	5	—	1
1846	15	—	9	—	9
1847	10	1	21	—	3
1848	6	—	17	2	—
1849	1	—	—	2	—
	58	1	66	4	15	(8)

It is obvious that crime was at its peak during the famine years of 1846-48.

The law relating to poinding, made it perfectly clear that all who possessed land had to herd their stock so that they might not cause damage to a neighbour's property. The penalty for neglect was half a mark for every beast that trespassed, in addition to having to pay for any damage done. It was perfectly legal for the person whose land had been trespassed on to detain the animals until his claim for damage was paid. (9)

Each farm or tack had a poind, *am priosan dubh,* the black prison, a small walled enclosure, sometimes only twenty feet by twelve feet, where stray animals were kept. This enclosure was often so tightly packed that the animals could hardly move. If the animals were not claimed, it was not possible to sell them until certain procedures had been complied with. In the first instance, an announcement of the intended sale had to be made at the church door on three successive Sundays, and also at the Chamberlain's office.

The animals did not always stray accidentally on to farms or tacks. The herds often allowed them to cross the boundary dyke if the herbage was better there. In one such instance, a boy who had allowed his animals to stray, attacked the farmer's dogs which had been sent to bring them to the poind. When the shepherd came to their rescue, he was also attacked. The boy, who was a powerful youngster, was taken to Court, and fined £1 for the assault. He refused to pay the fine, and so spent the night in gaol. In the morning, after paying the fine, he was released, but instead of returning home, he enlisted. As a Colour Sergeant at the Battle of the Modder River in South Africa, he was decorated for his gallantry. Later he rose to commissioned rank, and took part in the Gallipoli Campaign.

Poinding was a source of revenue to farmers, and often the fine was paid with articles like blankets, plaids, wool, grain, potatoes etc. when money was scarce.

A letter to Mr Adam, the factor, in 1822, reads as follows:

Dear Sir,
   Our horses went over the way of Tong yesterday, and Donald Murray has put them in the penfold, and we were over today for them, and we offered what we had ourselves, potatoes, some of our advyse till we would get money and he would not give us the horses and we are come to see you and we are promising to pay you faithfully the first money we will get in our hands or to pay them by work any time you think proper.
                                        Your M.H. Servants
                                        William Macrae
                                        John Macdonald. (10)

The Sheriff Court had also to deal with many cases of small debts. In 1818, an Uig pensioner sued another pensioner from the same village for the £1.13/-he had lent him in Fort George seventeen years earlier. He also claimed 18/-interest on this sum.

Many country people fell into debt with the Stornoway merchants. Here is one such debt of 1823:

2½ yd. cotton stripe, 1/1 a yd.	2/9
1 bonnet 2/-; 1 piece leather 10½	2/10½
3 pieces leather	1/4
Sugar and roll tobacco	1/5
2 oz. indigo	2/-
1 hat 8/6; 1 knife 1/-; 1 snuff box 4½d.	9/10½

Cash 6d; soap 5d.	11
1 waistcoat	2/-
Horse-hair 9d; 3 ½ yd. cotton stripe 2/9	3/6
2 doz. buttons 10d; biscuits 5d	1/3
10 oz. roll tobacco 6d; soap 5d.	11
	£1/8/10

The non-payment of rent often led to the sequestration of the defaulters' possessions, or at least that portion of it which would pay the debt.

Many of the sequestrated could easily have paid their rents. Many examples of this came before the Sheriff Court.

Colin Mackenzie, the tenant of Molchaigle in 1817, whose possessions were sequestrated, seems to have been in comfortable circumstances, owning 40 sheep with 12 lambs, 3 wedders, 20 milch goats with kids, 1 buck and 3 he-goats, 2 black milch cows with calves, 1 brandered cow, 1 red cow, 1 brown cow 2 years old, 1 red cow two years old, 1 black and white cow 2 years old, 1 year old quey and 1 brandered 3 year old heifer.

Increasing contact with the outside world has not benefited Lewis morally, and it is a sad reflection on the Welfare State, that crime generally, has steadily increased in recent years throughout the whole country including our own Island.

Drink is the cause of most of the cases which come before the Sheriff in Stornoway today. At one time it was regarded as disgraceful for a woman to be seen entering a pub, but the war years altered that. Rightly or wrongly, the Islanders have acquired an unenviable reputation for drinking.

However, in spite of all these criticisms, Lewis still has one of the most law-abiding communities in the United Kingdom.

EDUCATION

Although the arrival of St Columba in Iona in 563 A.D. heralded the dawn of education in Scotland (and much progress was made during the intervening centuries, both by the Celtic and Roman Catholic Churches), it was not until after the Reformation in 1560, that any serious attempt was made to create a national system of education.

In John Knox's First Book of Discipline, the importance of education was stressed, "seeing that God hath determined that his Kirke here in earth shall be taught, not by angels, but by men, and that men are born ignorant of God and all Godlinesse".

The young people of Scotland had to be educated, so a clearly defined plan was formulated to cater for them from the age of five until the University stage. Pupils with an aptitude for learning were to be encouraged to continue their studies, no matter what their station in life might be, while those with little ability were to be put to a trade. Colleges were to be provided in large towns, and those who could afford it, paid their children's expenses, while scholars from poorer families were financed by the Church. Unfortunately, the State was not forthcoming with funds for this far-reaching scheme, chiefly due to the rapacity of certain individuals, so a complete implementation could not be achieved.

It took a long time for Knox's idea of education for the masses to reach Lewis, where, according to the records of the Privy Council, there was a great need for it. In the last quarter of the sixteenth century, the Island was torn by fratricidal strife, and was constantly in trouble with the Crown, who regarded the Islanders as absolute barbarians, "guilty of such beastly and monstrous cruelties as were unheard of even among the Turks and other infidels, (1) an island possessed by a set of lawless and godless people, who, being brought up in all kinds of wickedness, were unlikely ever to be reformed to lead quiet and useful lives." (2) Even the Chief, Roderick Macleod, was unable to sign his name on a deed of 1573. Ronald Anguson, the parson of Uig signed on his behalf, "because he could not write himself, his hand led on a pen." (3)

When Bishop Knox of the Isles managed to coerce the Island Chiefs and important gentlemen of the Hebrides to agree to the Statues of Icolmkill (Iona) in 1609, they had difficulty in accepting the sixth statute. This proposed that everyone possessing sixty cattle should send his eldest son (or if he had no son, his eldest daughter) to a school in the Lowlands, to learn to read, write and speak English. The statute was largely ignored, and in fact, Macleod of Lewis was not even present at the meeting. (4)

In 1616, Parliament ordered that a school and schoolmaster was to be provided for every parish in Scotland, with the landowners making the school available and paying the schoolmaster's salary. In the same year, it was decided that Gaelic, which they considered to be the cause of the continued "barbarity and incivility" in the Highlands and Islands should be abolished, and replaced by the "vulgar English toung." (5)

Further Acts connected with education were passed in 1633 and 1646, but as these proved to be rather ineffective, another Act for the Settling of Schools, was passed in 1696. Once again, this stipulated that landowners had to provide a school and a schoolmaster at a salary of 100 to 200 merks. Those who failed to comply with this stipulation were to be punished.

However, there were schools in the North of Scotland before this date at such places as Fortrose, Fearn, Inverness, Beauly and Kingussie. Stornoway was not far behind these early centres of learning, for there was a school there before 1680, according to John Morrison of Bragar who wrote at this time:

> Onlie the time the country is possessed and safely governed by the Earle of Seaforth, by whose industrious care and benevolence, the people, formerly inclined to rudeness and barbarity, are reduced to civilie, much understanding and knowledge, by the flourishing schools planted and maintained by the said Earls all the tyme in the town of Stornoway, and not only the people of Lews, but those of the next adjacent isles, the gentlemen's sons and daughters, are bred in that school, to the great good and comfort of the people; so that there are few families but at least the maister can read and write. I do remember in my tyme, when there was not three in all the county that knew A b by a Bible. (6)

In other words, the children of the tacksmen, the ministers and other important gentlemen were catered for, but not the rest of the community. Education, was not for them. The Stornoway school was still functioning about 1695, when Martin Martin visited the island. It was a grammar school, where Latin and English were taught, but shortly after, it experienced financial difficulties. In 1743, the Stornoway Presbytery complained, that Lord Fortrose, the proprietor, had stopped paying the £100 annual grant which had been paid by his predecessors. Subsequently, this once flourishing school in the Parish of Stornoway which also catered for children from the rural areas, closed. (7) However, the Royal Bounty (a sum of money which George I donated in 1724 to the Church of Scotland for the reformation of the parts of the island where Popery and ignorance prevailed) came to the rescue and, before long, the school at Stornoway was once again in operation. The importance of the school may be gauged by the fact that in 1750, there was a suggestion that the Kirk Sessions of Uig, Barvas and Lochs, should each pay 13/6 for the repair of the Stornoway schoolhouse, the Stornoway Kirk Session contributing £2. Two years later, the ministers of these same parishes agreed to pay William Mackenzie, the schoolmaster of the Bounty School at Stornoway a small bonus. (8)

In a report to the General Assembly, attention was drawn to the need for schools of a 'higher type' than the ordinary parochial schools in the Highlands and Islands, for the instruction of the young in the learned languages, and in assisting those who intended to become students of Divinity. For this purpose, the schoolmaster of Fort Augustus, James Mackenzie, was transferred to the Bounty School at Stornoway, where he was instructed to use such time as he could spare from catechising. (9)

On the appointment of a young schoolmaster, Thomas Notman, to this School in 1774, the Presbytery drafted the following regulations for his guidance: (10)

1. To train up the youth in the principles of religion and morality, being the most essential part of education, it is recommended to the master to labour diligently therein in his teaching, discipline and by his

example. For this purpose he is every day to begin and dismiss the meeting of the school with prayer.

2. He is to set apart two afternoons each week for catechising his scholars in the principles of Christianity, and for teaching and explaining the Shorter Catechism, together with the old Psalms and other portions of the Holy Writ, also for teaching and explaining such forms of prayer as may be best suited to the age and capacity of the scholars.

3. The master is to inspect the morals of the scholars, not only during the time they are in school, but also while they are abroad at their diversions, particularly that they abstain from lying, cursing, swearing, pilfering, and profanation of the Lord's Day, for which purpose he is to appoint censors who are to report whatever they see their fellow-scholars do amiss, either in or out of school.

4. If any scholar shall continue vicious and obstinate after all habile methods are used for reclaiming him, he shall be extruded lest his bad example should debauch the morals of the rest.

5. It is recommended to the master to use all mild methods his prudence will suggest for the due exercise of his office, before he proceed to correction, but if he find that mild methods are ineffectual, he is to correct with temper and moderation, and he is inhibited from receiving any scholar to his school whom his parents or guardians will not put in his power to correct if necessary.

6. From the first of October to the first of February, the scholars are to convene at 8 o'clock, to be dismissed at 10 forenoon, to convene again at 11, and to be dismissed at 3 afternoon. During the rest of the year, they are to convene at 7 in the morning, to be dismissed at 9 forenoon, to convene again at 10, to be dismissed at 12, to convene again at 2 o'clock and to be dismissed at 5 afternoon.

7. On such Sundays as there is a sermon at Stornoway, the scholars are to convene in the school at 11 o'clock to repeat such questions as were subscribed the evening before, and then to walk along with the master to Church. When the length of the day admits, they are to convene again at 6 o'clock afternoon to give notes of the sermon, or for such other exercise as the master shall direct and to be dismissed at 7. On such Sundays as there is no sermon at Stornoway, the scholars are to be convened at 12 noon, and to remain till 2 p.m., in such exercises as the master shall judge expedient.

8. The scholars are to be arranged into classes, the first class of English Scholars to read Masson's Spelling Book, the second the New Testament and Dictionary, the third the Bible, the fourth The Economy of Human Life, Milton's Paradise Lost, and an English Grammar. The Latin and Greek classes will be recommended to the master as they are needed.

9. Every scholar must be possessed of a copy of the book read by the class he belongs to, otherwise he is not to be received.

10. The school fees are eighteen pence for teaching English and Writing, two shillings for Writing and Arithmetic, and half-a-crown for Latin and Greek, all by the quarter. (The Presbytery recommend to the parents of the scholars to pay the fees of every preceding quarter at the beginning of the next).

11. The master is to give at school hours such a number of lessons in Church music in the week to his scholars as he shall judge proper, or,

if between and after school hours he shall attend other persons for that purpose, his scholars shall also attend and be taught gratis.

Gaelic was not included in the curriculum.

Meanwhile, in 1700, a number of philanthropic gentlemen in Edinburgh, anxious to improve educational facilities in the remote areas of the Highlands and Islands, decided to solicit subscriptions to establish a fund to supply schools in districts where there was no parish school. (11) In 1709, the subscribers were elected into a body corporate, by letters-patent from Queen Anne, as the Society in Scotland for Propagating Christian Knowledge.

By 1711, five schools, including one on the far off Island of St Kilda were in operation, and before the end of the century, the number had reached two hundred.

Owing to demand, the Society decided to make their schools ambulatory, only staying in one place for about two years, or until such time as the scholars had learnt to read the Bible in English. All the schools were supervised by the Presbyteries in which they were situated.

The high standards set for parochial schoolmasters were not required of the S.S.P.C.K. schoolmasters, who were chosen more for their piety than for their educational attainments. The Society felt that their efforts should be concentrated "towards the cultivation of unperverted and uncorrupted youth" rather than in "employing unavailing efforts to instruct and reclaim untoward age." (12)

The curriculum was confined to teaching the principles of religion, reading, writing, arithmetic and psalm tunes. The teaching of Gaelic was forbidden under the threat of instant dismissal. This ban was not rescinded until 1767, when after half a century of restriction, it was realised that by prohibiting the teaching of their native language, the children showed a general lack of interest in education and experienced great difficulty in acquiring English.

In 1739, a Gaelic and English vocabulary by Alexander Macdonald was printed. The Mother's Catechism, in Gaelic, followed in 1758, but the New Testament was not translated until 1767. All these books were printed at the expense of the S.S.P.C.K.

All the stations for the schools were carefully chosen, with the Society insisting that, before one of their schools was established, proper provision must be made for the accommodation of the teacher by way of a dwelling house and a schoolhouse, as well as a kailyard, fuel and a cow's grass (sufficient pasture to maintain a cow for a year).

Later, as some landowners were slow to establish parish schools, it was decided that no charity school would be placed where there was no parish school, (13) since the former was meant to supplement the work of the latter and not to replace it.

In 1738, the S.S.P.C.K. applied for and was granted a second patent, which allowed it to give instruction in agriculture, trades, manufacture and housewifery. Salaries were to be paid to school-masters' wives and other females who were capable of teaching spinning, sewing and knitting.

The first S.S.P.C.K. schools erected in Lewis were at Barvas and Keose on 1st May 1737, with James Thomson and John Maclennan as their respective teachers. Mr Thomson was paid a salary of £5 from the S.S.P.C.K., and £4 from the Royal Bounty, while Mr Maclennan also received £5 from the S.S.P.C.K. but only £1 from the Royal Bounty.

A school was also placed in Bernera, but the schoolmaster, having been without a single scholar for twenty-seven months, was moved elsewhere. The teacher at Nether Coll only lasted a year at his post before being transferred to North Shawbost, where the Lochs minister felt his influence might counteract the frivolity of the youth there, who had built a house specially for fiddling and dancing, which was exceptionally well patronised on Saturday nights.

The first Spinning School to be established in Lewis was in 1763 with a Fife lady as mistress. The women were at first rather chary of attending, as it was rumoured they might be sent to the American plantations. However, as soon as this report had been discredited, they proved to be quick learners, and, instead of it taking three years, as was expected, to train one hundred and fifty of them, this task was completed in a year. A period of about three months was found to be sufficient to train a set of fifty pupils, ages ranging from nine to twenty-five, to acquire sufficient dexterity.

In spite of this initial success in the town of Stornoway, many obstacles were encountered in the rural areas, and it took all of Mrs Mackenzie's (later Lady Seaforth) patience and perseverance to overcome the women's unwillingness to attend the Spinning Schools.

The pupils at these schools were taught free of charge, were given 10d. for every spindle spun, and were supplied with wheels at a low price. If the girl was poor, sometimes the spinning wheels were given without charge. Mrs Mackenzie also provided each of them with two pounds of coarse lint to begin with, and organised competitions in the various schools with prizes for the best performers. (14)

These schools were so successful, that for many years, the Island had an annual export of thousands of spindles of linen yarn, and this was done by women, most of whom, ten years before, had not seen a spinning wheel. (15)

In 1796, schools based in the four parishes were as follows:

TYPE OF SCHOOL	STORNOWAY	BARVAS	LOCHS	UIG
Parochial	1	vacant	1	1
S.S.P.C.K.	1	1	1	1
Spinning	1	1	2	3

Teachers' salaries were not very high at this time. The parochial schoolmaster in Stornoway earned £25 per annum, and his assistant £15. In addition, the schoolmaster received whatever fees he was able to collect from his pupils, along with a dwelling house, a garden, and some land, rent free, from the proprietor. (16)

The S.S.P.C.K. schoolmaster was paid a salary of £17 and his assistant £8, but he had a schoolhouse of stone and lime, recently built at Seaforth's expense. (17)

The Spinning School mistress was paid £6 per annum by Lord Seaforth, and £4 by the S.S.P.C.K. She also had a garden and a slated house. (18)

In the other parishes, where the cost of living was expected to be less, the Spinning School mistresses' salary was £6, paid jointly by Mrs Mackenzie of Seaforth, and the S.S.P.C.K. This was expected to keep them comfortable, in conjunction with the goodwill of the people, who would be kind and attentive to them. (19)

In the Stornoway Parish School, the fees per quarter were as follows. English and Writing 2/6; English and Arithmetic 3/; Latin, Writing and Arithmetic 4/-; a course of Geography 10/6; Navigation £1.1/-; and for each set of Book-keeping 10/6. In all, there were forty pupils. (20)

The fees in the Society's school were much cheaper, the quarter fees were:

Reading 1/6; Writing 2/-; Arithmetic 2/6; Book-keeping 5/-; Mensuration 5/-; Navigation 10/-. There were 129 pupils at this school. (21)

As one would expect, the Spinning Schools were far more popular in the country than either the parochial or society ones, and at one time, there were ten such schools in operation. As a result, schoolmasters' wives, sisters, or any other women capable of doing so, were able to earn a little money teaching knitting and sewing.

In his report to the S.S.P.C.K. in 1800, Dr Macleod, the minister of Harris, who was superintendent of the Society's schools in the Synod of Glenelg, gave a very gloomy account of the Lewis people's attitude to education.

> The common people seem to have a rooted aversion to education. They and their fathers having never been taught letters, they cannot conceive of what use they can be to their children: they think that as literature brings no pecuniary advantage, so it is attended with this great loss, that it entices the children to leave them and their mean domestic employments at home. . . . The prospect of advantage from school appears to the crofter at best, distant and uncertain. The service of his child, so soon as he can herd a cow, or handle a spade, he considers as a present good, and looks no further into consequences. (22)

At various times, the S.S.P.C.K. had schools operating at Stornoway, Knock, Bayble, Nether Coll, Swainbost, Carloway, Bernera, Balnacille and Keose; but in spite of their efforts, these schools had very little effect, and the little support they had, practically ceased with the advent of the popular Gaelic Schools.

On 16th January 1811, there was formed in Edinburgh, a society, whose express purpose was to teach the inhabitants of the Highlands and Islands to read the Scriptures in their mother tongue. (23) It was called the Edinburgh Society for the Support of Gaelic Schools, a society, whose work over the next three decades did more to influence the minds of the people of Lewis than any other agency before.

Similar societies came into being in Glasgow in 1812, and in Inverness in 1818, but it was largely the Edinburgh Society which supplied the schools for Lewis. The Glasgow and Inverness Societies taught English as well as Gaelic in their schools, but it was only towards the end of its career that the Edinburgh Society did likewise.

Although the S.S.P.C.K. supported many schools throughout Scotland at this time, the Edinburgh Society realised how much more remained to be done, especially in the North, and they felt the best way to remedy the situation was to plant circulating schools in the most needy regions to teach the people in their own language. From the very beginning, the society concerned itself more with religious matters than with the various branches of education.

Very definite regulations were drawn up for the organisation of these schools. They were to be in the charge of men who were selected for their piety rather than for their intellectual ability: God fearing men of high moral standards, who could convey the blessings of the Gospel by reading the Scriptures and setting an example of Christian living. Although they were allowed to read the Scriptures, these men were forbidden to preach. This was not wholly due to ministerial jealousy, but chiefly because subscribers to the Society's funds were of all denominations, and these schools were intended for all children.

The schools were to remain in one place for a period of not less than six months and not more than eighteen months. (24) These schools were established for adults as well as children, and adults who could not attend during the day were accommodated during the evenings and on Sundays. In this way, everyone was catered for, and, it was hoped, as more and more people learnt to read, they would give assistance to the schoolmaster. (25)

The Society estimated that for a sum of 12/- per annum, or 18/- for eighteen months, a person could be taught to read the Scriptures. The expense of running a school was £30 per annum.

> For this sum, scarcely sufficient to buy the most insignificant article of luxury in food or raiment, you furnish to an immortal soul, the key which unlocks the treasures of salvation; you give his bosom a companion exempt from the failings of humanity, you introduce him to immediate communication with his God. (26)

The books to be used were —a First and Second Book in Gaelic (1d. and 2d. respectively), a Psalm Book (1/4d.), the New Testament (1/10d.), the Bible (4/6d.), as well as some extracts from the Scriptures (4d.)

The schools were to operate during those periods of the year when the people had most leisure time, carefully avoiding spring-time and harvest-time.

The year was divided into two sessions, the first of five months, from 1st November to 1st April, and the second of three months, from 15th June to 15th September.

In May 1811, the extent of illiteracy in the Island may be gauged from information supplied to the Society by the Rev. Colin Mackenzie, the minister of Stornoway. His Parish, he said, was divided into three districts, the town of Stornoway, the districts of Uidh, Eye or Point, and the Gress district. Of two thousand souls in Stornoway, only a third could read English, some imperfectly, while scarcely twenty could read Gaelic. One thousand one hundred and thirty three could not read English or Gaelic. (27) Uidh had eight hundred souls. Twenty could read English, and about six could read Gaelic. Gress, which stretched from Tong to Tolsta, contained seven hundred souls. Six could read English and two could read Gaelic. Uidh and Gress had to be content with a sermon every five weeks, along with the labours of two catechists, so that apart from those people who could afford to board their children in town, no benefit was gained from the Parish and S.S.P.C.K. schools there. (28)

Of the first five schools founded by the Edinburgh Gaelic Schools Society in the Highlands and Islands, one was stationed at Bayble in Lewis, with an Angus Macleod, a Skyeman, as schoolmaster. (29) Mr Macleod began teaching in Mid-December, 1811. His first day was not very encouraging, for only three pupils turned up; the following day twenty appeared, and before long, he had sixty on the roll. He taught without a break for ten months, and seldom had fewer than fifty scholars. His time-table makes one wonder how he managed to survive, far less conduct himself to the satisfaction of the whole community. In winter, he began work regularly at 7.00 a.m. by candlelight, dismissed his pupils at 9 or 10 a.m. for an hour's break, they assembled again at 10 or 11 a.m., and continued to work till 4 p.m. The school re-opened again at 5 p.m. to accommodate other pupils and continued until 10 p.m. or even midnight. (30) His adult pupils were so anxious to learn, that they would sit up night and day if possible. (31)

In fifteen days, the people built Mr Macleod a large schoolhouse 35 feet in length, but on many occasions, it could not accommodate all the people who gathered on Sundays to hear the Gospel. One Sunday he had three hundred eager listeners. Those who could not squeeze inside, lay on the roof to listen. (32)

In July 1812, Mr Macleod informed the Edinburgh Committee that he had one boy reading Genesis, four in the New Testament, eighteen reading the Psalm Book, with a number of others about to begin. He also had six scholars who had been at an English school, but had been unable to understand a single sentence of what they read. They were now making good progress. (33)

One lady told him how strange it was to see so many Psalm books in Church. Formerly, there had only been four, the minister's, her own, and two others. (34)

Mr Macleod was removed to Gress in 1813, leaving behind him people who were both able and willing to carry on the work which he had so successfully pioneered.

When Mr Macleod arrived in Gress, there was a schoolhouse ready waiting for him. He had brought one of his scholars with him from Bayble, and on the first occasion that the minister came to preach, this lad, to the amazement of the congregation, precented and also read the Gaelic Scriptures. This so impressed the congregation, that Mr Macleod promptly sold all the books which he had the foresight to bring with him. (35)

His period of service at Gress was as successful as his stay at Bayble. When he arrived, only six people in the district were able to read English, and only two could read Gaelic, but such was the desire to learn to read the Scriptures, that before long, one hundred and fifty were in attendance at his school. When Mr Macleod left Gress, the people were sincerely dismayed to see him go.

A correspondent in the Stornoway Parish was so impressed by the influence of the schools at Bayble and Gress, that he wrote to the Committee saying that these schools had done more good in spreading knowledge and in warming the hearts of the common people to true religion than all the other means which they had enjoyed for the last century. Two years before, they used to gather in groups on the Sabbath and talk about every kind of nonsense. They now met regularly every Sabbath, when the boys of the school read a chapter of the Old and New Testament alternately.

By 1815, there were eight Gaelic Schools on the Island, at Ness, Melbost, Tolsta, Shawbost, Bragar, Barvas, Valtos (Uig) and Balallan. As soon as the teachers arrived, they were warmly received and they began to teach immediately, even if there was no accommodation or books available. In Bragar, the school initially met in a barn, and even when the new school was built, it was a barn-like structure, with the usual double walls of unhewn stone or turf, thatched with straw, fern or heather. The fire, for which the pupils brought peats, was in the centre of the floor with a hole almost directly above it. It was really a pocket edition of the ordinary black house without the *todhar,* byre. The small windows were, at first, simply holes in the thatch on the wall-top, and admitted little light even in summer, while in winter, it was dark, for these openings had to be closed to keep out the wind, the rain and the cold. The peat smoke, thus denied egress, made visibility very poor. The floor, which was of bare earth or beaten clay, had heaps of stones lying here and there for seats.

A favourite punishment, was for a recalcitrant scholar to be made to stand on top of one of these heaps of stones with a basin on his head. If the basin fell, he was punished. Needless to say, the victim's classmates amused themselves by aiming *caorans,* bits of peat, at the basin, and in trying to dodge these, the basin often clattered to the floor with the attendant result.

The furniture was equally simple, a desk or table for the schoolmaster, and a plank or planks placed on stones or logs for the scholars.

As a rule, the Estate supplied the roof timber for these dwellings, as wood was always scarce. The Gravir people got their school when a fir log, suitable for roofing, was washed ashore.

Before long, the fame of these schools, *Sgoilean Chriosd,* The Schools of Christ, as they came to be known, spread throughout the Island, and the ministers, as well as the townships in some cases, vied with one another for priority, each claiming to be in a more necessitous condition than the rest.

The ministers derived great benefit from the services of these pious, self-sacrificing teachers, for not only did they read the Scriptures and catechise the people on Sundays, they also kept Sunday Schools, visited the sick and the dying, and laboured unceasingly for the temporal and spiritual welfare of the community in which they temporarily resided. Their salary of £12 per annum was later increased to £25. One minister wrote:

> I labour alone, without a catechist or useful teacher within the bounds of my Parish. Pray that notwithstanding these inconveniences and disadvantages I may not be alone, but that I may be graciously supported by the Head of all gracious influences, seeing that He giveth power to the faint and to them who have no might He giveth strength. I am in hopes that any teachers the Society may be pleased to favour us with will prove pious and judicious as without that, I am convinced, that they cannot be useful in this place. (36)

An example of the unselfishness of these devoted teachers is the case of Alexander Anderson, the Barvas schoolmaster, who asked the Society for a dozen pairs of spectacles for the use of poor old scholars, stipulating that unless some benefactor paid for them, the price was to be deducted from his salary. (37)

The scholars were of all ages and of both sexes, although there were more men than women. In one school, there was a great grandmother and a child of five. With few exceptions, married couples attended regularly, mothers with children at their breasts came, and in some classes, children sat next to their fathers and grandfathers.

One example of how eagerly the people took advantage of the opportunity to learn to read the Scriptures was that of Donald Macritchie, a father who could not read when the school in the village was opened. He gave a neighbour's boy a lamb for coming to his house every morning and evening, to read to him at the time of family worship. Before long, both this man and his wife were able to read a little, and a young daughter of theirs, about ten years of age, precented and read the chapter at family worship, while her father raised the tune and prayed. (38)

Examination day in the school was a cause of much excitement. It was regularly conducted by the minister, often accompanied by the tacksmen, or one of the Society's inspectors. The parents listened eagerly to the questions and the answers.

The questions asked of eight-year old John Macdonald of Back, during one of these examinations, illustrated the type of teaching that took place.

"How many Kings were in Israel?"
  "Nineteen."
"In Judah?"
  "Twenty".

"Were more of the Kings evil or good?"
"More evil!"
"Where is Bethel?"
"In Israel."
"Why did Josiah go to Bethel to destroy the altar seeing it was situated in Israel?"
"There was no King in Israel when Josiah reigned in Judah: the ten tribes were carried captive." (39)

All those who visited the schools were surprised how quickly the scholars learnt to read Gaelic, and to their utter amazement they also discovered that by learning to read their own language, they also became interested in reading and speaking the English language; actually, it was the best way to start learning English, a fact which some parents and educationists still ignore.

In 1840, Mr Knox, the factor, claimed that the Gaelic teachers were the most useful people that ever came among the poor tenantry of Lewis, (40) while that prince of preachers, the Rev. John Macrae of Ness, *"MacRath Mor,"* expressed the same view in his own inimitable way. *"Cho fada agus a bhitheas bainne geal aig bò dhubh, cha bu choir do mhuinntir Leodhais'di-chuimhn' 'a dheanamh air na Sgoilean Gaidhlig."* "As long as white milk comes from a black cow, the people of Lewis should not forget the Gaelic schools."

The subscriptions for the upkeep of these schools came from individuals, associations, and from Bible classes all over Britain and abroad. The people of Stornoway and of rural Lewis were also generous. Even the soldiers of the 78th and the 93rd Highlanders sent contributions to the Society, but as the years went on, the associations became less interested in providing educational facilities. With the introduction of National education, the Gaelic schools, having laid foundations for sensible education, ceased to function.

General Assembly Schools came into existence as a result of an enquiry made by the General Assembly of the Church of Scotland into the state of education in its sixteen synods. It was discovered that, of these, there were six synods, including the Synod of Glenelg, which required at least two hundred and fifty schools. (41)

Every minister in the Church was given particulars of the large number of uneducated people in these six synods, with the result that in a couple of years, a fund of almost £5,000 was raised from Parish collections, donations and annual subscriptions. (42)

Landowners of needy areas were asked to provide a schoolhouse, a dwelling house, a kailyard, and a cow's grass and fuel before a school could be established in a district.

The teachers were permitted to charge the same fees as those charged in the Parish schools. The first of these schools to be opened in Lewis was at Cross in Ness, in 1829. Later, another was opened in Stornoway.

The following details of education in Lewis in 1833 shows many changes since 1796. The Parish of Stornoway had at this time no fewer than thirteen schools. The S.S.P.C.K. had, however, only one school on the island, while the Gaelic Societies supported eleven. The Spinning Schools had disappeared by this time.

TYPE OF SCHOOL	STORNOWAY	BARVAS	LOCHS	UIG
Parochial.	1	1	Vacant	1
S.S.P.C.K.	1	—	—	—
Edinburgh Gaelic Soc.	2	2	4	3

Inverness Educ. Soc.	—	—	—	1
Female School, jointly endowed by the Hon. Mrs Stewart Mackenzie and Mary Carn Mackenzie.	1	—	—	—
Self. Supporting Schools (Tenants)	2	—	—	—
Schools supported jointly by the Hon. Mrs Stewart Mackenzie and Tenants.	3	—	—	—
Adventure Schools (unendowed).	3	—	—	—
Private School (Fee-paying) Discontinued.				
	13	3	4	5 (43)

The Female School was very popular, with a roll of sixty pupils who were taught to read, write and sew. Mary Carn Mackenzie, whose father had been the local postmaster, jointly endowed the School with the Hon. Mrs Stewart Mackenzie. Mary Carn Mackenzie was completely illiterate, yet her brother, Colonel Colin Mackenzie, was India's first Surveyor-General.

The teacher in charge of the Seminary had undergone teacher training in Edinburgh, but she had been reared in a family which had given over twenty years' service in Lewis Schools. Her father was an S.S.P.C.K. schoolmaster.

The fact that tenants in some villages were prepared to give financial support to schools, shows the awakening desire for education.

In December 1835, the list of persons engaged in teaching, apart from the four parochial schoolmasters, was:

STORNOWAY PARISH
BACK: A lad paid by the tenants.
MELBOST: Donald Ross, Gaelic School Society.
KNOCK/SWORDALE: Malcolm Macritchie, Gaelic School Society.
GARRABOST: Murdo Mackenzie, a teacher of English, paid £5 by the Hon. Mrs Stewart Mackenzie.
BAYBLE: Malcolm Macleod, paid by the tenants.
SANDWICKHILL: A teacher from the Edinburgh Gaelic Schools Society.
BAYHEAD: John Mackay, paid by the tenants and £5 from the Hon. Mrs Stewart Mackenzie.
STORNOWAY CHURCH: John Macmaster, paid £20 by the S.S.P.C.K.

LOCHS PARISH
LOCH SHELL: Mr and Mrs Neil Macleod, S.S.P.C.K. and paid £5 by the Hon. Mrs Stewart Mackenzie.
RANISH: Murdo Mackenzie, paid by the Glasgow Auxiliary Society and £4 by the Hon. Mrs Stewart Mackenzie.
MARVIG: Angus Mackay, Edinburgh Gaelic Schools Society.
SHIELDINISH: Angus Macfarlane, Edinburgh Gaelic Schools Society.
CARLOWAY: John Shaw, Edinburgh Gaelic Schools Society.
SHAWBOST: Alexander Munro, S.S.P.C.K. with a lot of land at an annual value of £5.

UIG PARISH:
VALTOS: Mr and Mrs Cameron, £15 from the Hon. Mrs Stewart Mackenzie.
CALLANISH: Mr and Mrs Matheson, £15 from the Hon. Mrs Stewart Mackenzie.
DOUNE: Mr and Mrs MacPherson, £15 from the Hon. Mrs Stewart Mackenzie.
BRENISH: Hector Morrison, Edinburgh Gaelic Schools Society.
CAPADALE: Donald Macfarlane, Edinburgh Gaelic Schools Society.
BERNERA: Angus MacIver, paid by the tenants.
TOLSTA CHAOLAIS: Alexander Macdonald, Inverness Gaelic Society.

BARVAS PARISH:

LOWER BARVAS:	A lad from Back, paid by the tenants.
UPPER BARVAS:	John Munro, Edinburgh Gaelic Schools Society.
MID BORVE:	Murdo Macleod, paid by the tenants.
NORTH GALSON:	Alexander Macleod, Edinburgh Gaelic Schools Society, formerly paid £8 by the Hon. Mrs Stewart Mackenzie.
SOUTH DELL:	Donald Mackay, paid by the tenants.
CROSS:	Donald Macdonald, Assembly schoolmaster, paid £3 by the Estate for the upkeep of a cow.
FIVEPENNY NESS:	Murdo Macdonald paid by the tenants.
ARNOL:	Schoolhouse had just been newly built. (44)

Even before the Disruption in 1843 when the Free Church of Scotland came into being, there were ominous signs that some of the teachers of the Edinburgh Gaelic Schools Society were frustrated at not being permitted to preach the Gospel which they taught their scholars to read.

Two of these teachers, John Macleod and Angus Maciver, were dismissed from their posts because of their strong conviction that they should preach to the people among whom they laboured, and there is no doubt that they influenced the rest of their colleagues. When the Disruption came, all, with the exception of the Stornoway parish schoolmaster, cast in their lot with the Free Church.

Over the years, the Church of Scotland had been most zealous in the cause of education, and the newly established Free Church became even more so. It felt that no matter what it cost, the youth of the country had to be educated, and the teachers who accepted their principles, and so lost their posts, had also to be provided for. The provision of new schools for these two purposes was of prime importance, and for this reason, an Education Scheme was set afoot for the purpose of raising £50,000 to erect 500 schools. (45)

This appeal was so successful, that by 1845, two hundred and eighty schools had been established throughout Scotland, a number which was increased to 650 by 1847. Some of these however, though attached to the Free Church, were not supported by it, such as the Schools of the Edinburgh Gaelic Schools Society.

This unexpected progress caused Dr Candlish, one of the principal Free Church leaders, to proclaim in 1847, that when that Church separated from the State in 1843 "she obtained the services, in her educational department, of the very elite, the very flower of all the educational bodies in all broad Scotland. She got the flower of the parochial teachers, she got the flower of the Assembly teachers, and by an act of infatuation, during the past year, the Establishment has given us the flower of that valuable body of men—the teachers of the Society for Propagating Christian Knowledge." (46)

By 1867, Lewis had twelve of these schools at Back, Tong, Barvas, Tolsta Chaolais, Callanish, Shawbost, Ness, Maryhill, Stornoway, Valtos (Uig) and Carloway. (47)

From 1871, the number of Free Church Schools in Lewis decreased. In 1874, the only ones left were at Back, Callanish, Shawbost and Stornoway, and these were discontinued as the national system of education took over the responsibility. (48)

At the Disruption, the Free Church found itself confronted with the problem of supplying ministers for a hundred and fifty congregations in the Highlands, and it was in an attempt to remedy this deficiency, especially of Gaelic speaking preachers, that the Edinburgh Ladies' Highland Association was formed in 1850. (49)

The aims of this Association were:

(1) An increase in Aid-schools in the most necessitous districts in the Highlands.
(2) To give assistance to promising young men in prosecuting their studies for the ministry.
(3) To provide an agency to combat the Popery which still existed in many Highland districts.
(4) To provide clothing for poor people which would enable them to attend Church and school. (50)

By April 1851, the Association began its work by opening five schools in Harris, but it was not until 1854, that the first *Sgoilean nan Leidies,* Ladies' Schools, as these schools were called, were established in Lewis in Uig and Gravir.

The plan of operation for these schools was that from April until late Autumn, they were to be taught by Highland students who would attend college during the winter months to train for the ministry, leaving the schools for the rest of the year in the charge of some promising pupil who would act as a paid substitute. Many of these substitutes later became student teachers and ministers.

Many of these schools were poorly built and badly equipped. The building was usually badly thatched with an uneven clay floor and it was very dark inside. A former pupil remarked that in wet weather, his school was like a watchmaker's shop with a tick coming from every corner of the room as the rain came dripping through the roof.

However, some schools were quite comfortable due to the generosity of the proprietor, Sir James Matheson, and possessed some equipment. Other schools could not even practise writing as they had neither desks nor slates. In fact, slates were so precious, that in one school in Lochs, the pupils carried them slung round their necks.

Owing to the poverty of the people, no fees were paid, except in Stornoway and by one person in Barvas, but the teacher was supplied with whatever the people could afford in the way of fish, mutton, eggs, fowls and butter.

Visitors to the schools were always impressed by the excellent behaviour of the pupils.

The perfect quietness and order in the schools were most striking, and though the children were often sadly crowded in the small inconvenient houses, the absence of all jostling, pushing and quarrelling is most remarkable, whilst with the greatest life and spirit, they gain and lose places in the classes, sulky looks and cross words are unknown.

It is truly affecting to see the happy looks of children in school, standing with bare feet on cold damp floors, and coming long distances over moors, poorly fed and scantily clad, they seem to forget all discomfort in the pleasure of acquiring knowledge. (51)

You can imagine a boy with a jacket—the original article having totally disappeared in the process of patching, with only an apology for shoes, demonstrating a proposition in Euclid with fluency and intelligence, and translating Vergil like one sympathising with the Roman Poet.

I can only attribute their generally high character to the prevalence among the teachers of something of that missionary spirit which I have elsewhere spoken of, as demanded in these regions. They are young men, and though many of them have received no special training as teachers, they often make up for want of it, by a large amount of the earnestness and activity still more essential to the life of the school. (52)

The curriculum seemed to depend on the teacher and contained elements of Reading, Writing, Grammar, Arithmetic, Geography, Natural History, Latin, Greek, Algebra, Geometry, Geology, Interest, Discount and Book-keeping. Very little attention was paid to Gaelic except for translation purposes.

Most schools had at some time or other a Sewing School attached, taught by a lady capable of teaching knitting and sewing. These ladies worked wonders with the girls, with the result that they began to make their own clothes and take a pride in their appearance. Some of these sewing mistresses gave their girls work to do while they herded cattle on the moors or the machairs, work which was carefully examined on their return to school.

One teacher combined the reading of Gaelic with her work; others had hymn singing, which caused some Point girls passing one of these schools one day to walk in and join the youngsters, as it reminded them of the "Rest" in Yarmouth which they visited during the East Anglian fishing season.

In 1864, Lewis schools sustained by the Edinburgh Ladies' Highland Association, in addition to English and Arithmetic, taught the following subjects:

SCHOOL	Teacher	Roll	Present	Latin	Greek	Maths	Sewing
Aird	D. Matheson	106	90	4	—	—	—
	Miss Matheson	—	—	—	—	—	17
Bayble	J. Murray	80	72	1	—	—	—
	Mrs Martin	—	—	—	—	—	21
Knock	R. Macdonald	34	32	—	—	—	—
Laxdale	A. Macdonald	67	50	—	—	—	—
	Miss Macdonald	—	—	—	—	—	16
Tolsta	D. Macgregor	50	43	3	—	—	—
Lionel	M. Macphail	80	75	7	—	6	—
	Miss Macpherson	—	—	—	—	—	16
Bragar	M. Beaton	65	60	—	—	—	—
	Mrs Beaton	—	—	—	—	—	12
Carloway	R. Ross	92	92	5	—	3	—
	Miss Ross	—	—	—	—	—	18
Bernera	J. Watt	34	31	—	—	—	—
	Miss Maclean	—	—	—	—	—	14
Brenish	M. Morrison	56	52	5	1	1	—
	Miss Morrison	—	—	—	—	—	15
Achmore	M. Matheson	40	28	—	—	—	—
	Miss Matheson	—	—	—	—	—	10
Cromore	J. Macneil	41	31	1	—	—	—
	Miss Macneil	—	—	—	—	—	8
Gravir	H. Cameron	82	79	3	—	—	—
	Miss Cameron	—	—	—	—	—	22
Balallan	J. Macmillan	56	50	6	—	1	—
	Miss Macmillan	—	—	—	—	—	20

When Sheriff Nicolson visited Lewis in 1865, he was highly perturbed at the state of education there. Some adults were able to read the Scriptures in Gaelic, but the number able to read English was small, and few could write it.

Some of the school buildings were thatched houses, and many of them were in a deplorable state. Of the forty-seven schools which he enumerated, fifteen were good, fourteen were tolerable, while the remaining eighteen were bad or inadequate. The latter could not "by any standard of comfort or fitness, above that of a troglodyte, be considered suitable for having the work of education carried on in them, or any work indeed, to which the prevalence of smoke and moisture are unfavourable.''

The proprietor, Sir James Matheson, did his utmost to provide educational facilities for his tenants. In 1864, he was reported as having contributed £135/3/6. in money and land, £107 in cash to four other schools, as well as the salaries of four parish schoolmasters. The Government had only spent £159 to build a Free Church School in 1852.

Sir James considered charging fees at one time, a proposal with which the Presbytery of the Established Church as well as the members of Lewis Educational Association were in complete agreement. The fees were to be one shilling a quarter for each child, where the number of children in a family did not exceed three, and threepence per quarter for each child in excess of that number. (53)

Although the Education Act was passed in 1872, it was not until 1878 that the first Board Schools came into operation. In that year, thirteen of the Ladies' Highland Association schools were closed, but other schools were opened in the more remote parts of Uig. By 1881, H.M. Inspectors paid occasional visits to these Ladies' Schools, but showed very little consideration for the welfare of the pupils.

Mr Malcolm Macleod described his experience when he brought seven of his eleven pupils from Kinresort School to be examined in a foreign language at Carishader in June 1883.

> We first thought of taking them all, but decided to leave the younger ones at home, as they were so weak and the distance so long. Mr Mackenzie (a parent) went with us and took a cart from Morsgail after walking over four miles of moorland, and even though they had the cart, they were quite exhausted when they reached the schoolhouse. The weather was very warm, and we had to leave at six in the morning. We were back at Kinresort at night. (54)

When the new Board School was opened at Carloway in 1881, the Association decided that as there was no longer any need to provide education for children of school age, facilities should be made available for children who had not a place in the Board School, and who were anxious to continue their studies, to prepare themselves for Grammar School Bursaries which were now available, or to remedy the deficiencies in their early education. The only qualification required of a pupil for this new type of school was age: attainment was not taken into account. (55) This new experiment was so successful, that by 1885, a Carloway pupil was awarded a Macphail Bursary for Aberdeen Grammar School. This was only the first of Carloway's many successes.

A similar experiment was started at Crossbost in 1883, so there were now two schools in rural Lewis providing secondary education. By 1894, Carloway was functioning as a department of the Board School, but the Crossbost experiment was never really a success, and terminated in 1900.

The Association, nothing daunted, began a similar experiment the same year in Bayble, which finally ended in 1917, as did the experiment at Carloway in 1920.

The Schools of the Ladies' Highland Association and those of the Gaelic Schools Society, did what the S.S.P.C.K. and the Parish Schools failed to do, make the people aware of their need for education, and also realise their own intellectual abilities.

The Rev. George Campbell of the Lochs Free Church once said that these schools were agencies for the godly upbringing of the young, centres of spiritual influence for young and old, and fountains of knowledge and learning. (56)

"The Omniscient only knows", said a report, "what some of these poor, half-clad Highland boys may come to when furnished with the elements of a good education" (57) The Omniscient knows now!

With the passing of the Education (Scotland) Act of 1872, the Government accepted complete responsibility for education, a responsibility which it had formerly left to private individuals or associations.

School Boards were established in every parish or burgh in Scotland, which had to provide schools and education for the pupils in their specific areas. Attendance at school was compulsory for all children, and fees were to be paid.

The four Lewis School Boards met for the first time in the Spring of 1873, with the Factor in the Chair. Unfortunately, they ran into trouble immediately. There was jealousy among the members (few of whom were from the crofter class), there was a lack of school accommodation, a lack of experienced teachers and parental support, especially in the rural areas, where they were content to maintain the status quo. Those parents felt their children received as much education as was necessary for them from the two Edinburgh Agencies, free, and looked on the national system as being another imposition, a completely unnecessary interference with their way of life, for which they had to pay.

Education encouraged their children to leave them, a matter which had the full support of the estate officials. Parents had not forgotten that, a few years before, the first prize offered in a competition for all the Island schools was a single ticket to Australia. There were no competitors.

The Board of Education, whose powers were later taken over by the Scottish Education Department, ignored the suggestions made in the Education Commission Report of 1866 that special arrangements should be made for the Highlands and Islands. In view of their isolation, the lack of communication between the various regions, and particularly owing to the language difficulty, regulations devised for the Lowlands were not likely to be suitable for these areas.

In the parishes of Barvas, Lochs and Uig, many schools were required, and they were all built to the same design, a *rùm mor,* long room, and one or two smaller ones attached to a two storey schoolhouse.

The first of these Board Schools was opened in 1878, and before long, the School Boards found themselves in financial difficulties. As the Napier Commission of 1883 said, "The Education Act of 1872 has laid a burden on the people, quite beyond their strength."

The Scottish Education Department believed that much of the Board's trouble was due to the irregular attendance of the children, which affected the amount of the parliamentary grants given, as well as the non-payment of fees.

By 1888, the School Boards of Barvas, Lochs and Uig, unable to meet their obligations, applied to the Scottish Education Department for special assistance to meet their educational requirements. (58) This was not surprising, as from 1882, "the year in which the corn was scattered by Autumn gales", until this time, poverty was rife, land agitation had taken a firm hold on the people and there were several instances of law-breaking. Rents and rates, as well as school fees, remained in many instances unpaid, and one inspector carried a revolver during one of his visits. (59)

Before the Department would consent to give any further assistance to these Boards, it insisted on having some control over their administration. (60)

The Boards agreed to this, and Dr J. L. Robertson, H.M. Inspector of Schools, was appointed as the Department's administrator. (61)

With the abolition of school fees by the Local Government (Scotland) Act of 1889, one of the parents' main objections to sending their children to school was removed, with the result that the Department, in its report of 1890-91, was able to report that the School Boards were now solvent.

The rural schools, so long under Church management to a great extent, passed smoothly into the new educational system, although the Church had some misgivings about this.

In the town of Stornoway, which had more opportunities for education, things were different. Here, there were five schools in existence, two maintained by Sir James Matheson, Mackay's School, and the Female Seminary; two supported by the Free Church and the Established Church, and one, the Nicolson Institution, under the management of Trustees. (62)

It was several years before the various schools were combined in one central school, the Nicolson Institute. The General Assembly School was discontinued in 1876, the Free Church School was transferred to the School Board in 1896: the Female Seminary became part of the Nicolson Institute in 1901, while Mackay's School was the first to become part of the Nicolson Institution. (63)

The Nicolson Institution, which opened in February 1873 under the leadership of Mr John Sutherland, owed its inception to the generosity and far-sightedness of a Stornoway engineer, Alexander Morrison Nicolson, who died as a result of a boiler explosion in Shanghai in 1865. In his will, he bequeathed one third of his entire property to the most approved Charitable Institution in his native town for the education and rearing of destitute native children, in the hope that he might be the indirect means of rendering some assistance to the children of some of his oldest acquaintances. His two brothers, Angus and Roderick, selected Mackay's School as the one to benefit from the bequest of £1,898. (64)

Sir James Matheson, always generous where education was concerned, decided that in view of this bequest, Mackay's School should be placed "on a more permanent footing under a 'Public Trust' and should be known as the Nicolson Institution."

As the buildings occupied by Mackay's School were felt to be unsuitable for such an important and permanent institution, it was decided by the proprietor and the Rev. Roderick Nicolson, that a new school and teacher's dwelling house should be erected out of the Trust funds. Sir James agreed to give a site for the school at the corner of Matheson Road and Sandwick Road, for a nominal sum, and to give an endowment of £35 a year, in perpetuity, to supplement the headmaster's salary. (65)

The original name "Nicolson Institution" was changed in 1888 to the "Nicolson Public School", and to "Nicolson Institute" in 1901.

The staffing of these schools presented the Boards with a very difficult problem. Trained teachers, with a knowledge of Gaelic, were scarce, so English-speaking teachers, with no knowledge of Gaelic, were imported to teach children who had no knowledge of English. "Native teachers, with even barely passable competence, are much preferable to a type that tends to migrate to the Highlands and Islands after many years of service in Southern parts." (66)

It took the S.S.P.C.K. half a century to realise that the chief obstacle to the success of their schools was the Society's opposition to Gaelic, "the rude speech of a barbarous people" and that children could be taught to read what they could not understand. It took much longer for the same lesson to be learnt by our latter-day educationists, some of whom have still to appreciate this fact.

It was also realised in these distant days, that teaching a child to read in his native language led to a quicker understanding of English.

In the national schools, Gaelic was not taught, and the books inflicted on the children dealt with topics outwith their experience. One of the first lessons stated "The cat sat on the mat", as if there were mats for Lewis cats to sit on in front of grated fires.

The nursery rhymes were equally foreign. "Jack and Jill" going of all places "up a hill for water," and then Jack "breaking his crown" made no sense whatsoever, nor did "Jack Horner", who "sat in a corner eating his Christmas pie" with plums in it. The celebration of Christmas had not reached Lewis in the early years of this century, and as for plums—if potatoes had been substituted it might have made sense.

The repetition of English poems and psalms were equally incomprehensible to these children who used to say:

Up the hairy mountain, down the rushing glen
In parcels green he leadeth me, the quiet quarters by.

Still the teachers persevered, and in spite of all this, progress was made.

As we have already seen, the Ladies' Highland Association Schools at Carloway and Crossbost provided a certain amount of secondary education, (67) but those who wanted education beyond the island standard were forced to go to mainland schools.

Towards the end of the nineteenth century in Scotland, people became more aware of the importance of providing further educational facilities, and this led to the creation of the Leaving Certificate Examination in 1888, but it was not until 1894, that an attempt was made by Mr William J. Gibson, the headmaster of the Nicolson Public School, a teacher and administrator of outstanding ability, to establish a Secondary Department there. In this new venture, Dr J. L. Robertson gave Mr Gibson his full co-operation and support.

In 1898, two of the pupils from the school, one from the town and the other from the crofting township of Bragar, passed direct to the University. The former, graduated with First Class Honours in Classics at Edinburgh University before proceeding to Oxford, where he was equally successful, taking a First Class in Moderations, and a First Class in Greats. The latter, took First Class Honours in English at Aberdeen University. (68) Later, he became headmaster of Boroughmuir Secondary School in Edinburgh.

The trail blazed so successfully by these scholars in 1898 led to a desire for higher education throughout the island. This meant that most children who wanted advanced education, would have to spend forty weeks away from home each year, while those living within fifteen to eighteen miles could go home at weekends to collect a change of clothing and a week's supply of provisions.

This living away from home was too expensive for the majority, but the granting of bursaries partly solved this problem. In the first instance, these bursaries were awarded on the results of a competitive examination, but when it was realised that this method meant the selection of only the best children from the best schools, while equally capable children from poorer schools were unsuccessful, a new system was adopted. Students were then nominated by a Secondary Education Committee on the report of the school managers and teachers. (69) The amount awarded to successful students was barely sufficient to support them in Stornoway. In 1919, it was £18 per annum; £6 at the end of each term.

Children who had to walk home as far as eighteen miles on Friday evenings and the same distance back to school on Sunday afternoons, endured much hardship. During the school year, some travelled from 1,200 to 1,400 miles, mostly on foot, with the occasional ride in a cart or gig.

Those who stayed in lodgings in town, were fortunate in having a Welfare Officer from the Edinburgh Ladies' Highland Association to take an interest in them in times of sickness, and in the promotion of social activities in the hall of the Sandwick Road Building on Friday and Saturday nights. Later, hostels were provided for pupils who had to stay in town.

For a long time, there were no continuation classes in Lewis. Young lads who joined the Militia were given instruction in the three R's, but the girls were not given any instruction in subjects necessary to them such as Cookery, Housewifery and Needlework. (70)

By 1910, some classes in Navigation were held in schools like Knock, where ten pupils were learning navigation and signalling. Similar classes were held in Breasclete, where the sole teaching aid was a mariner's compass. (71) Gardening was also taught in some schools.

The two World Wars made the young men and women realise the importance of technical knowledge, and as a result, the Domestic Science College for Girls at Duncraig, near Kyle, and the Lewis Castle Technical College, came into being. The latter seemed destined to be of even more benefit to the people of Lewis than the more academic Nicolson Institute.

Former pupils of the Nicolson are now to be found in all branches of education, industry, commerce, and the services. Quite a few have held or are holding Chairs in universities at home and overseas, and the grandson of a crofter, the late Mr Iain Macleod, became the Chancellor of the Exchequer. Wherever one goes in the world, old Nicolsonians are to found holding positions of authority.

At long last, it looks as if John Knox's ideal of pupils being educated according to their abilities is being realised.

EVICTIONS

The people of Lewis, in common with most Highlanders in the nineteenth century, firmly believed that they had a definite right to the land they occupied, as long as they paid their rents regularly, and performed the services demanded of them by either tacksmen or proprietor. This may have been due to the tradition of the udal system of land tenure (where there was no feudal superior) which probably prevailed in the island when it was under Norse domination. However, the real reason was more likely to be that the arable land had been reclaimed by the relentless toil of their ancestors.

The people were always closely associated with the land, and this is clearly indicated in a report written between 1577 and 1595, possibly for King James VI, in which it was estimated that Macleod of Lewis could put seven hundred fighting men into the field, over and above the tillers of the soil who had "to remane at hame to labour the ground." (1)

After Culloden in 1746, the Highland chiefs were deprived of certain privileges, but this had little effect on the relationship between the rulers and the ruled, as far as Lewis was concerned. Everything on land, sea or air belonged to the proprietor, who could treat his tenants as he wished, for successive Acts of Sederunt had given him legal sanction to do this. By these Acts, tenants could be removed from their lands as if they were animals, provided a warning of removal had been given, or an action brought against the individuals concerned, before a judge, at least forty days before the Whitsunday term. (2) Such legal actions did not trouble the Lewis factors unduly. In 1818, one of them considered it sufficient warning if the ground officer gave the tenants a verbal intimation of removing. (3)

There were three main reasons why summonses of removal could be issued to tenants. The first of these, and the one which accounted for nine-tenths of all summonses, was for arrears of rent. This did not mean immediate eviction, for other legal proceedings had to be undertaken before this could take place. However, during the nineteenth century, every Lewis tenant expected to receive at least one of these summonses during his life-time, a privilege which cost them anything up to thirty shillings.

The second reason for issuing a removal summons, was for a breach of the peace between individuals or townships. There were many instances of this, of which a few may be cited.

In 1797, Allan Morison, a Ness tacksman, complained to the factor about a woman who not only threatened to set his house on fire, but also abused his wife because her son had been conscripted into the Militia. The tacksman also alleged that the woman's husband, John Roy, was so unruly a character, that he did not feel safe anywhere near him. Needless to say, John Roy and his wife were evicted.

In Gravir in 1825, the factor wanted a troublesome occupant who quarrelled with all his neighbours exchanged for a notorious thief from Eishken, (4) while about the same time, the ground officer for Barvas supplied the factor with a list of persons he considered should be evicted. One was suspected of sheep stealing as well as being in arrears with his rent; another had absconded for fear of being punished for sheep stealing, and a third was a 'great thief', who had been detected fleecing a neighbour's sheep on the moors. (5)

The third reason, and the one from which there was no possibility of evasion, was for the sake of land 'improvement', which simply meant the clearing of townships to make way for sheep farms.

Although the Lewis evictions did not receive the same publicity, nor were they on the same scale as those of Sutherland and other Highland districts, the dispossessed suffered similar hardships, and endured the same harsh treatment at the hands of the Estate officials; migration or emigration was their lot. The deserted villages on the Island, especially in Park and Uig, bear testimony to the wholesale evictions which occurred.

The Mackenzie proprietors left the government of the Island chiefly in the hands of the factors, who showed little consideration for the people entrusted to their care. As these proprietors seldom lived on the island for any length of time, they may not always have known the indignities their unfortunate tenants suffered.

As they had no security of tenure, being merely tenants-at-will, under a presumed verbal lease, terminable at Whitsunday, any tenant who fell foul of the factor or ground officers, had little chance of escaping eviction. (6) The threat of *"Cuiridh mi as an fhearann thu"*, "I shall evict you", was no idle threat, and it lost nothing of its terror through constant repetition.

As early as 1793, Mr Francis Humberston Mackenzie, later Lord Seaforth, advertised the whole parish of Uig for letting as a sheep farm, much to the amazement of Colonel Colin Mackenzie of Stornoway, the first Surveyor-General of India, who wrote to the factor from Hyderbad in 1794, expressing concern regarding the future of the inhabitants to be removed, but hoping that Seaforth would supply them with land and employment elsewhere. (7)

As Seaforth's financial affairs deteriorated, the number of removing summonses increased. In 1796, there were no fewer than 358 issued, 150 for Barvas, 133 for Uig, 44 for Lochs, and 31 for Stornoway. (8) In addition, 36 of the Goathill tenants were ordered to appear before the Sheriff-Depute of Ross-shire, Mr Donald Macleod of Geanies, or his substitute, "to hear the Decreet and Sentence of Removing given furth and pronounced against them." (9)

Between 1780 and 1813, the summonses of removal were in excess of 500, but during the years 1818-32, the number rose to over 2,300. This was mainly due to the collapse of the kelp industry, which led to the introduction of sheep farming on a large scale, and the expansion of the fishing industry, where it was hoped to employ those evicted.

It was not only the Sheriff-Depute and his Substitute who issued removal summonses. The factor, who was also Baron Bailie, could do likewise. In 1826, he handed out a total of 422 summonses for arrears of rent and for sheep-stealing.

Although every tacksman could evict a sub-tenant, some were more likely to do so than others. The most notorious of these men were Lewis Maciver of Gress, Dr Macaulay of Linshader and Crossbost, and Archibald Stewart of Park. Stewart's favourite excuse for getting rid of his sub-tenants was for sheep-stealing. He was a most aggressive man, who had no hesitation in manhandling his tenants or anybody else for that matter who happened to cross him. On one particular occasion, he ill-treated some fishermen he found ashore on the Shiants, then part of his tack, as he thought they were there to steal sheep. It was also said that he, and some others, severely manhandled the

Breabadair Mor, the Big Weaver, a native of Seaforth Head, who had gone to Valamos after some poinded horses.

Stewart, with his brother Alexander, a much more respectable man, is believed to have arrived in Park with only 60 sheep, 50 of which were ewes. (10)

The arrogant and litigious Dr MacAulay, "a land grabber and oppressor with an insatiable appetite", (11) made life extremely difficult for his tenants, exacting his 'pound of flesh' whenever possible.

Lewis Maciver of Gress, seldom needed an excuse for removing his tenants. A shrewd business man, he showed little consideration for anyone who interfered with his plans. His sub-tenants, in Back and Gress, led an unenviable, uncertain existence. In 1822, his tenants in Gress complained to Seaforth of having been dispossessed of their lands twice in as many years and sent to the "Edge of the Town" for no known reason, especially as they had paid their rents on "The Day". (12)

The irascible Maciver fought a duel with a Customs official in Goathill Park in 1835. (13) the last ever to be held on the Island. However, the fight was stopped, and the result declared a draw.

In 1833, Alexander Stewart, the factor, proposed a most ambitious plan for Lewis when he suggested that large scale improvements could be achieved by two simple arrangements.

Firstly, at the expiry of their leases, all the improvable land in the Parish of Stornoway would be lotted, on both sides of Broad Bay. Five or seven lines of crossroads would be made in Point, from sea to sea, Broad Bay to the Minch, parallel to one another, and the intermediate land lotted and let on suitable terms. This would afford several thousand people an opportunity to improve the land, and give them access to the fishing grounds, seaware and flatfish of Broad Bay, and ling and cod from the Minch. A similar operation could be carried out on the great tract of improvable lands in the parish, particularly round the town of Stornoway. The part of Ness, north of Galson, could be treated in the same way, with reclaimed land devoted to the growth of barley for the production of whisky.

Secondly, to populate these new allotments, the inhabitants of Uig ought to be transferred there. The pasturable districts of Lochs, whether Carloway or Lochs proper, could also be relieved of their present occupants, and the whole two parishes let as grazing farms. (14)

Evictions began in earnest in Uig about 1823, when Kirkibost and Little Bernera were cleared to become part of Linshader Farm. (15) By 1825, the families in the townships behind Mangersta and Mealista, Ceann Chaolais, Hamnaway, and Aird Bheag, were settled at Kinresort, and Aird Uig settled as a crofting community. A sheep farm was formed beside Loch Resort. (16)

From 1825-28, the Uig tenants were deprived of their wintering islands and much of their moorland pasture. The houses of the Timsgarry tenants were "rased out" in 1826 to make a glebe for the Rev. Alexander Macleod, an act which met with a hostile reception from the tenants, and which made the minister unwilling at first to have any of their land in his glebe, as some of them blamed him for their removal, and this might render his gospel ministrations unsuccessful with those concerned.

Mealista, the largest of the townships in West Uig, was cleared of its inhabitants about 1838. Some were sent to already crowded Brenish, and other places on the Island, but the majority went to Canada. Those left behind on the Island, always remembered the cries of the children as they were forced to leave their humble homes.

About 1851, the inhabitants of Gisla were removed at their own request, but those of Carnish, Reef and Ballyglom had no option but to leave their homes. They were removed to other districts or sent overseas.

In 1872, the people of Bosta and those of Mangersta were likewise removed at their own request, the former to Kirkibost, as their peat supplies were running out, and the latter to Doune Carloway, because of the open position of the village. The Croir tenants were sent to Hacklete, in 1880, along with some others from Tobson, because of overcrowding. (17)

The following list of deserted Uig townships, though not complete, gives some indication of the depopulation which occurred in that parish:

Kinresort, Crola, Torraidh, Aird Mhor, Aird Bheag, Tamnabhaigh, Ceann Chuisil, Beinnisbac, Mealista, Ceann Chaolais, Bhuidhe Mhor, Pabbaidh Mhor, Bhacsaidh, Bernera Beag, Croir, Breidhbhig, Bosta, Cleidir, Baile Ghriasaich, Beiridhro, Berisaidh, Erista, Timsgarry, Bail'na Cille, Penny Donald, Capadal (Ardroil), Balnicol, Knockmagem, Drovernish, Earshader, Strome, Ceann Thulabhaig, Cleitihog, Berve, Linshader, Sgealasgro, Morsgail, Dùn and Sandwick.

The Parish of Lochs, excluding the Carloway portion, was always sparsely populated, particularly the area known as Park. It was here that the first sheep farm was formed, early in the nineteenth century by a group of Skyemen, including Lachlan Mackinnon of Corry. Their manager was a Donald Stewart, who became tenant in 1816. On taking up an appointment in Harris, he was succeeded in the tenancy by his two brothers, Alexander and Archibald, who held it until 1842. These were years of sore affliction for the Park tenants, and even yet, the name of Stewart is anathema among the descendants of those whom they evicted. A Walter Scott held the farm from 1842-57, when it was let to a Michael Scobie, who removed the Steimreway crofters to re-settle in Lemreway, which had been cleared many years before. Mr Scobie made over his lease to a Mr Sellar, until its expiry in 1883. It was then unsuccessfully advertised for letting, and finally let as a deer forest to Mr Joseph Platt. (18) Both Mr and Mrs Platt were very popular in Lochs, so much so, that Mrs Platt came to be called "Lady" Platt, and her Christian name, Jessie, was bestowed on many children.

The original Park Farm was fairly small, consisting chiefly of the area round Valamos, where the first farmhouse still exists. In 1823, in addition to Valamos and the Shiant Islands, the Stewarts had only managed to gain possession of Scaladale Mor and Beag, and Ceann Chrionaig. (19)

Some of the Park townships were probably cleared before the arrival of the Stewarts. They were all small villages containing from about two houses, as at Bun Chorcabhig, to twenty-three in Lemreway which was later re-settled in 1857. Before 1830, well over a hundred families, something like five hundred souls, were uprooted to make room for sheep. Lemreway was cleared in 1831, Orinsay in 1838, and Eishken and Ceann Loch Shealg in 1843. (20) Steimreway, as already stated, was cleared in 1857.

The cleared townships were: Valamos Beag and Mor, Caolas an Eilean, Bagh Ciarach, Ceannamhor, Scaladale Beag and Mor, Stròmas, Brinigil, Bàgh Reimsabhaigh, Smosivig, Gleann Claidh (the deepest, the most desolate, and to the superstitious natives, the most fearful glen in Lewis), (21) Brollum, Ceann Chrionaig, Mol Truisg, Mol Chadha Gearraidh, Ailtenish, Budhanais, Ceann Loch Shealg, Eilean Iubhaird, Isginn (Eishken), Steimreway, Orinsay, Cuiriseal, Gearraidh Riasaidh, Bun Chorcabhig, Gilmhicphaic, Ceann Sifiord. (22)

Other places cleared in Lochs were: Crobeg, Cleitir, Shildenish (later re-settled), Ardintroime, Aline, Valtos, Keose (part), Swordale (for the minister's glebe), Crò Gearraidh, Ceann na Cairidh, Dalmore and Dalbeg.

When Isginn and Ceann Loch Shealg were cleared, the fires on the hearths were drowned by the Estate officials, and the inhabitants fined for not evacuating the villages on the appointed day. (23)

The evicted were given little consideration. They were dealt with as if they were sheep. There were no roads in South Lochs, so in most cases, the people had to carry their young children and their goods and chattels on their backs over moorland, while driving their stock before them. Some were more fortunate than others in not having to travel so far to their new homes.

Overcrowded Balallan received many unfortunates; others went to Crossbost and to Tong, where they were not exactly welcome, while some made the long trek to Glen Tolsta and Tolsta. In this case, the women and children drove the stock while the men sailed with the roof timbers and other heavy articles to their allotted places. On arrival, they slept under their upturned boats until they had built new turf-walled homes.

The parishes of Barvas and Stornoway had fewer evictions as there was more arable ground there. Upper Barvas was cleared about 1827, to make it into a minister's glebe. Owing to the nature of the soil, it was a double glebe, containing thirty acres of land formerly in the possession of the crofters. (24)

South Galson lost its sub-tenants because it was the ground officer's tack, but North Galson was not cleared until 1863, at the tenants' own request. As in the case of Balmeanach and Melbost, the ground was added to South Galson. Altogether, 108 families were removed from these townships over a period of twenty years. Many people went to Canada.

Prior to 1844, the cleared villages in the parish of Stornoway were: Gress, Upper Coll, Gearraidh Ghuirm, Tong, Aignish, Holm, Melbost, and Stoneyfield, and after 1844, North Tolsta, Goathill, and the *Gearraidh Chruaidh,* Castle Grounds.

It must have been heartbreaking to see these people leave their homes. Some incidents are still remembered, like that of the Bernera widow who, on being evicted, was rowed across to the mainland and then, accompanied by her three children, and carrying all her wordly goods on her back, walked to Cliascro, where she built a bothy for herself and her family.

A four year old Tolsta boy, John Macdonald, carried the tongs when his parents had to leave their home in 1852. The family had to flit once again the following year to the Moine, unreclaimed peat land on the outskirts of South Tolsta. The factor was extremely generous, for he did not charge rent for this bog-land for the first two years. In 1922, seventy years later, the boy returned to the village from which he had been evicted as a child.

Angus Maclean, one of those evicted from Reef, was sent to Lochganvich, but he was not there long before he had to emigrate. The estate officials came and quenched his fire, and sent him away to the waiting emigrant ship. His only cow was left standing at the back door. (25)

Alexander Macleod from Laxay was reported as having had to abandon three different holdings and three different homes in three consecutive years. Two of these houses were at Seaforth Head and Ardintroime. Another Laxay resident, an Angus Morison, was said to have been chased by "deer and sheep", from Uig to Dalmore before arriving at his present destination. (26)

A John Smith, born in Eishken, was compelled to go to Brinigil, from where he was removed to Cleitir before finally being settled in Balallan. (27)

A Mr Craig, writing to Mr Stewart Mackenzie, in 1828, gives some idea of what these poor, uprooted people had to suffer.

Until I saw the actual situations of the new lotters in the Aird of Tong, I had no idea of the great hardship and privation that the poor people endure who are forced into new allotments, without matters being previously arranged for their moving. The situation of the new lotters on the Aird of Tong, at this moment, beggars description. It is worse than anything I saw in Donegal, where I always considered human wretchedness to have reached its very acme. The roofs of the present hovels on the Estate might, in general, stand for a few years if they were let alone, but the act of taking them down, breaks and injures them so much that they are of comparatively little value in roofing their new homes—fresh timber is therefore necessary, and the exorbitant price demanded is so great as to more than exhaust their means.

I am therefore deeply of the opinion that whenever a general move of the people is ordered by you from one part of a farm to another, you ought to present them with the timber necessary to roof their buildings, and besides, good access should be made to the site of the proposed habitations before they be required to leave their old: for lack of such an arrangement at Aird of Tong, the poor people at the new lots there, are suffering the greatest hardship, many of them dead, I am told, from disease brought on, I have no doubt, from the unwholesome situation in which they have been forced to plant themselves.

To erect their cabins, the sward has been taken off the whole line of the intended road which has now become a morass, dangerous for both man and beast, to set their foot upon: how the children contrive out and in of their cabins baffles my comprehension, for the men have literally to step up to the knee in mud, the moment they quit their threshold. (28)

There were many places worse than Aird of Tong, with no one to describe the conditions. Even New Shawbost, where most of those evicted from Reef were placed, was not much better.

By 1850, the farms formed from the deserted townships were: South Galson, North Dell mill and land, Dalbeag, Gress, Coll, Melbost, Holm, Stoneyfield, Arnish, Aignish, Goathill, Crobeag, Valtos (Lochs) and Eilean Torray, Mealista, Ardroil, Timsgarry and Eilean Vacsey, and the largest of all, Linshader. (29) Most of those were occupied by farmers from the mainland.

Other farms were created later. Dalmore was added to Dalbeag in 1853, Manor Farm in 1851, North Tolsta and Tong in 1853, and Mangersta in 1873. Park, Aline, Morsgail and Scaliscro became deer forests, Park in 1866, and the others about 1850. (30)

Mr Mackay, the factor, might say that it was not for the sake of profit that Sir James Matheson cleared any one township, but because the crofters could not make a living from it and so were unable to pay the rent. (31) This may be true, but the fact remains that successive Lewis proprietors did evict their tenantry, forcing many to leave the island, while others were sent to places "where hardly a snipe could live." (32)

EMIGRATION

During the eighteenth century, Stornoway was a port of call for many ships trading with North America, so the Islanders were not entirely ignorant of conditions on the other side of the Atlantic. The few soldiers who returned from service in America during the Seven Years' War, as well as the time-expired servants of the Hudson Bay Company, all contributed to their knowledge of conditions overseas.

Early emigration from the Island was entirely voluntary, and was chiefly confined to the tacksman class and their dependants, as well as a few tradesmen.

In 1773, no fewer than 840 people emigrated from Lewis, causing so much consternation, that the proprietor, Lord Fortrose, who spent most of his time in London, rushed to the Island to try and stop any further departures. His tenants told him that they would only stay if they were given the land at their former rents, the excess rental for the previous three years refunded, and the immediate dismissal of the factor. (1)

Lord Fortrose evidently paid little attention to their demands, for the following year, 1774, two ships, the *Friendship,* and the *Peace and Plenty,* sailed from Stornoway for Philadelphia and New York respectively, carrying over a hundred emigrants between them, among whom was the future Canadian explorer, Alexander Mackenzie, then aged twelve. Along with his aunts, he was on his way to join his father and his uncle John "Ready Money" Maciver, in New York. Some Morisons, descendants of the Brieve, also emigrated at this time. (2)

In 1776, the outbreak of the American War of Independence checked the tide of emigration. When it was eventually resumed, Canada was the main destination.

In 1803, three ships sailed from Stornoway for Pictou, Nova Scotia.

This steady loss of manpower was not all to the liking of the lairds. As long as the kelp trade was profitable, the more people employed in it meant larger revenues. In 1803, they managed to have an Act of Parliament passed which severely curtailed this movement of population. By 1811, regulations were eased slightly, and in the same year, seventy-six people, mostly from Skye, left Stornoway for Pictou and Prince Edward Island.

For some years, the Hudson Bay Company had an agent in Stornoway to recruit men for the fur trade in Canada, locally called the *Talamh Fuar,* Cold Land. These men were engaged for a minimum period of three years, and were given free passages there and back. Many lads took advantage of these terms, and in 1811, one hundred and nine sailed the Atlantic, not all of whom returned home again. The life in Northern Canada appealed to many of them, as they got on well with the Indians and the Eskimos. Some married Indian girls, and in any case, there was not much difference between a beehive shieling in Lewis and a wigwam or an igloo in Canada. Some of those who returned brought their families with them. Perhaps the most outstanding athlete the island ever produced had a Red Indian mother.

As the kelp industry declined, emigration was encouraged. Redundant kelpers were regarded as a burden, and every encouragement was given to evicted crofters to cross the seas. Many were willing to go, but lacked the finance.

In 1826, the Hacklete tenants threatened to emigrate unless they were given a lease of their holdings. Such a mass exodus was not to the liking of the proprietor, as he knew it would be the most active who would leave, and the poor, the old and the weak, who would be left behind. (3) Discontent was rife, and in 1832, 248 individuals sailed for Cape Breton Island, forty-eight for service with the Hudson Bay Company.

After the spate of clearances in Park and Uig from 1827-32, emigration slowed down, chiefly due to poverty, lack of English, and the most potent reason of all, an unwillingness to leave aged dependants to the mercy of others. Seldom, however, did a ship sail round Arnish Point without emigrants on board.

The famine of 1837 led to further emigration, and in 1838, sixteen families, about seventy individuals, were forced to go to Canada. Despite the fact that their rents had been regularly paid, their townships were being converted into sheep farms. (4)

John Mackenzie of Stornoway, the agent in charge of this last group wrote:

They were probably the poorest crowd that ever left the Highlands. With being so late in sailing, the harvest was past before they arrived, and only the cold forbidding Canadian winter ahead of them.

After examining a fair amount of territory, about sixteen families settled at Bury, where nobody lived—and where there was not even a road. They got the land for eight shillings an acre, to be paid over a certain number of years.

Winter was approaching, and heavy snow had fallen when the poor Lewismen began to fell their first trees, a work at which they were not very skilful, but the British American (Emigration) Company kindly sent two or three men to teach them how to go about it.

In this condition the meal they had taken with them from Scotland became exhausted, and the British American Company had to provide them with meal or they would have perished: they came to collect this meal, and carried it on their backs, owing to lack of roads, a distance of ten miles, and glad they were to get it. With this, and the price of the wood ash, worth six shillings a bushel, they passed the first winter in gloom. However, in spite of poverty, fatigue and hardship, before seed-time came in spring, there was not a family but had ready for planting, from six to ten acres. They spent the summer partly in preparing or clearing their land, or in making roads. When autumn came they were in no-one's debt—Providence blessed the work of their hands with outstanding blessing. When the second winter came, not one was in want, as long as oats, barley, potatoes, cabbage and carrots lasted, and they were not without roads.

Two years after their coming over, the Lewismen had from eight to twelve acres cleared for each family, and fully cropped, without mentioning cattle, sheep and pigs.

When they saw how well off they were, they naturally wrote to advise their poor kinsfolk to follow them. These invitations encouraged more than a hundred to come over in 1841, but it happened that they also came rather late, so that they had to be supported by their friends all winter. (5)

These unfortunates were accompanied by a minister to look after their spiritual needs. Perhaps they expected Canadian manna to sustain them through the long, cold winter, for apart from having their passages paid for them, no other provision was made. It was only through the charity of the St Andrew's Society of Montreal, and the ready and willing support of friends, that these poor, uprooted people were saved from starvation.

In 1841, a statement to the Select Committee on Emigration by Mr Knox, the Lewis factor, inferred that a good deal of compulsion was being applied in order to make people emigrate. He said that between 6,000 and 7,000 individuals could be removed, and that the proprietor was willing to participate in any plan connected with the emigration of the redundant population, as the lands so vacated would become sheep walks. (6) The following year, more than one hundred and twenty individuals crossed the Atlantic.

During the famine years of 1846-50, emigration was given high priority, not only because of the need to reduce the population, but also because it was financially beneficial to the proprietor, who, as a result of the new Poor Law Act, was responsible for supporting his poor tenants. Even the Rev. A. Macleod of Uig thought that emigration was the only solution to the population problem, as the people would not be comfortable, even in a good season, unless a third of them was removed. The lands vacated could be allocated to those who remained. (7)

In 1850, in Lewis, there were 12,829 individuals in receipt of charity. This caused the new proprietor, Sir James Matheson, to offer to pay the passage of all destitute people to Quebec or Ontario. At the same time, he promised to forego all arrears of rent and meal, to buy their stock at valuation, if they could not otherwise dispose of it, and provide clothing where necessary. How they were to survive after landing in Canada was given little thought.

From 1851-55, 1,772 people took advantage of this offer. Many of them settled in Quebec Province, round the town of Sherbrooke, south of the St Lawrence River, a district which later became known as "Scotch County". It was here, that small villages came into existence with famliar names like Stornoway, Balallan, Galson, Tolsta, Bosta and Gisla. Here also were found Gaelic names like A' Bheinn Ruadh, An Abhainn Ruadh, Druim a' Bhac and Beinn Nis.

In 1852, three Lewis settlers in this district decided to go in search of Government land. They were William Macleod from Branahuie, a former Hudson Bay trapper, and two brothers, Ruairidh and Murdo Maciver from North Tolsta, all from the township of Lingwick. After three days' trek, they reached the shores of Lake Megantic, where they spent some time in exploration. The following Spring, they visited the Lake again, which was about thirty miles from Lingwick, carrying with them three bushels of potatoes for planting.

In the Spring of 1854, the three pioneers, now accompanied by a third Maciver brother, John, set off again for Lake Megantic, each carrying a bushel of barley which was sown along with potatoes from the previous year.

In the Spring of 1856, these four men set off through the forest on the six day journey with their families and all their goods and chattels and stock, camping out at night. When they reached Lake Megantic, they started to sow barley and plant potatoes immediately. Once a month, some of them went to the township of Winslow to buy necessities like tea and tobacco. By 1858, there were thirteen families in the new settlement, among whom was Malcolm Mackay who was believed to possess second sight. (8)

167

Among the early settlers on the shores of Lake Megantic, was a Murdo Morrison, Murchadh Thormoid, from Reef in Uig, who was married to *Siobalag a' Bhreabadair,* Isobel the weaver's daughter from Barvas. Their son Donald was handsome, gallant and loyal, but unfortunately became known as "The Megantic Outlaw" after killing a man in a gunfight, but he was no real outlaw. His remains lie buried near his home in the beautiful cemetery at Gisla, Quebec.

Many of these early settlements in the *Coille Ghruamach,* Gloomy Forests, in Nova Scotia, Prince Edward Island, Quebec and Ontario, were in many cases, only temporary resting places, for the descendants of the original settlers moved steadily westwards or southwards, as the American continent developed. The Lewis villages in Scotch County have, in many cases, been taken over by the French speaking population of Quebec. The old names have been preserved however, but it may not be long before the town of Stornoway becomes St Ornoway.

Between 1851 and 1854, letters arrived in Lewis from emigrants, extolling their present state compared with the conditions back home. Wages were from 3/6 to 4/6 a day, and there was plenty to eat. A Peggy Maciver from Sherbrooke, writing to her father, Angus Maciver in Barvas, mentioned that her table was as well furnished as the minister's, while another settler told of how a year old heifer had a calf and a year old ewe a lamb. In 1866, a John Macdonald who left Callanish in 1851, became the Mayor of Whitton, Lake Megantic. (9)

From around the turn of the century, a steady stream of islanders took part in the settlement of the Prairie Provinces and of British Columbia, following the trail once blazed by Sir Alexander Mackenzie of Stornoway, a former emigrant and refugee from New York, the first white man to cross Canada in 1793. Another Lewisman, the equally indomitable John Macleod, was the hero of the defence of the Red River Colony, Winnipeg, when it was attacked by half-breeds in 1814.

The Government sponsored the formation of two settlements in Manitoba, one at Killarney, where 183 people from Lewis and Harris, were settled in 1888, and the other, the following year at Saltcoats, where 282 persons were also settled. Only the Killarney settlement was a success, and one of its settlers, an Angus Macdonald, wrote to his parents as follows:

> If you could see the crop that is in Manitoba you would say that you never saw a crop before. You were telling me that . . . was giving you a bad account of the place that we came to but you can tell him that he is a liar. There is not a better place in the whole world; there is not a better land under the sun than what it is here. We got a very good land. I broke fourteen acres of my land and if I be spared I shall have forty broke next year. I got a splendid ox and a good cow and a heifer calf, plenty of milk and butter, and plenty to eat of everything. I got 200 lbs. of pork, and six bolls of flour, and three of oatmeal, we got that, and I am expecting 100 barrels of potatoes. I planted an acre and it is looking splendid, we can get new potatoes already, but we had old potatoes. I am telling the truth in everything. We got the house already; they are good houses. You were wanting me to tell you was it difficult of getting firewood and water. No, nothing of the two. I can take home in a day as much as last me two months, and we have very good water, nearly as good as that water that is in widow D. Mackenzie's land. Dear parents, I would wish you all out here if you can get out. The harvest will soon commence here now. We

will get two dollars a day and our board then. The lads that came out with us are doing splendid.

An A. Graham wrote home in a similar vein, praising the beauty of the landscape, the richness of the soil and the kindness of the inhabitants. On their arrival in Quebec, Highlanders flocked to meet them, and gave them provisions and tobacco.

Every place and station we passed friends came to us and encouraged us. When we reached Killarney every head of a family got a team of oxen, plough, wagon, a house, a stove, provisions for three months, consisting of oatmeal, and flour, pork, tea, sugar, syrup, pepper, tobacco, matches; and pots, frying pans, dishes, cake-pans, and many other articles required for American cookery and domestic work. Sir William Collins, Glasgow, supplied each family with two Bibles (Gaelic) . . . William Macleod's house is only a few hundred yards from my home. The winter is not so very cold as they say in Lewis. Of course it is a little colder than the old country. Mrs John Campbell, Back, had a boy last week, the first Scots-Canadian born among us. . . . I would advise you to come here, you would get on far better than in the old country; but yet I would not like you to come if it would break my mother's heart. This is one of the most healthy countries in the world. (10)

Although Canada was at first the Mecca for most emigrants, it did not remain so for long, as people settled in other parts of the world. Many chose the United States, and during the first quarter of this century, South America, the *Ceann a' Deas,* South End, as it was called, attracted many lads from the parish of Lochs, who went out there as shepherds. Nowadays, there are many Chileans, Peruvians and Argentinians with names like Macleod, Maciver, Martin, and Smith, of Lewis extraction.

The collapse of Lord Leverhulme's schemes in 1921, led to mass unemployment and emigration. In April 1923, the *Metagama* sailed with 300 emigrants. In April 1924, the *Marloch* carried away 290, and a few weeks later, the *Canada* left with 270 more, a total of 860, mostly youngsters who had never been out of the island before.

It is almost impossible for people nowadays to understand the hardships and frustrations experienced by early emigrants. Weary travellers often had to wait a long time for transport while their limited stores of provisions ran low. There was also the agony of parting with loved ones for ever, and the fear of what lay ahead.

Aboard most ships, conditions were deplorable, especially by the end of the six weeks' voyage across the Atlantic. Each passenger's accommodation was similar to that provided for the transport of African slaves. Dirt, disease and overcrowding were common, and when bad weather forced the passengers to stay below deck, there was utter chaos. Dysentry was rife, and mortality, especially among children, was high.

One mother, who had seen children being buried at sea, was determined that this would not be the fate of her dead boy. She told nobody that her son was dead, and carried the body with her wherever she went for a couple of days, pretending the child was still alive. When the truth was discovered, and the reason explained, the captain was so impressed that he placed the body in the long-boat until the first point of land was reached, when the boy's body was taken ashore for burial. Not all captains were so considerate.

In 1840, the *Kingston* embarked most of her passengers in the Larach, near the south end of Raasay, and completed her loading in Stornoway before sailing to Prince Edward Island with 365 emigrants, excluding children. Three days out of port, the weather deteriorated, and the *Kingston* began to leak. Some of the passengers helped to man the pumps, but their efforts were in vain as the water gained on them. The skipper was asked to turn back, but he refused, and a seaman, Johnston by name, took charge, telling the mate as he took the wheel, "Give me the course and I'll take her back if she stays afloat." The skipper was ordered not to interfere. Those battened down below were naturally badly frightened with the water swirling round their feet. One nervous passenger, on seeing his sack of potatoes sink in the water, grabbed it to his chest. A neighbour told him he shouldn't worry, for quite soon, he too would be in the depths. A mother with a three months' old baby, placed the child on the bunk of a man noted for his piety, saying, "Murdo, take him to heaven with you." The *Kingston* finally made Stornoway. (11)

A Mrs Maclean, emigrating from North Tolsta gave birth to her child aboard one of these boats in 1852, the day before the vessel docked in Quebec, and there must have been many other similar incidents.

Like most Highlanders, the Lewis emigrants proved themselves able, self-reliant, versatile colonists, but they never forgot the island of their birth, as their songs testify.

Donald Morrison's song is a good example of how these emigrants must have felt.

> *O's laidir na bannan 'tha'm tharruing a null*
> *Gu Eilean Beag Donn Mhicleoid;*
> *Gu'n stiuirinn gun solus do d'chala mo long*
> *'Nuair ruigeas mi ceann mo lò.*

> O strong are the cords that are drawing me over
> To the little, brown island of Macleod;
> I would steer my boat in the dark to your harbour
> When my end is drawing nigh. (12)

LAND AGITATION

In spite of the vast amount of money Sir James Matheson spent in Lewis, not all of it was for the benefit of his tenants. During the lifetime of Sir James and Lady Matheson, there was much discontent among the people, chiefly due to the fact that he left them to the mercy of his factors, the ground officers, and the hated *earraidean,* estate messengers, whose tyrannical behaviour made even the wholesale eviction policy of the previous proprietors seem lenient in retrospect.

By far the worst of these factors was the autocratic Donald Munro. A Ness crofter once said that he believed it was his policy from the first day of his factorship to extirpate the people of Lewis as far as he could. (1)

Munro had absolute sway over the whole Island, holding no fewer than seventeen public offices, naturally the most important ones, while his clerk held the others which were too trivial for his attention.

The crofters' main grievance was the small size of their holdings, which had to be constantly cropped owing to the number of people dependent on their produce. This caused them to become poorer every year, while the adjacent farms, formed from the best land, had plenty of once cultivated tracts now only used as pasture. In addition, they felt that too many encroachments had been made on the arable and pasture areas of the townships. Farms had been enlarged, and new crofts created to absorb those people who had been evicted, without any compensating reduction of rent to the existing occupants.

The lack of security of tenure made the crofters' position precarious at all times, and this left them completely at the mercy of the Estate officials. As a Stornoway lawyer once said, "They (the crofters) positively shudder at the everyday threat, 'I'll deprive you of your land'. Frequency does not rob this threat of its terrors (indifferent as their lands sometimes are). They get off lightly by paying thirty shillings as the law costs of a removing". (2)

The constant friction between crofters and neighbouring farmers over boundary dykes and straying stock was a further source of annoyance. Poindings were common, and were a profitable source of revenue for those who had them. Iain Mor Macrae's poind can still be seen near Timsgarry, where the Valtos and Crowlista cattle used to be impounded. In Uig, on one occasion, the blankets from the beds and the women's plaids had to be handed over to pay the poinding dues, (3) while a poor woman who had nothing with which to pay the fine was asked by the farmer what were the three things she feared most. She replied, *"Ròs na maidne; currag na beinne; agus an Taoitear Taileach"*, "A red dawn, mist-shrouded hill-tops, and the Tutor of Kintail". The farmer was of Kintail extraction, but he gave her back her cows, free.

Rackrenting, kain money and road money, paid by people who in many cases had no roads, could also be added to the long list of grievances.

Though the people were law-abiding and docile, the time came when their patience was exhausted. It was inevitable that Donald Munro should be responsible. This happened when he served summonses of removal on fifty-six Bernera crofters without the proprietor's knowledge.

171

For centuries, the district between Lochs Langabhat and Resort, in Uig, were the summer pastures of the Bernera stock. The animals may even have been left out there until late in the year when they were sent to the islands in Loch Roag. (4) When the Uig Deer Forest was formed, about 1850, this mountainous pasture was taken from the crofters, and a dyke had to be built to separate the Forest from the remaining common pastures and kept in repair for twenty years at the crofters' expense. (5)

In 1872, more grazing land was taken from the crofters, and they were given in exchange, the moorland between the road and the sea, which at one time formed part of the Earshader tack, (6) long in possession of the Uig ground officers. Again the tenants had to build a dyke between the new summer pastures and the Forest, but they were not allowed to put a beast on them until the five or six mile long dyke had been built, once more at their own expense. (7)

In 1874, after having had this area for two years, Donald Munro, the factor, informed them that they were to be deprived of these grazings, and in future, their stock was to be confined to the Island of Bernera. Naturally, the people were upset at this latest interference with their pastures, and refused to co-operate. "Shah" Munro came to see them, but they refused to obey him. This unexpected resistance so annoyed the despot, that he decided, not only to deprive them of the Earshader grazings, but to have them removed from Bernera completely.

Summonses of removing were served on the crofters by the Sheriff Officer, who was accompanied on this occasion by the ground officer, and a Customs officer. Some *plocs,* pieces of turf were thrown, and the following day, there was a slight disturbance during which a garment was torn.

Some days later, one of the men involved in this altercation, was arrested in Stornoway, and this, on top of the summonses of removing, so angered the people, that between two and three hundred of them marched to Stornoway to confront Sir James, who sympathised with them, and no further action was taken.

Munro was annoyed with this interference, and three of the Bernera men who had been the most conspicuous during the disturbance were ordered to appear in court on a charge of assaulting the said officer in the execution of his duty.

In July 1874, when the men appeared for trial, they pleaded not guilty to the charge. Their lawyer, Charles Innes from Inverness, made great play on the number of public positions held by the factor, and on the unlimited power he held over the people.

While being cross-examined, Munro freely admitted that he was not in the habit of consulting the proprietor about every small detail of estate management like removing fifty-six families. The men were found not guilty, and the factor lost his post.

This verdict was a first victory for the Island crofters against officialdom, and emboldened them to agitate for the reform of the land laws and to become more active in their demand for the return of lands which had once belonged to their forebears.

As already stated, the Park district of Lochs began to be cleared of its inhabitants very early in the nineteenth century, and the process was completed in 1857, when the Steimreway people were removed to Lemreway. As a result of these evictions, there was much overcrowding in the villages of Lochs, and in 1833, it was reported that there was not sufficient food

172

produced in the parish to support its inhabitants, who were glad to have a spot of ground at any price to grow food for the ensuing year. (8)

The situation steadily deteriorated, and each year saw the crofters and cottars becoming more and more impoverished, as they looked with envious eyes at the formerly cultivated lands now under sheep, and although the Estate officials maintained that no part of Park was suitable for crofters, except a small area round Loch Shell, they knew that this was not so. Park had been cleared, not because of its unsuitability for crofters, but because it was suitable for sheep rearing. Many people were still alive who remembered how comfortable they had been before eviction. An example of this is given in the case of *Calum Taillear,* Malcolm Smith, of Brinigil, who in 1822, possessed four cows, three heifers, one stirk, two tups, thirty ewes, ten wedders and fifteen hoggs. (9) There were other tenants even better off.

Knowing that the lease of Park Farm was due to expire on Whitsunday 1883, in November 1881, thirty-two fishermen from Gravir, Calbost and Marvig, petitioned the proprietrix, Lady Matheson, to let them the lands of Orinsay and Steimreway at such terms as could be arranged. At the same time, they promised to obey all the rules and regulations of the Estate. (10)

On 5th December, 1882, having had no reply to their letter, they sent another, this time addressed to the Chamberlain, requesting a reply to their petition so that they could consider what further steps to take. (11)

We expect that the prayer of the said petition has been favourably received by Lady Matheson and all concerned, and that our very distressing condition, which is become more and more serious, may induce you to give us an opportunity of earning an honest livelihood in our native land, specially when such a suitable opening occurs. (12)

No reply was received to either of these letters, but the Chamberlain did state, verbally, that the petition had been refused.

On 23rd December, 1882, the petitioners wrote to Lady Matheson once again, enclosing a copy of their original letter. In one paragraph, the hope was expressed that they might not be led, reluctantly, to take such steps as many of their unfortunate countrymen were forced to adopt. This annoyed Lady Matheson intensely, (13) and brought an immediate response.

Her Ladyship regrets that the above named respectable class of Lewis men should have been led to address her on a subject of such importance as that contained in their petition by adding to it a letter which causes her to set aside their request, as Lady Matheson is too devoted to her Queen and the laws of which Her Gracious Majesty is the representative, to listen for one moment to a petition accompanied by a threat from them to infringe the law by which all are governed, and by the support of which, as individuals, the well-being of the land and its communities at large can alone be promoted. (14)

Their hopes of acquiring land were again dashed when the Crofters' Holdings (Scotland) Act of 1886 was passed, for although it granted many benefits to crofters, including facilities for enlarging holdings, it did nothing to help them in their immediate need. When, in the same year, the Park Farm became a deer forest, and the former townships of Orinsay and Steimreway were added to Crobeg Farm, they became extremely angry, and the sop of granting Seaforth Head to six crofters did nothing to pacify them.

The landless men of Lochs, now militant as never before, found a leader in the recently appointed schoolmaster of Balallan, Mr Donald Macrae. Soon plans were formulated at meetings in Mr Macrae's school, for the invasion of Park Forest by groups of cottars and squatters, to shoot and drive away the deer, thus drawing attention to their miserable plight. Everybody in Lochs knew of the scheme, but few believed it would ever materialise.

Early on the morning of 22nd November 1887, there was tremendous excitement in the villages from Crossbost to Gravir. Several groups of men, totalling more than a hundred, made their way to the appointed rendezvous at Seaforth Head. Some were armed with muzzle-loading rifles, while others carried spars, sails, and cooking pots.

The deer drive started immediately. A few animals were shot, and towards the evening, camp was set up in the deserted township of Stromas, the most beautiful of all the evicted hamlets of Park. There, a large tent, about 100 yards long, and other smaller tents, were pitched, their fronts open to the huge fires which provided heat and light, and roasted and boiled the venison.

When supper was ready, an old patriarch from Marvig rose to say Grace in which he beseeched Almighty God for a blessing on the food which He had so graciously provided, and also on those gathered around him. He hoped that the day would come when a church would stand on the spot where they now stood.

Mr Platt, the lessee of Park was not at home at the time, so it was left to Mrs Platt to go and meet the raiders, and although they admired her for her many sterling qualities, they now completely ignored her. However, her gamekeepers and gillies noted the names of the men they recognised.

The next morning, Mrs Platt wired her agent in Edinburgh, asking him to see the Lord Advocate about sending soldiers. At the same time, she gave warning that any delay would prove fatal.

On the second day, the raiders employed the same tactics, but had to spend a miserably wet night encamped at the ruins of *Airigh Dhomhnuill Chaim,* One-eyed Donald's Shieling. There, they had time to digest what was implied in the Riot Act that had been read to them earlier in the day by Sheriff Fraser of Stornoway, an active and resourceful man.

This combination of circumstances dampened the raiders' spirits and lessened their desire for further action. They began to drift back, singly and in groups, to their respective villages. Unfortunately, one of those travelling alone, a Donald Mackinnon, met Superintendent Gordon, whom he threatened with his gun before running away. Realising what he had done, Mackinnon raced to Stornoway, where he reported all that had happened in Park, and gave the names of the ringleaders, information which led to the arrest of sixteen men who were taken to Stornoway, but later released.

The day after the collapse of the raid, eighty men of the Royal Scots arrived in Stornoway. The Navy was also called in to help but H.M.S. *Ajax* on her way from Greenock with four hundred marines on board, met with an accident on the way, and was unable to continue. However, H.M.S. *Jackal* (Jackass to the locals), did arrive, to be followed, shortly afterwards, by H.M.S. *Seahorse,* with forty marines on board who had been issued with 100 rounds of ball cartridge per man. (15)

On 13th January 1888, a large crowd gathered on the pier in Stornoway when the deer raiders left for Edinburgh on the *S.S. Lochiel.* The Crown witnesses were escorted on board by the police.

Donald Macrae, the Balallan schoolmaster, Roderick Mackenzie, a Balallan merchant, Murdo Macdonald of Balallan, John Matheson of Gravir, Malcolm

Mackenzie and Donald Macmillan of Crossbost, were charged in the High Court in Edinburgh, with mobbing and rioting.

The Counsel for the accused was able to convince the jury that there had been no mobbing or rioting, and that nothing more serious than trespassing and poaching had taken place. Fifteen deer had been killed, he granted, but he was certain that, but for the three witnesses who, he suggested, were the actual leaders of the raid, and who had turned King's evidence, there would have been no case for the Crown.

The men were found not guilty, and Mr Macrae was carried down the Edinburgh High Street, shoulder high, by a jubilant crowd.

On their arrival in Stornoway, the men were greeted with loud cheering by a large crowd waiting for them on the quay. (16)

At this time, the whole Island was very unsettled. Poverty had rendered the people desperate, and the Park Deer Raid, abortive though it had been, was destined to be the forerunner of similar occurrences in the other parishes.

The Point cottars and squatters often looked with envious eyes on the fertile farm of Aignish as they passed on their way to or from Stornoway. The sight of such excellent arable land under pasture made their own small plots seem even meaner than they were.

Eventually, on Christmas Day 1887, a meeting was held in the old Eye Churchyard, and it was decided that a deputation should interview the farm lessee, a Mr Newall, to inform him that if he did not vacate the farm with his entire stock, within a fortnight, they would drive every beast off the land. Mr Newall was completely unmoved by the threat, for he did not believe the men were in earnest. Soon he was subjected to a series of petty harassments with fences and dykes being destroyed, and stock allowed to stray. The police were informed, and one of three men who was engaged in this destruction was caught, after being partly stunned with a baton.

Shortly after, a crowd arrived at Aignish Farmhouse demanding the prisoner's release, and threatening to destroy the farm steading. When Mr Newall appeared with a gun, the men dispersed.

Everyone throughout the Island knew that Monday, the 9th January, 1888 was the day set for clearing Aignish Farm of its stock. The Authorities in Stornoway, after their experience in Park, and the strong criticism of their inaction at the time of the Deer Raid, which they did not try to prevent, although they had advance information about it, decided to check any lawlessness by declaring the proposed assembly illegal. Anyone taking part in it would therefore be guilty of the crime of mobbing and rioting, even if not participating in any act of violence.

Before dawn on the chosen morning, thirty-six men from H.M.S. *Seahorse,* which happened to be in Stornoway, were landed quietly in Sandwick Bay. As they made for the farm, a company of the Royal Scots moved quietly from Manor Farm to Melbost Farm. Sheriff Fraser, with Police Superintendent Gordon, Deputy Procurator-Fiscal Ross and a couple of policemen were also in Aignish Farm awaiting developments, and prepared to deal with any emergency.

The raiders came with the dawn, and immediately began driving the stock in the direction of Stornoway. On seeing this, Sheriff Fraser, a Gaelic speaker, went out to meet them. His earnest appeal to abandon their project fell on deaf ears, as they continued to drive the beasts away. Sheriff Fraser called for the Marines, but the raiders paid little attention.

About noon, a party of the raiders clashed with the Marines, and eleven of them were taken into custody. When the incensed crowd attempted to free their comrades, it took the bayonets of the Marines to keep them at bay. Missiles of all kinds began to fly, and the situation appeared ugly.

It was Sheriff Fraser, ably assisted by Superintendent Gordon, who, by his coolness and tact, prevented a dangerous confrontation from having tragic consequences. Many of the raiders were Militia men or Royal Naval Reservists, trained in the use of firearms, and quite capable of taking drastic action against the Marines, a branch of the Services never popular with the Islanders. There is no doubt that if a single shot had been fired, there would have been much bloodshed.

The Sheriff finally read the Riot Act, and explained its provisions in Gaelic, but this seemed to make no impression on those assembled. The arrival of the Royal Scots, however, made them realise there was little more they could do. Tempers began to cool, and all that the raiders could do was to return home, while the prisoners, strongly guarded by Marines and soldiers, were marched to gaol in Stornoway.

Early on the morning of 13th January, the prisoners, handcuffed in pairs, and carefully guarded by police and soldiers, were escorted aboard H.M.S. *Jackal,* and taken to Edinburgh. They were tried before Lord Craighill, and found guilty of the crime of mobbing and rioting. His Lordship sent them to prison for periods ranging from twelve to fifteen months.

It was not until 1905, that Aignish Farm was given over to crofting.

The troubles in Park and Aignish seem to have added fuel to the fire of discontent which smouldered throughout the Island, and Barvas was the next district where the people demonstrated their grievances. In January 1888, three hundred men from the villages of Borve, Shader, Barvas, Brue and Arnol, set off for Stornoway. They petitioned Lady Matheson to make Galson Farm into crofts to be given to them at a fair rent, as it was impossible to support their families on the crofts they presently held. Lady Matheson refused to see them, and informed one of their number, who had been allowed into her presence, that until their arrears of rent were paid, she would have nothing to do with them, especially as Mr Helm, the present tenant of the farm paid his rent promptly.

Galson Farm was not the only land the people were interested in. They also wanted a re-arrangement of the boundaries of the Barvas minister's glebe. They maintained extensions had been made to this some time before, at the expense of their own pasture lands, without any reduction in their rents.

The Authorities, anticipating trouble, stationed policemen at Galson, Barvas and Dalbeg Farms, whose tenants had been warned to move out.

Fences and dykes on Galson Farm began to be destroyed by nocturnal invaders so that stock could stray. It was not long before the police and the night-hawks met, and a short, sharp mêlée occurred. (17) The police, who were outnumbered, were forced to retreat, with three of their number slightly hurt.

A messenger was immediately sent to Stornoway with news of the affray, and the Authorities there decided to try a pincers move against the law-breakers. H.M.S. *Seahorse* set sail for Port of Ness, carrying Sheriff Fraser and a strong contingent of police and Marines, while a party of Royal Scots and some Marines marched to Borve.

Before dawn the following morning, acting on information received, the police, with military protection, unceremoniously entered the lockless houses, to the great alarm of the inmates. Five men were arrested, and marched, handcuffed, to Port of Ness, from where they were taken to the gaol at Stornoway.

The five men were taken to Edinburgh, and tried in the High Court, accused of mobbing and rioting, but on a plea of alibi, they were found not guilty.

Meanwhile, the men of Barvas were busy diverting the river there into its former channel, alleging that it periodically flooded some houses and land, as well as desecrating the graves of men who had been killed and buried there long ago. The people of the adjoining village of Brue were not too pleased with these activities and, in the end, the law intervened, and the work was abandoned.

In spite of a spate of requests for more land and reductions in rent, an uneasy kind of peace settled over the Island for a while. Perhaps the MacNeill Inquiry into the condition of the crofters, and the Government's expressed intention to improve the lot of the Islanders had something to do with this. As circumstances, especially those of the cottars and squatters, steadily deteriorated, a new attempt was made to acquire land by force, again in Lochs. This time, it started in the village of Crossbost, formerly a tack, to which many of those evicted from Park had been sent, some of whom were still alive.

In March 1891, eighteen men sailed from Crossbost with the intention of re-settling Orinsay. On arrival, they roofed three of the least ruinous of the old houses with spars and sails.

This township of Orinsay was now part of the farm of Crobeg, and men from Marvig and Gravir had previously applied for it. Their request had been refused, partly because Lady Matheson thought there was an element of threat in the petition.

This latest batch of land seekers were unfortunate from the start, for the weather steadily deteriorated to blizzard conditions the day after their landing, making their makeshift dwellings more or less untenable. They had no desire to interfere with any stock, at least in the first instance. All they wanted was the peaceful possession of the land of their forefathers.

The people from the adjacent villages of Calbost and Gravir decided that they could also do with more land. Ten men from Gravir, and some from Calbost, invaded the deserted township of Steimreway.

In both settlements, some attempt at tillage was made, with the planting of potatoes, but the weather was so inhospitable, and the law moved so rapidly, that they were able to accomplish very little.

Twelve of the Orinsay raiders were tried under the Tresspass (Scotland) Act of 1865, in the Stornoway Sheriff Court, and were found guilty. However, being first offenders, they were only sentenced to fourteen days' imprisonment in Inverness.

Four days later, a second lot of fifteen men was tried in Stornoway, all of whom pleaded guilty. Nine were released on promising that they would never again trespass on Orinsay Farm, except to collect whatever implements they had left there, nor to take part in any more land raiding. The other six refused to give such a promise, and were sent to prison for fourteen days. (18)

THE LEVERHULME PERIOD

Shortly before the outbreak of the 1914-18 War, the Board of Agriculture for Scotland prepared schemes in accordance with the provisions of the Small Landholders (Scotland) Act, 1911, for dividing into crofts, farms with a rental in excess of £80, or 150 acres. There were at least 800 people from Lewis who applied for crofts at this time, but the outbreak of war caused these schemes to be shelved, as many of the applicants were on active service. The farms being considered for conversion were, Gress, Galson, Carnish/Ardroil, and Orinsay/Steimreway.

In 1917, the Board proceeded to make arrangements for the implementation of their plans immediately the war ended. These plans had the full approval of Mr Munro, the Secretary for Scotland.

In 1918, Lord Leverhulme purchased the Island from Lieut.-Colonel Duncan Matheson, and upset the carefully prepared plans, so the Board immediately opened up negotiations with the new proprietor, hoping that they would have his full co-operation for the execution of their schemes. (1)

This turned out to be wishful thinking on the Board's part, for Lord Leverhulme had plans of his own for his newly acquired property, in which the extension of the crofting system had no part. He considered Gress and Galson Farms as being vital to the success of his projects, by providing milk for a considerably increased population in the town of Stornoway.

Lord Leverhulme visualised the Island as a huge landing stage for the development of a thriving fishing industry which would require not only the provision of increased harbour facilities, but also the establishment of ancillary industries such as fish-canning, handloom weaving, land reclamation, afforestation, basket making, poultry keeping and the making of roads and railways. He wanted to have a happy and prosperous resident population, with each family earning, as a result of his development schemes, as many pounds as they then earned in shillings. He was horrified to discover that the women carried 80 lb. creels of peat when the women of the Congo were only allowed, by law, to carry 44 lb. (2)

Lord Leverhulme considered the Board's schemes, estimated at a cost of £57,000, to be a sheer waste of public money. (3) They provided for only 153 holdings or enlargements to satisfy the demands of about ten per cent of the Island's population. All of these holdings would be uneconomic, and of no permanent value to the community. He made it quite clear that he needed these farms, not for sporting purposes, for he placed more importance on people than on grouse or deer, but for the benefit of the islanders.

His Lordship refused to co-operate with the Board, and threatened to abandon his development plans if they proceeded with their proposals. The Board ultimately decided that, in view of the considerable sums of money Lord Leverhulme was prepared to spend, to defer its undertaking until the people realised it was to their advantage to participate in the proprietor's schemes and abandon their demand for small holdings. The Board was also quite certain that the people of Lewis would force Lord Leverhulme to deal with the land problem.

By the beginning of 1919, the Lewis development works were in full swing. Houses were being built; the road to Arnish, and the Tolsta-Ness road had been started; old roads were being repaired; a canning factory was in the course of erection, and the harbour facilities were being steadily improved. Never before had Lewis so many people engaged in lucrative employment. Transport was being revolutionised, with lorries and cars replacing carts and gigs.

In spite of this unprecedented prosperity, some of the ex-servicemen continued to demand land. They thought the government preferred Lord Leverhulme's plan to their justifiable claims. They knew that land settlement was taking place in other parts of the Highlands and Islands, and could see no reason why the same was not happening in Lewis. They were becoming impatient at the Government's delay in fulfilling its promises. The fact that Lord Leverhulme was spending about £200,000 a year in the Island meant nothing in their eyes, in comparison with the possession of a croft.

Threats to raid farms were frequently heard in many of the villages, especially those of Back and Coll. A letter from some ex-servicemen to the Rt. Hon. Robert Munro, the Secretary for Scotland, illustrates very forcibly their determination to get a croft at any cost.

Sir,
We thought it necessary to inform you of our firmly Determination concerning small holdings in the Island of Lewis. Shortly there is going to be a Lawful or Illegal action to be taken by us regarding Coll Farm. Of course we would rather have it lawful but time and space can't allow us to wait any further, and we are determined to take it by force, without Delay to Fulfil the promise granted by the Government to Demobilised soldiers and sailors, the land ought to be in wait for us we are anxious to know where does the Obstacle Lay's as we are in wait on the land. As propitors are not willingly to give us land suitable for Cultivation we inform you that there isn't a landlord or even a Duke in the British Isles that will keep the land from us, that has been promised to us by the Primier and the Country at Large without bloodshed. As it is in your power we sincerely hope that you will grant and fulfill the promise made by the Government and at the same time giving us our wish and saving us from any trouble that's liable to come round concerning small holdings. We desire every farm great or small to be cut down as long as there is any of us without a piece of Land able to call his own with Fair Fixity of Tenure and compensation for improvements we have forwarded a copy of this letter to the Prime Minister and Dr Murray, M.P. for the Western Isles.

Early in March 1919, raiding began on the farms of Tong, Coll and Gress, an example which was soon to be repeated in the other parishes. Lord Leverhulme went down to Gress to meet the raiders, and in an eloquent address, described how he hoped to develop the fishing industry in the Island and the benefits which the whole population would enjoy as a result. He was given a tremendous ovation when he finished, an ovation which he accepted as an endorsement of his schemes. However, Allan Martin, one of the leaders of the raiders addressed the assembled crowd in Gaelic, translated as follows:

Come, come, men! This will not do! That man with his silver tongue would make us believe that white is black and black is white! We are not concerned with his fancy dreams that may or may not come true. What we want is the land—and that is the question I put to the landlord. Is he willing to give us the land? And is he willing to give it now? (4)

The crowd roared their approval, but Lord Leverhulme, without hesitation replied, "The answer is NO."

Again Lord Leverhulme re-stated his plans for the future prosperity of Lewis and its people, but again he was interrupted. A John Smith asked permission to speak, and said:

We give credit to your Lordship for good intentions in this matter. We believe you think you are right, but we know that you are wrong. The fact is, there is an element of sentiment in the situation which it is impossible for your Lordship to understand. But for that we do not blame you; it is not your fault but your misfortune that your upbringing, your experience and your outlook are such that a proper understanding of the position and of our point of view is quite outwith your comprehension. You have spoken of steady work and steady pay in terms of veneration—and I have no doubt that in your view and in the view of those unfortunate people who are compelled to live in smoky towns, steady work and steady pay are very desirable things. But in Lewis we have never been accustomed to either—and strange though it must seem to you, we do not greatly desire them. We attend to our crofts in seed-time and harvest, and we follow the fishing in its season—and when neither requires our attention we are free to rest and contemplate. You have referred to our houses as hovels? but they are our homes, and I will venture to say, my Lord, that, poor though these homes may be, you will find more real happiness in them than you will find in your castles throughout the land. I would impress on you that we are not in opposition to your schemes of work; we only oppose you when you say you cannot give us the land, and on that point we will oppose you with all our strength.
It may be that some of the younger and less thoughtful men will side with you, but believe me, the great majority of us are against you—because we want to live our own lives in our own way, poor, it may be, but clear of the fear of the factory bell, and free and independent. (5)

Lord Leverhulme, often referred to by the people as *Bodach an t-Siabuin,* the Soap-man, began to realise how much the possession of a croft meant to the people. He was certain however, that if he were allowed to proceed with his schemes, even if they did not create more crofts, they would initiate new industries, and bring such prosperity to those employed, that, in ten years' time, the people would have a different attitude to life and land. (6)

He tried to impress on the people that his industrial proposals were completely different from the picture many conjured up as consisting of huge iron-works, cotton factories and machine shops. Such alien industries, he told them, could be no more successful in Lewis than an attempt to grow bananas and coconuts. The Islanders were faced with a choice between two plans, the Government's or the proprietor's. The Government was in a dilemma. If it did not fulfil its promise of giving small-holdings to ex-servicemen, it was bound to incur some odium for going back on its promises. On the other hand, it was naturally reluctant to offend Lord Leverhulme, whose works had already brought a great deal of prosperity to the Island at no cost to the Treasury.

180

The Secretary for Scotland hoped to persuade Lord Leverhulme to continue his schemes, while at the same time, allowing the sub-division of farms to proceed. His Lordship was, however, adamant that he needed the farms to supply milk to the town of Stornoway, and he would not agree to any modification of his plans.

The majority of the Islanders had no doubt that, if the farms were broken up and the proprietor forced to abandon his operations, mass emigration would result. At the same time, if his proposals were put into effect, an efficient fishing industry could be established, for, in the proprietor's own words, the sea had no seed-time or ploughing time, while its harvest could be reaped, in one way or another, every week of the year. (7)

During the whole of 1919, the parties to the dispute became more entrenched in their views, and yet it was evident that unless some measure of agreement was reached, chaos would ensue.

In the Spring of 1920, raids on a larger and more determined scale took place. At Coll, twenty-nine men seized plots and began building operations, while at Gress, twenty-one men did likewise.

The managers Lord Leverhulme had placed in charge of those farms after the farmers had left, had their horses unyoked from the ploughs and returned to their stables.

The proprietor had interim interdicts served on several of the raiders, but these were completely ignored. On being cited to appear in the Stornoway Sheriff Court for breach of interdict, the raiders failed to appear, as they were too busy planting potatoes. Warrants were issued for their arrest, but these were never served, and this met with the disapproval of most of the Islanders, who were annoyed that a few men should be allowed to wreck the future prospects of prosperity for the Island.

Lord Leverhulme's refusal to sanction the serving of the arrest warrants was partly due to the advice of the Secretary for Scotland, who did not want a confrontation at this time, and partly due to a remark attributed to the same, by which his Lordship understood that even if the raiders were imprisoned, he, the Secretary, had the power to order their release. (8)

Lord Leverhulme was so incensed at this new outbreak of raiding in the Back district, that in February, 1920, he ordered sixty men from Back, Vatisker and Coll townships to be dismissed from his employment.

This gesture pleased the raiders, who thought it was a splendid example of what could happen to those who allowed themselves to fall completely into Lord Leverhulme's power. Many of those dismissed were intensely annoyed at losing their jobs through the activities of a few men.

The proprietor was quite prepared to re-employ the sacked men, without their suffering any financial loss, but only if the raiders stopped their illegal operations.

The raiders were not influenced by what had happened to their countrymen, nor by the strong feelings throughout the Island that Lord Leverhulme should have them arrested. They believed they had paid a dearer price for the land than Lord Leverhulme, in many cases, with their flesh and blood. (9) As for the stones from the dykes which they used in their housebuilding activities, they considered they had as much right to them as they had to the land, since they had been placed there by their forefathers at a time when the crofters had no legal protection, and could be forced to work for the tacksmen without wages. (10)

Efforts were still continuing to reconcile the various parties in the dispute. The Board thought that the raiders might be persuaded to withdraw, if Lord

Leverhulme made certain farms over which they had no compulsory control available for sub-division. This proposal was not accepted, as it was felt that the withdrawal should be unconditional, especially as the proprietor was prepared to grant quarter-acre sites for house building, with loans up to eighty per cent of the cost. He was also ready to ask the Land Court for the resumption of part of the common grazings in order to form ten-acre small holdings. It was felt that the area between Tolsta and Ness, now being made accessible because of the new road being made, would be very suitable for this purpose. (11)

The raiding still continued, and by April 1920, there were eight raiders on the Carnish/Ardroil farm, thirteen on Reef, six on Orinsay/Steimreway, nineteen on Gress, and twenty on Coll.

In May, Lord Leverhulme stopped all his Island operations, to the utter consternation of those who were thus suddenly deprived of their livelihood.

On 21st May 1920, the Coll raiders wrote to Mr Munro, the Secretary for Scotland:

> Right Honourable,
> A crowded meeting of landless ex-servicemen was held at Coll on 19th inst. and the meeting was unanimously agreed to give the land to the landless ex-servicemen without delay and unanimous. Protested against the one-sided meeting that was held at Stornoway on the 14th inst. The said meeting was formed by Crofters, Drapers, and Fishcurers, and a great many of Con—objectors and many was blind and lame, and full of consumption until the war was over but after the Peace was Proclaimed they were all right. Now after we fought and bleed for King and Country and conquer the enemy on account of the great Victory won and the promise was made to be fulfilled that is to say to give land to Soldiers and Sailors and proper Homes but as we took 4½ years . . . conquering the Germans it seems to us it is going to take longer before the British Government shares out the land for the few was left to tell the tale. But our main object is this. We took possession of Coll Farm on account of our extremities circumstances and more than that we only claim our rights as matters is not in such as it was anticipated. We have to help ourselves the best way we can.
> Now the Government bear in mind that the land was promised to Sailors and Soldiers and also was passed by Act of Parliament as you are well aware of, if it goes by votes from ex-servicemen we are sure to get the majority. We object to take Druggists and Dentists and Fishcurers votes. . . .
> We hope the Government will look into our circumstances without delay and get the Land Act to work in Lewis. (12)

In view of what the cessation of work meant to the Island, the Secretary for Scotland was urged to adopt the continuance of Lord Leverhulme's scheme. "The economic salvation of Lewis can come only from the sea and that by appropriate means. No crofting policy offers a practical solution." (13)

The following telegram was despatched by Provost Smith to Mr Munro, on the 8th June 1920.

> Desperate situation in Lewis compels me to wire you; abandonment of Lord Leverhulme's development schemes causing widespread discontent; hundreds demanding employment and out of work benefit;

fishing also failure up to present; can you do anything to get Lord Leverhulme persuaded reconsider his decision? (14)

The Stornoway Town Clerk also wired Mr Munro suggesting that in view of the seriousness of the situation, Lord Leverhulme should be given any reasonable pledge which would bring about a resumption of the improvement schemes. (15)

The raiders' lawyer, Mr Donald Shaw of Edinburgh, who felt that a way out of the impasse had to be found immediately, not so much in Lord Leverhulme's interests as in those of the poor people who had been thrown out of employment, also contacted Mr Munro. (16)

Mr Munro replied to Mr Shaw, thus:

> The loss of employment . . . which is bringing suffering on a large number of the Islanders is directly attributable to the action of the raiders, and I think you would be on good ground if you were to appeal to their sense of honour and to their local patriotism, to induce them to abandon a course fraught with so much injury to the interests of their friends and neighbours. (17)

Mr Shaw promptly informed Mr Munro that the men were not likely to abandon their position, for which they had fought so hard over the last few months, unless something was done about their settlement. Lord Leverhulme's failure to reinstate his dismissed employees did not help the situation. The raiders, he affirmed, viewed with indignation his attempt to avenge their acts on their innocent neighbours, especially as Coll and Gress farms were absolutely unnecessary for his schemes.

Mr Shaw said:

> Lord Leverhulme may be entitled to withhold employment, but the Government are not entitled to assist him in the boycott, by withholding the land which is the sheet anchor of the community. The present stoppage only proves how very precarious would be the lot of the islanders if they were silly enough to give up their rights to the land. (18)

By June 1920, Lord Leverhulme was prepared to offer the farms of Reef, Mealista, part of Timsgarry, Dalbeag, and Carnish/Ardroil for crofting purposes. (19)

Relations between the Secretary for Scotland and Lord Leverhulme, never very cordial, became more strained, and in August 1920, the former reminded the latter that, unless he was prepared to resume his schemes, there would be no longer any justification for the Government to refrain from exercising the statutory powers possessed by the Board of Agriculture to meet the demand for land holdings. These powers had been held in abeyance in order that Lord Leverhulme be given the opportunity he wished to proceed with his schemes. (20)

Lord Leverhulme insisted that, before he resumed operations, the Government should give him an assurance that there would be no raiding for the next ten years, and that the raiders would vacate the farms.

In October 1920, the Lord Advocate visited the raiders at Back and Coll, to discuss matters with them. Some of the men were willing to leave, providing he gave them a guarantee that the farms would be made available to them the following Spring. The Lord Advocate could not give this guarantee, but the raiders thought that the outcome would be in their favour, and accordingly, they left the farms.

Meantime, support was steadily mounting for Lord Leverhulme. The following resolution was endorsed by practically every township in the Island, including Back, Coll and Vatisker, and a copy sent to the Secretary of State.

> That this representative meeting of the inhabitants of . . . heartily appreciate the development schemes for Lewis, voluntarily offered by the Rt. Honourable Lord Leverhulme and welcome the prospect of an early settlement, satisfactory to both parties of the present unfortunate position brought about by the illegal raiding and occupation of certain farms on the East and the West coast of the island.
>
> Further we, the inhabitants of the above-named townships undertake for at least ten years, not to take part in the illegal raiding of any farm lands in the Lewis, so as to give his Lordship the necessary opportunity and support he requires to make his schemes a success. (21)

As a result of these resolutions, Mr Munro concluded that Lord Leverhulme's policy was endorsed by a very large section of the community, and that the only thing necessary for the resumption of the work was the Government guarantee asked for.

He accordingly informed his Lordship that having considered the problem with great care, he believed that it was in the best interests of the community as a whole that such an assurance, as he sought, should be given.

> Accordingly, if you proceed with the various schemes . . . I am prepared, on behalf of the Government, to undertake that the compulsory powers for taking your land for small holdings shall not, while your schemes go on, be put into operation, and that land settlement under the auspices of the Government shall only proceed upon the land which you have agreed to make available to me, and any other land which you may hereafter place at my disposal for this purpose.
>
> *Should your development schemes for any reason not proceed, the hands of the Government will, of course, be free.* (22)

Lord Leverhulme replied to this communication by stating that, providing raiding ceased and was not likely to re-occur, he was prepared to resume operations by the end of March or early April, and only awaited assurances from the raiders and their friends. (23)

The Board of Agriculture was not very sanguine about the future developments, so a partial scheme of land settlement was prepared in which due regard was paid to the interests of both landlord and crofters, knowing full well that the raiders' withdrawal was only a temporary measure in order to allow the Secretary for Scotland and the Board to have a free hand in their negotiations with Lord Leverhulme.

By January 1921, Lord Leverhulme was in financial difficulties, with the result that when the work was resumed in April on a much reduced scale, there was a feeling of uneasiness, and a sense of imminent disaster, throughout the Island.

The Coll and Gress raiders, when they saw their houses on the farms being demolished to repair the dykes, promptly raided the farms again.

This was the last straw. Lord Leverhulme's patience was finally exhausted, and all work throughout the Island was brought to a standstill. On 31st August, he announced the indefinite suspension of all his projects.

With almost indecent haste, Mr Munro reminded Lord Leverhulme that the pledge of non-intervention by the Government had been granted on condition that his schemes were in operation, but, in view of the fact that these schemes had been suspended, there was now no reason why land settlement should not be undertaken.

Lord Leverhulme was annoyed at the way Mr Munro took immediate advantage of his announcement of suspension of operations, owing to his financial difficulties, and he complained that the Scottish Office had not given him its full support for his development plans, especially with regard to the farms of Coll and Gress, for, he contended, that without these two farms to provide milk for the industrial centre of Stornoway, it was impossible to bring the complete scheme which he had originally contemplated, into operation. (24)

By the end of 1921, there was much distress, owing to the cessation of Lord Leverhulme's projects. Relief work had to be started. Early in 1922, the Lewis District Committee was given a grant of £38,000 by the Board of Agriculture for this purpose, of which, £10,000 was to be spent on the breaking of road metal, and the re-surfacing of existing roads. The balance was to be used for making new roads, such as the one from Balallan, round by Shildinish to South Lochs. It was no uncommon sight at this time to see men by the roadside hammering away, breaking stones for road metal. The Board were well aware of the fact that they could expect no local contributions to relieve the sufferings of the people, and that the only outside help they might get would be, of all people, from Lord Leverhulme, who might lend tools and huts and even the services of his officials. (25)

What a shock for the economy of the Island—a grant of £38,000, when Lord Leverhulme had been spending £200,000 a year!

The Scottish Office and the Board of Agriculture might still salve their consciences by saying that it was never suggested that the Lewis croft provided a livelihood, and that these crofts which eked out other sources of income, and provided necessities when these other sources failed, formed a normal feature in Lewis. To extend their numbers, was both practical and desirable. The fishing was often a failure, and it might be observed, that the suspension of Lord Leverhulme's industrial schemes had given added weight to the Lewisman's desire for the security which the crofts alone could give. (26)

An official of the Board of Agriculture also rather naively informed the Scottish Office that he could not understand how the Board had prevented the adoption of Lord Leverhulme's industrial schemes, as the Board had welcomed them, and the Secretary for Scotland had delayed action in regard to Land Settlement for a long time in order to allow these industrial schemes to develop. The only reason that he could think of for such an opinion, was that the Board pressed the necessity for the settlement of Gress and Coll, when Lord Leverhulme wanted to keep these farms for the milk supply of a potentially industrial Stornoway. (27)

Therefore, due to the action of a few ex-servicemen, a very small percentage of the ex-servicemen in Lewis, the actions of the Scottish Office and the Board of Agriculture, combined with that of outside organisations which knew very little of the conditions prevailing in Lewis at that time, and the stubbornness of Lord Leverhulme to modify his plans, the schemes for a prosperous Island came to nothing, and the Islanders were left destitute. Inevitably, emigration followed.

In disgust, Lord Leverhulme transferred his schemes to Harris, where they were generally welcomed.

In 1923, His Lordship finally decided to give the Island of Lewis to the people. He proposed the formation of a Stornoway Trust to administer the Parish of Stornoway, with the freehold of all the crofts, with the exception of those occupied by the ex-raiders, to be offered as a gift to their present occupiers.

With minor exceptions, the rest of the Island was to be given to the Lewis District Committee, and the crofts there offered to the crofters on the same terms as those in the Parish of Stornoway.

The Stornoway Town Council accepted his offer, but the Lewis District Committee refused it, as did the majority of the crofters, because of the rating difficulty. Only forty-one of the crofters accepted his gift.

Bit by bit, parts of the Island were sold to individuals or syndicates until, by 1925, its dismemberment was complete, and nothing remained connected in any way with Lord Leverhulme. Perhaps, after all, Lord Leverhulme's assessment of the Lewis character, as given during an address to the people of Stornoway in 1920, was not far wrong.

I cannot claim a thorough knowledge of the average Lewisman, but I am firmly convinced on a few points; first that they are a very fine people, and that I am very fond of them, notwithstanding that they are a little difficult at times; the next is, that you may lead a Lewisman with a hair, but you won't drag him with a cable. (28)

To quote an old proverb:

"Is treise Tuath na Tighearna"

"Tenantry are stronger than Laird".

DESERTED ISLANDS

North Rona, lying about thirty eight miles north-east of the Butt of Lewis, is the most attractive of all the islands round the coast which were formerly inhabited.

Captain Burnaby, who surveyed the island in 1852, compared it to a long-necked decanter, the neck portion, the low flat area called Fianuis, lying towards the north, and a similar tract, Sceapull, lying to the south-west. The highest point, the Tòbha, north of Sceapull, rises to a height of 360 feet, and on a clear day, Lewis and Cape Wrath can be seen from this point. The soil is good on North Rona, and with the exception of about 50 acres, is arable with no peat moss. (1)

According to tradition, the island was a bone of contention at one time between the men of Ness and those of Sutherland. To settle the question of ownership once and for all, two well-manned boats left Cape Wrath in Sutherland and Port Chealagmhol in Ness at the same time, as both places were thought to be equi-distant from Rona.

The Sutherland boat arrived at the island a few yards ahead of the men of Ness, an indication that they had a shorter distance to row. In any case, the men from Sutherland threw burning peat ashore at Geodha Stoth to claim the place, but a quick-witted Ness-man hacked off one of his fingers and threw it ashore. As blood is more potent than fire, it was amicably agreed that Rona would belong to Lewis.

There are many seals on North Rona, especially on Fianuis, and it is probably due to this fact that the Island was named Rona, the Island of Seals, and not after the Culdee monk, later called St Ronan, who spent some time there.

There are many stories about Ronan, and one tells how he came to Rona. It seems he used to live in Eoropie, but like so many of his profession, preferred solitude to the company of the attractive, but talkative ladies who were his neighbours. The poor man prayed fervently to be transferred elsewhere so that his meditations might not be interrupted by feminine frivolity. Being a saintly person, his petition was granted sooner than he expected. On three successive nights, he was awakened by a voice ordering him to go to the shore at Cunndal where *an t-each iomchair,* the transport horse, was waiting for him. After the third summons, he obeyed the call, and taking his sister Brianuilt with him, he made for Cunndal, where a huge whale took them on its broad back to Rona.

However, his troubles were not yet over, for he found himself faced with a pack of huge dog-like beasts, which threatened him with menacing snarls. Undeterred by this welcome, the intrepid Ronan advanced, and the beasts retreated towards the cliffs until at last they slipped backwards into the sea at *Leac nan Scrob,* Ledge of the Scratches, where marks, supposedly made by their claws, are to be seen.

Dean Munro, who visited the Western Isles in 1549, tells that the Island was then "inhabit be simple people, scant of any religion". They were well-fed, for any stock, surplus to their souming (allowance), had to be eaten or used to pay their dues to Macleod of Lewis. Fish, especially cod, ling and coal-fish, were plentiful, as were whales. (2)

When sheep were killed, their skins were peeled off as if they were rabbits and used as sacks to take the flour-white barley, smoke-dried meat and fowls across to Lewis. (3) The people told the Dean that when a person died, a spade was left in St Ronan's Chapel, and the following morning, they found the site of the grave marked. (4)

There was a tradition in Ness, that early in the 17th century, all the men on Rona were drowned during a whale-hunt in Port Heallair, and that their families were six months on the Island before being rescued and taken to Lewis.

Tradition also tells of a woman living on Rona who wanted to test the truth of the old belief that fire was never quenched there. She soon found out that this was a fallacy, but when she discovered her fire extinguished, her fervent prayers brought it to life again. (5)

The writer Martin Martin, who toured the Western Isles about 1695, was told by Mr Daniel Morison, the minister of Barvas, whose tack included Rona, that when he visited the Island, he was received with the greatest courtesy. "God save you, pilgrim, you are heartily welcome here", he was told, "for we have had repeated apparitions of your person among us, and we heartily congratulate your arrival in our remote country". (6)

Mr Morison was not so courteous. When one of the men walked round him *deiseil,* sunwise (a demonstration of regard) while wishing him every happiness, he told the man to stop such a heathenish practice. (7)

A house was provided for the minister's comfort, with a bundle of straw to sit on. Each of the five families then killed a sheep, filled their skins with barley meal, and presented them to their guest for favouring them with a visit.

Every Sunday morning, these people assembled in St Ronan's Chapel, where they repeated the Lord's Prayer, the Creed and the Ten Commandments, but at the same time, they regarded with respect the stones set at one foot intervals in a ten foot plank on the altar. To each stone was attributed a special power. One for instance, was believed to help a woman in childbirth. (8) These people had few wants, and as long as they had food and clothing, they were content.

About this time, two men were courting the same girl. When she married one of them, the other suggested to the minister that he arrange matters so that they could have her to wife on alternate years. Mr Morison said he could not permit this, but promised to send him a wife from Lewis the following year, which he duly did, a duty he also performed for another man who gave him a shilling to buy him a bride.

Martin also relates that about 1680, a swarm of rats came ashore (9) and ate all the corn on the Island, and shortly after, some sailors stole their bull. As if this were not enough misfortune, the yearly supplies from Lewis failed to arrive, and when the St Kildan factor was storm-driven to Rona, he found, in the shelter of a rock, a woman with a child on her breast, both dead. The whole population had perished. The minister later had it re-settled. (10)

The fate of this new colony is unknown, for by 1796, a shepherd and his family were the only inhabitants of Rona, which was then rented by a Ness tacksman at £4 per annum. (11) A large boat was sent regularly to bring back corn, butter, cheese, a few sheep, sometimes a cow, as well as wild fowl and feathers.

When Dr MacCulloch visited Rona in 1815, the only occupants were the shepherd, Kenneth MacCagie (MacGuigan), his wife and three children, and his old, deaf mother. When the visitor approached, they all ran away until they realised he meant them no harm. (12)

The shepherd had six to seven acres planted with barley, oats, and potatoes. There was certainly no scarcity of food, with grain, potatoes, meat, and cheese made from sheep's milk. On average, the tacksman received an annual eight bolls of barley, eight stones of gannet feathers, and the wool from fifty odd sheep. The shepherd was indentured to serve on this lonely island for eight years, with an annual wage of £2 in addition to his food. His wages were not paid in cash but in clothing. (13)

MacCagie was not allowed a boat in case he deserted, so he could only fish with a rod. However, fish were plentiful, so he had sufficient oil for his crusie lamp. There being no peat, his fire was carefully tended, for if it went out, they had to wait for the annual visit from Lewis to have it re-lit. (14)

The shepherd's house was similar to those in use at the time of Mr Morison's visit over a century before. To withstand the gales, it was built partly underground, with the walls only about two feet above ground level and the roof composed of slabs of turf covered with thatch. A turf rampart was also built round it as a further protection.

> The entrance to this sub-terranean retreat is through a long, dark, narrow and tortuous passage, like the gallery of a mine, commencing by an aperture not three feet high and very difficult to find. . . . The interior strongly resembles that of a Kamchatchan hut; receiving no other light than that from the smoke-hole, being covered with ashes, festooned with strings of dried fish, filled with smoke, and having scarcely an article of furniture. (15)

The last solitary shepherd, Donald Macleod, "The King of Rona" left the Island in 1844.

In 1824, the Lewis factor, Mr Adam, proposed that a fishing crew should be based in Rona, each of whose six members should pay £5 per annum. By the middle of the century, several crews were fishing from the Island.

The next arrivals on Rona were two men from Ness, Malcolm Macdonald (Calum mac Mhurc' Dhughaill) and Murdo Mackay (Murchadh Bhragair) who arrived there on 20th May, 1884, and decided to settle after having had some religious difference with their minister at home in Ness. Although two attempts were made that year to persuade them to return home, they refused to do so. In April of the following year, 1885, another party went to see how they were faring, only to discover both had died. Malcolm Macdonald was found lying at the door of their house, and his companion was by the fire-place covered with a tartan plaid. The bodies were buried in the old graveyard, but rumours began to circulate that the men had not died from natural causes, so the Stornoway Procurator-Fiscal and two doctors were sent to Rona where the bodies were exhumed and a post-mortem carried out. It was found that Mackay had died of acute inflamation of the right lung and left kidney, and Macdonald from cold, exposure and exhaustion.

The proprietor offered the Island to the Government in 1850, gratis, for use as a penal settlement. Today, although uninhabited, it is still used as a sheep farm.

Sulisgeir or Gannet Rock, lies about eleven miles south-west of Rona. It is about half a mile long by a third of a mile wide with cliffs rising steeply from the sea in most places. The only landing place is at Geodha a' Phuill Bhàin, where a ring is fixed in the rock for securing boats.

There have never been any permanent residents on this rock, as there is neither soil nor water, but there is a great variety of sea fowl, especially gannets and eider duck.

Brianuilt, the sister of St Ronan, was said to have been transported to this island (in the same way as she and her brother had been carried to Rona from Eoropie) and built the Sulisgeir Temple, the *Tigh Beannaichte,* Blessed House there. It is also related that a man named Maoldonaich was marooned here by the people of Rona as a punishment for thieving, but he only survived for five or six weeks. (16)

From time immemorial the daring men of Ness have gone to Sulisgeir every September to kill gannets. In the eighteenth century and long afterwards, they travelled the forty miles in an open six-oared boat, without even a compass. Before the ring was fixed in the cliff to secure a boat, some of the crew had to stay on board sheltering on the lee-side of the island, while the rest were ashore killing the gannets, which were so tame that they could be slain with sticks. (17) Nowadays, the gannet or guga hunters are taken to Sulisgeir by motor-boat and fetched back on an appointed date. During their stay, the men live in five stone huts which lie close to each other.

Before the introduction of the tacksman system, the Ness men went every September to kill gannets without having to seek anyone's permission, but afterwards, gannets and feathers became a source of revenue to the tacksman, minister or layman, who owned the land. With the arrival of the Mackenzies, it was the annual boat to Rona that officially called at Sulisgeir for gannets and feathers. The Nessmen thoroughly objected to being deprived of their ancient rights, so gannet poaching was practised in the appropriate season.

A crew who visited Sulisgeir in 1811 and returned with a considerable cargo of birds and feathers, were ordered by the tacksman to pay him £5 as compensation for the loss he had suffered. The men refused, and even threatened to repeat the operation. Finally they were taken to court, where they were ordered to pay £5 to the tacksman, a further £5 fine and about £10 legal expenses. (18)

In 1821, a Eoropie crew, heading for the Skerries, were forced by bad weather to shelter in the lee of Sulisgeir, where they naturally killed some gannets. On returning home, the tacksman threatened to charge them £1 apiece, £7 in all, unless they made a return trip, partly at his expense. They returned to Sulisgeir in August 1824, on a trip which lasted seven days: two days' preparation, and seven days work, for which they received nothing. (19)

In spite of the danger attached to such expeditions, there were comparatively few accidents. One accident occurred in 1800, when a boat insecurely moored, was wrecked. The crew were forced to remain on the island for about six weeks, before a passing vessel rescued them and put them ashore on Rona, from where they later returned to Lewis.

In 1912, another crew set off for Sulisgeir in very unsettled weather. When they failed to return as scheduled, a search was made for them on the stack, and it was presumed they were lost. While their relations and friends were mourning for them, Donald Campbell and his crew were busy on Sulisgeir which they had eventually reached after having been forced by the weather to shelter for some time on Rona. Port of Ness has seldom witnessed such a scene of jubilation as when the storm-battered boat returned to harbour with a rich harvest of gugas.

Pigmies' Isle lies to the west of the Butt of Lewis, near Cunndal. A small race of people was believed to have once lived there. It was also called *Eilean nan Daoine Beaga,* the Island of Little People. Many small bones were unearthed, but were later identified as animal. (20)

Dean Monro reported that there was "ane little kirk in it of ther awn handey wark." (21)

The Shiant Isles, twelve in number, lying off the south-east coast of Lewis, are locally known as the *Eileanan Mora,* the Large Isles. Six of them have some vegetation. The largest are *Garbh Eilean,* Rough Island; *Eilean an Tighe,* House Island; and *Eilean Mhuire,* Mary's Island. The first two are connected by a long, narrow, shingly beach, which is sometimes covered at high tides.

The Shiants lie about a third of the way between Lewis and Skye, and were often cursed by sea-sick travellers crossing from Kyle of Lochalsh to Stornoway. It was believed at one time that the turbulence of the sea in their vicinity was caused by the playful antics of the Blue Men of the Minch, who had their abode in these waters.

The terrain of the Shiants is wild and picturesque. Some cliffs rise to a height of 500 feet above sea level, and are a home to thousands of sea birds.

Eilean Mhuire is the only one of the three large islands which is wholly arable, the other two being partly arable and partly heathy pasture. At one time there was a chapel on this island dedicated to the Virgin Mary, hence its name, (22) and a priest is said to have lived here during the Reformation upheaval. Although there are ruined bothies (probably belonging to fishermen) on the three main islands, Eilean Tighe, as its name suggests, seems to have been the only one permanently inhabited.

At one time, sheep and cattle were grazed on these three islands and some of the other smaller islands were suitable for sheep. About 1760, five families had their homes on Eilean Tighe, but by 1796, there was only one, and by 1843 it was uninhabited. (23)

Towards the end of the eighteenth century, the steep cliffs of Eilean Tighe brought tragedy to one shepherd's family. His wife and son were killed while chasing sheep, and his daughter fell to her death while collecting eggs. (24)

The Shiants, now regarded as part of Harris, were for a long time part of the tack of Park, in Lochs, and when the brothers Alexander and Archibald Stewart of Valamos had the tenancy, they meted out swift physical punishment to any fisherman who had the temerity, even during bad weather, to land on any of their islands, believing, rightly perhaps, that the sole motive for such a transgression was the theft of sheep.

Isle Iubhard, a small island at the entrance to Loch Shell, once had the privilege of providing shelter for the royal fugitive Charles Edward Stuart who was in hiding from his enemies. In May 1746, the Prince had a fruitless visit to the neighbourhood of Stornoway in search of a vessel to carry him to safety.

Five families once lived on Isle Iubhard in the Seann Bhaile and in Tigh a' Gheumpail, but it has now been deserted for a long time.

The Flannan Isles or The Seven Hunters, although fourteen in number, lie eighteen miles west of Gallon Head, in Uig. There is a certain amount of vegetation on half of them, much enriched by the droppings of innumerable sea-fowl.

In 1549, Dean Munro referred to the Flannan Isles as the Seven Haley Isles and there is no doubt that they have been vested with an aura of sanctity since very early times. Those living on the west side of Lewis are believed to have made an annual pilgrimage to St Flannan's Chapel on Eilean Mor. Any neglect of this custom, even after the Reformation, was believed to invite misfortune. (25)

The two main Flannan Isles are Eilean Mor and Eilean Tighe. On Eilean

Mor are two ruins, *Bothain Chlann 'ic Phail,* Macphail bothies and the small corbelled chapel of St Flannan. A lighthouse was built on the island in 1899.

On Eilean Tighe, there are only the ruins of houses.

These islands have always had the reputation of fattening sheep, and at one time, the sheep there belonged to no-one. Nowadays, they are owned by the Bernera crofters.

In Martin's time, a strict code of conduct was prescribed for all who landed on Eilean Mor, and to avoid any breach of this, any novice in the crew was given exact instructions on how to conduct himself ashore. To ensure that he behaved properly, each newcomer was paired with someone familiar with the recognised practices.

When they arrived on the island, it was regarded as unlawful to kill a fowl with a stone before disembarking, or to disembark before the usual preliminaries had been observed. They were also not permitted to relieve themselves where the boat lay, as this was supposed to bring misfortune to the crew. It was also unlawful to kill a fowl after evening prayers. No sheep suet was to be taken back home, it being too fat, nor was anything to be eaten by one partner without the other's knowledge.

On reaching the level part of the island, the hunters uncovered their heads and made a *deiseil*, or sunwise turn, at the same time thanking God for taking care of them. When they were within twenty paces of the altar in the chapel, they stripped themselves of their outer garments and placed them on a stone. They then prayed three times before they started fowling. The first prayer was offered as they went towards the chapel on their knees; the second as they went round it, and the third when they were close to the chapel, a performance which was repeated daily morning and evening.

The Flannans had to be referred to as "the country". Certain other objects were similarly treated; *uisge,* water had to be called "burn"; *creag,* rock was called *cruaidh,* "hard". (26) This practice was also common in Lewis where *bradan,* salmon is still referred to as *biasd,* "beast".

In 1900, the year after the lighthouse was erected on Eilean Mor, the three lighthouse keepers mysteriously disappeared. The lighthouse tender *Hesperus* paid its routine visit on 26th December 1900, and as it approached the island, the crew became somewhat apprehensive when there was no sign of life. When the lighthouse was searched, no trace of the men could be found. Everything in the building was in order, the lamp was ready to be lit, the work of the forenoon of 15th December had been completed and logged, indicating that the men had disappeared that afternoon. There was ample evidence that they had experienced very bad weather, as the West Landing was damaged. They eventually concluded that the men, James Ducat, Principal Keeper; Thomas Marshall, Second Assistant, and Donald Macarthur, Occasional Keeper, had been swept away by a freak wave while trying to secure gear or examine the damage to the landing. (27)

For many years, the people of Lewis firmly believed that the keepers had been kidnapped.

The lighthouse now functions without keepers, and the Flannans have reverted to their former state, tenanted only by sea-fowl and sheep, and very rarely disturbed by man.

On St Columba's Isle in Loch Erisort, there are the ruins of a chapel and what was once supposed to be a monastery, as well as some other buildings. The chapel and the adjoining graveyard were once enclosed by a stone wall and it was here that corpses were brought from Lochs and even distant Park for internment. A reminder of this custom is the name *Port nam Marbh,* Port of the Dead on Loch Seaforth, opposite Airivruaich and on the island itself. Owing to overcrowding, it was closed in 1878, when it was replaced by the Laxay Cemetery.

Macleod of Lewis used to have an orchard on the island, which was probably started by a monk, whose gardener would have it rent free. (28)

The first of the Seaforth factors *Mac Mhic Mhurchaidh,* Murdo Mackenzie also lived here.

Mealista Island, which is about 300 acres, is half a mile off the mainland south of the deserted village of Mealista. There are some ruined houses on the island which provides good pasturage for the stock ferried over from *Leac Na h-Aiseig,* Ferry Ledge.

The former inhabitants of Mealista village were deprived of its use in 1823, when it became part of a sheep farm.

It was also once said that anyone born on the island would become feeble-minded.

Of the many islands in Loch Roag, once "inhabit and manurit", only Bernera Mor, which has seven villages, is still inhabited.

Bernera Beag which was once well populated, was regarded as one of the best islands in Lewis for providing not only good pasturage for sheep and black cattle, but also for crops, giving more than 200 bolls of barley a year. In 1831, the Edinburgh Gaelic School Society established a station there with a roll of 19 boys, 20 girls and one adult. Unfortunately, the school only lasted a year, being discontinued in May 1832, when the residents were moved to Dun Carloway.

Stac Dhomhnuill Chaim, Donald Cam's Stack, is a reminder of that doughty Macaulay warrior.

Other islands once populated are Kearstay, Bhuidhe Mhor, Bhuidhe Bheag, Bhacsaidh and Pabbay which once had a chapel.

Rory Macleod, Old Rory, resorted to Pabbay when "he wald be quyeit, or yet fearit." (29) He must have visited it regularly.

Four families once lived on the island of Pabbay which became part of Linshader Farm about 1827, when so many of the other islands, like Bhacsaidh and Flodaidh, were taken from the crofters.

In 1841, Bhuidhe Mhor had seven families, 25 males and 14 females.

All the islands on Loch Roag were noted for the production of kelp. Little Bernera had "infinite sea-ware on every stone", and during the kelping season, people lived in bothies on these little islands.

On the decline of the kelp industry, fishing became important, and the islands once again had their seasonal occupants, all engaged in the cod and ling fishing. Fishermen also came from outwith Lewis. In 1861, a crew from Rosehearty in Aberdeenshire, complete with a female cook, was living in a tent on Mealista Island. In the same year, Pabbay Mor had two crews of fifteen men and two female cooks from Banffshire, who all slept in a cave, while nine Uig men lived in a tent. (32)

YEARS OF CHANGE

The last three decades have seen a most remarkable transformation throughout Lewis. Most of the houses are new or modernised, complete with all modern conveniences undreamt of not so long ago; hot and cold water, bathrooms and toilets, electricity at the touch of a switch.

Street lighting has now been installed in some of the villages, a far cry from the days when people could only go visiting on moon-lit nights, or with the aid of a flaming peat stuck on a sickle point. Stray sheep also appreciate the street lighting, as it enables them to feed at night by the roadside. Paraffin lamps are only kept at hand for the occasional power cut.

Peat remains the main fuel, although coal and calor gas are also used. It is practically impossible nowadays, to hire people to cut peat, so this work is done on a communal basis.

The advancing tide of commercialism has swamped any attraction the croft ever held. It was never an economic holding, but has always been chiefly regarded as a homestead, to which one could return from seasonal or other work outside the Island. What was once arable land is hardly cultivated, and no longer do we see the different shades of green of growing potatoes, oats and barley in summer, or the golden autumnal hues of the ripening grain. Some kind of land reorganisation seems due.

With the decline of crofting, the cattle population has decreased, while the number of sheep has greatly increased. Very few cows are kept now, and crofters, especially in the Parishes of Stornoway and Lochs, have to depend on imported milk from the mainland, although a couple of local dairies do exist in the Parish of Stornoway, but there is a need for many more.

Rural shops, unless there is a post office attached, have difficulty in competing with the many vans on the road, selling groceries, bread and butcher-meat.

Fish, once the main dish on the Islanders' menu, is in short supply. Even the once humble herring, at one time so plentiful in the sea-lochs, now fetch fantastic prices. No longer are morning stragglers along the Stornoway quays given a *gad,* fry (a number of herring on a string) to take home. A little small-line fishing still persists in some villages. Perhaps some day, as in Japan, more use will be made of the sea produce around the Island's shores.

There is an air, perhaps a false air of prosperity in the Island today that seldom existed before, although the unemployment rate, at present, is very high. Government grants, subsidies, and the many benefits of the Welfare State, undoubtedly contribute to this.

During the day, the town of Stornoway is thronged with people from the outlying areas. The main shopping street, Cromwell Street, is then as congested as any city street, with the parking places filled with cars.

Men and women are still the chief export from Lewis, and are to be found abroad in ever increasing numbers, especially in Commonwealth countries. The restlessness of the ocean, constantly thundering along the Island's shores seems to have imbued the inhabitants with an insistent urge to travel the world, but always with the intention of returning home someday.

194

Though the Island may be remote from the mainland, it has always attracted people of diverse races to settle there. Nowadays, Italians, Pakistanis, Jews, English, Welsh, Irish and mainland Scots are to be found there. Red Indian blood runs in the veins of some Lewismen since the days when many Islanders served with the Hudson Bay Company. Today, the rapidly improving means of transport encourage both emigration and immigration.

The narrow macadamised roads are fairly adequate, and buses go to every part of the Island, although this service has had to be curtailed, owing to the ever-increasing number of private cars now to be found in the country districts. If, through time, this should lead to the discontinuation of the bus services, it will indeed be a calamity for many.

A ferry plies between Stornoway and Ullapool twice daily in the summer, and once in the winter. Another ferry runs between Uig in Skye, and Tarbert in Harris, which provides easy road access to Stornoway.

Planes leave Stornoway Airport, from what was once the Stornoway Golf Course, to Inverness and Glasgow. The flight to Inverness only takes about fifty minutes, or, as one old lady put it, the time it takes to suck a pan drop. The flight to Glasgow takes about one hour.

Public telephones have been installed in every village, and private subscribers are on the increase, all enjoying the benefits of S.T.D.

The rural areas have a mobile library, and a mobile bank, and tweed yarn is deposited, and the woven material collected by the mill lorries wherever such a service is required.

At one time, all the jobs in the town of Stornoway were occupied by locals, but this is not now the case, for a steady stream of commuters converge daily on the town from far and near. Gone are the days when the rural areas were only reservoirs for unskilled labour.

Improved communications have also improved the Island's social and cultural life, with villages no longer isolated from one another. Village halls and Community Associations are now common, and a ceilidh and dance in any township attracts people from miles away. There are three successful choirs at Laxdale, Lochs and Stornoway.

Dramatic groups have sprung up in some districts, and sport has become a common pastime. There are also opportunities for athletics, badminton, bowling, darts, golf, swimming, rugby, tennis and netball. Football has become a craze, with ten teams in the Lewis Football League, including one from Harris, each organised in a most professional way, and most of them coming from the country districts.

The girls are not so well catered for in this respect, although hockey is making some headway. Those who have never played hockey in a men's team, still think it is a game only fit for ladies. It is to be hoped that some day shinty, that most Highland of all games, will be re-introduced. An old Glasgow professor once remarked that he could never understand how the 51st Highland Division won such a high reputation for gallantry until he saw a shinty match.

There are now opportunities for boys to become Scouts, Sea Cadets, Army Cadets, or Air Force Cadets. For the girls, there are the Brownies and the Guides.

The re-organisation of Local Government in 1974 saw the formation of the Western Isles Islands Council, better known by its Gaelic name *Comhairle nan Eilean,* a name reminiscent of past Hebridean glories. All the islands from Barra Head to the Butt of Lewis are represented at its headquarters in

Stornoway and life seems to have acquired a new dimension. No longer are the inhabitants dependent on decision-making by committees in Dingwall. They know their councillors, and feel they have a say in controlling their own destiny. Comhairle nan Eilean has even a song composed about it, and a popular one at that. Few councils can boast of such an honour.

Nowhere is the enthusiasm engendered by this transference of power to the local people more evident than in the field of education, which seems to have become rejuvenated. It is a treat to visit the schools and see the children, intensely interested in their work, and their complete lack of inhibition when confronted by strangers. The teacher-child-parent relationship seems particularly close. The curriculum, with English and Mathematics no longer the all-important subjects, has been made much more attractive, and lessons are no longer confined to the classrooms.

Most important of all, Gaelic is once again coming into its own as a means of instructions in schools, thanks to the efforts of John Murray and his team in the bilingual education project.

The formation of *Acair,* Anchor, the first bilingual educational publishing company in the Western Isles, established in Stornoway in 1977, to meet the needs of Gaelic schoolchildren is a most important step, and already, several splendid new books have been issued. Acair is jointly financed by Comhairle nan Eilean, An Comunn Gaidhealach and the Highlands and Islands Development Board. Such positive steps to halt the decline of our native tongue, a decline hastened by centuries of hostility on the part of short-sighted critics, not all from the wrong side of the Minch, are to be congratulated. Our beautiful language must be preserved at all costs, and it is hoped, that before long, pupils transferring from primary to secondary schools, will be as literate in Gaelic as they are in English.

In 1954, to the amazement of many people, a team from the Nicolson Institute won the B.B.C.'s Top of the Form Competition.

The Church is still a dominant factor in the Island, and takes a keen interest in all aspects of community life. It is no surprise to find a minister, the Rev. Donald Macaulay, as Convener of Comhairle nan Eilean, and another minister, the Rev. John M. M. Macarthur, as Chairman of the Education Committee. Mr Angus Macleod is the Director of Education.

For many years, the Western Isles were represented at Westminster by a Labour Member of Parliament, but in recent years, there has been a strong swing towards Scottish Nationalism. The present Member of Parliament for the Western Isles is a Scottish Nationalist, ex-provost of Stornoway, the Right Honourable Donald Stewart, P.C., an extremely able, quiet-spoken, determined Lewisman, dedicated to the task of regaining Scotland's Independence. Mr Stewart is at present the leader of the S.N.P. Parliamentary group.

At one time, the aged and infirm were cared for by their relatives or friends, and this self-imposed duty was an indispensable part of Island life and seldom shirked. This intimate relationship is now changing, as it has throughout Britain, if not to the same degree. The introduction of the Welfare State has taken over, to some degree, the traditional obligation to the old. Stornoway now has homes for the old and the infirm as well as a Geriatric Unit in what was once the Sanatorium, when tuberculosis, now practically eliminated, was the scourge of Lewis.

The Lewis Hospital in Stornoway is well equipped and well staffed, and can call on mainland specialists when necessary. It is a happy hospital where even a ward maid will help an old bodach struggling to shave with an electric razor for the first time in his life. Gaelic is in constant use.

The Harris Tweed industry, the main employer of labour in Lewis, has saved the Island from mass emigration and poverty, and it is gratifying to note that in 1977, one of Stornoway's mills, Kenneth Mackenzie Holdings Ltd., was presented with the Queen's Award for export achievement, the only Scots textile firm to be thus honoured.

In spite of Government assistance in the provision of fishing vessels and the training of personnel, the Lewis fishing industry has sunk to a very low ebb. There are very few local boats operating today, and these only fish for a certain number of days a week. Successive governments must accept the blame for this, by not extending the country's fishing limits, and by failing to protect the industry from trawler depredation, both British and foreign. Fishing for clams, prawns, scampi and even crabs, once despised, has proved quite lucrative, but Ullapool and Mallaig on the mainland, are now more important fishing ports than Stornoway.

The few fishermen left are mostly full-time, for the old breed of crofter-fishermen has now more or less vanished. In 1976, there were only 234 such men left in the whole country. Bernera still has a thriving lobster industry.

Perhaps when the proposed new port at Breasclete has been constructed for the development of the fisheries to the west of the Hebrides, once so important, the fishing industry will be re-vitalised. There are other fish besides the blue whiting to be caught in these waters, but a sensible fishing policy must first be put into operation to make this venture a success.

There is also the prospect of oil in the Rockall area, and if this should be true, Breasclete could provide a suitable port for oil related activities, on a much more extensive scale than those engaged in at Arnish.

Perhaps the Loch Roag district may yet become a hive of industry as it must have been in Neolithic times when the Callanish Stones were up-ended by strangers from over the sea. Will the giants of industry intrude on land once associated with the mythological giants of Lewis, and oil-storage tanks lie cheek by jowl with the *Fir Bhreige,* False Men of Callanish?

Whatever the future may hold, one thing is certain, the men and women of Lewis will adapt themselves readily to changing circumstances, as they have done in the past. Their versatility, perseverance, and physical and mental stamina, will always enable them to cope with the stresses and strains of the morrow.

ABBREVIATIONS

A.F.	Agriculture and Fisheries
C.D.B.	Congested Districts Board
C.E.	Customs and Excise
CH 2	Stornoway Presbytery Records
GD 46	Seaforth Muniments
G.S.S.	Gaelic Schools Society, Edinburgh
H.R.B.	Highland Relief Board
L.H.A.	The Free Church Ladies' Highland Association, Edinburgh
N.S.A.	New Statistical Account
O.S.A.	Old Statistical Account
P.C.R.	Privy Council Records
P.S.A.S.	Proceedings of the Society of Antiquarians of Scotland
S.C.E.	Select Committee on Emigration
S.G.	The Stornoway Gazette
S.S.P.C.K.	The Society in Scotland for Propagating Christian Knowledge
T.G.S.I.	Transactions of the Gaelic Society of Inverness
O.N.B.	Old Name Book

BIBLIOGRAPHY

Anderson, J.	The Hebrides, 1784.	Edin. 1785
Anderson, J.	The Orkneyinga Saga.	Edin. 1873
Anson, P.	The Fisheries of Scotland.	Edin. 1938
Barron, J.	The Northern Highlands in the Nineteenth Century.	Ins. 1907
Brogger, A. W.	Ancient Emigrants.	Oxon. 1929
Brown, T.	Annals of the Disruption.	Edin. 1893
Buchanan, J. L.	Travels in the Western Hebrides, 1782-1790.	Lon. 1793
Burt, E.	Letters from a Gentleman in the North of Scotland	Lon. 1815
Carmichael, A.	Carmina Gadelica. 6 Vols.	Edin. 1928-71
Cregeen, E. (Ed.)	Argyle Estate Instructions, 1771-1800.	Edin. 1964
Cumming, C. F. G.	From the Hebrides to the Himalayas.	Lon. 1886
Darling, F. F.	West Highland Survey.	Lon. 1955
Davidson, Major H.	The 78th Highlanders.	Lon. 1955
Day, J. P.	Public Administration of the Highlands and Islands.	Lon. 1918
	Edinburgh Gaelic Schools Society, Annual Reports.	Edin. 1811-44
Elder, J. R.	The Royal Fishery Companies of the Seventeenth Century	Glas. 1912
Ewing, W.	Annals of the Free Church of Scotland.	Edin. 1914
Fenton, A.	Tools and Tillage.	Edin. 1969
	Scottish Country Life.	Edin. 1976
Geddes, A.	Island of Lewis and Harris.	Edin. 1955
Gibson, W. J.	Education in Scotland.	Edin. 1912
	History of the Nicolson Institute (MS).	n.d.
Goodrich Frier, A.	In the Outer Hebrides.	Lon. 1902
Gordon, Sir R.	The Earldom of Sutherland.	Lon. 1813
Graham, J.	Disruption Worthies of the Highlands.	Edin. 1877
Grant, I. F.	The MacLeods.	Lon. 1959
	Highland Folkways.	Lon. 1961
Gray, M.	The Highland Economy, 1750-1850.	Edin. 1957
Gregory, D.	History of the West Highlands and Islands of Scotland.	Edin. 1881
Handley, J.	Scottish Farming in the Eighteenth Century.	Glas. 1953
Headrick, J.	Report on the Island of Lewis.	Lon. 1800
Henderson, G.	The Norse Influence in Celtic Scotland.	Glas. 1910
Hutcheson, G.	Sixty-One: Reminiscences of the Lews.	Lon. 1871
Innes, C.	Origines Parochiales.	Edin. 1854
Iona Club	Collectanea de Rebus Albanicis.	Edin. 1847
James, W.	The British Navy in Adversity.	Lon. 1926
Johnson, S.	Journey to the Western Isles of Scotland.	Lon. 1926
Keltie, J. S.	A History of the Scottish Highlands, Highland Clans and Regiments.	Edin. 1874
Kerr, J.	Scottish Education.	Cam. 1910

Knox, J.	A View of the British Empire, especially Scotland.	Lon. 1784
	A Tour Through the Highlands of Scotland and Hebrid Isles in 1786.	Lon. 1787
Lacaille, A.D.	The Stone Age in Scotland.	Lon. 1954
Lamb, J. A.	The Fasti of the U.F. Church.	Edin. 1950
MacBain, A.	Early History of Lewis. Highland News.	Ins. 1896
MacCulloch, J.	The Highlands and Western Isles.	Lon. 1824
MacDonald, C.	Highland Journey.	Edin. 1945
MacDonald, Dr D.	Tales and Traditions of the Lews.	Storn. 1967
Macdonald, J.	General View of Agriculture in the Hebrides.	Edin. 1811
Macfarlane, W.	Geographical Collections.	Edin. 1907
Mac Gille Chaluim	Families of Lewis. Stornoway Gazette	Storn. 1956
Macinnes, J.	The Evangelical Movement in the Highlands of Scotland.	Aberd. 1951
Mackenzie, A.	Prophecies of the Brahan Seer.	Stirl. 1899
	The Highland Clearances.	Stirl. 1914
Mackenzie, Col. A. J.	The Soldiers of Uig. Stornoway Gazette.	Storn. 1956
Mackenzie, D.A.	Scotland, the Ancient Kingdom.	Glas. 1936
Mackenzie, W. C.	History of the Outer Hebrides.	Pais. 1903
	The Book of the Lews.	Pais. 1919
	The Western Isles.	Pais. 1932
Mackinlay, D.	The Island of Lewis and its Crofter-fishermen.	Lon. 1878
MacLeod, D.	Gloomy Memories in the Highlands of Scotland.	Glas. 1892
MacLeod, J. N.	Bardachd Leodhais.	Glas. 1916
Macphail, J. R. N.	Highland Papers, Vol. 2, S.H.S., Sec. Series.	Edin. 1906
Macphail, M.	Religion in Lewis. Oban Times.	Oban 1898-99
Macritchie, D.	Fians, Fairies and Picts.	Lon. 1893
Martin, M.	A Description of the Western Isles of Scotland, c. 1695, and containing Sir Donald Monro's Description of the Western Isles.	Stirl. 1934
Mitchell, A.	The Past in the Present.	Edin. 1880
Mitchell, D.	History of the Highlands and Gaelic Scotland.	Pais. 1900
Morrison, A.	The MacLeods, The Genealogy of a Clan.	Edin. 1976
Monro, Sir D.	See Martin Martin	
Muir, T. S.	Ecclesialogical Notes on some of the Islands of Scotland.	Edin. 1885
Munch, P. A.	The Chronicle of Man, trans. by Dr Goss.	Lon. 1860
	New Statistical Account; Ross and Cromarty	Lon. 1841
Nicolson, N.	Lord of the Isles.	Lon. 1960
	Old Statistical Account. Vol. XIX	Edin. 1797
Pitcairn, R.,	Criminal Trials, Vol. III	Edin. 1833
Pigott, S.	The Pre-historic Peoples of Scotland.	Lon. 1962
	Proceedings of the Society of Antiquarians of Scotland	Edin. 1853-94
Sacheverell, W.	An Account of the Isle of Man.	Lon. 1702
Sage, D.	Memorabilia Domestica.	Edin. 1889
Scott, H.	Fasti Ecclesicae Scoticanae.	Edin. 1928
Skene, W. F.	Celtic Scotland.	Edin. 1880
Smith, W. A.	Lewisiana.	Lon. 1875
S.S.P.C.K. Reports.		Edin. 1755-1800
Sturlason, S.	Heimskringla Saga, trans. by S. Laing. Everyman's Lib.	Lon. 1930
	Transactions of the Gaelic Society of Inverness	Ins. 1879-1900
Wade, M. S.	Mackenzie of Canada.	Edin. 1927
Walker, J.	An Economical History of the Hebrides and the Highlands of Scotland.	Lon. 1812
Watson, W. J.	Scottish Verse from the Dean of Lismore.	Edin. 1937
Whyte, D.	A Dictionary of Scottish Emigrants to the U.S.A.	Baltimore 1972

OFFICIAL SOURCES OF MATERIAL

Scottish Record Office, H.M. General Register House

Seaforth Muniments, G.D. 46.
Agriculture and Fisheries Reports, A.F. 67/104-278.
Lewis Presbytery Records of the Church of Scotland. CH. 2/473.
Privy Council Records for Scotland.
Stornoway Customs and Excise Records. CE. 86.
Stornoway Sheriff Court Records. SC. 33.

Reports

Select Committee on Emigration (1841)
Sir John McNeill on the State of the Highlands and Islands of Scotland. (1844).
Royal Commission on the Condition of the Crofters and Cottars in the Highlands. 5 parts. (1884).
The Condition of the Cottar Population of the Lews by Sheriff Fraser and Sir Malcolm McNeill. (1888).
Commission to inquire into certain matters affecting the Population of the Western Highlands and Islands. (1890).
Royal Commission to inquire into the possibility of certain sporting and grazing subjects in the Crofting Counties being occupied by crofters or small tenants. (1892).
Crofters' Commission Report on the Social Condition of the People of Lewis in 1901, as compared with twenty years ago. (1902).
On the Sanitary Condition of the Lews. (1905).
Home Industries in the Highlands. (1914).
Congested Districts Board. (1899-1912).
Royal Commission on the Ancient and Historical Monuments of Scotland, (No. 9), "The Outer Hebrides, Skye and the Small Isles." (1928).

Newspapers	Periodicals
Edinburgh Courant	Celtic Magazine
Edinburgh Scotsman	Celtic Monthly
Glasgow Herald	Cuairtear nan Gleann
Highlander	Gairm
Highland News	Guth na Bliadhna
Inverness Courier	Lewisman
Mac-Talla	Scots Magazine
Oban Times	Scottish Studies
Stornoway Gazette	

NOTES

PRE-HISTORIC LEWIS

1. Ordnance Gazetteer, Scotland, u.d., Vol. IV, 508.
2. Heimskringla Saga, Everyman's Edition, 193, 261.
3. J. L. Black, Scottish Forestry, Vol. 20, No. 1. Jan. 1936, 37.
4. P.S.A.S., Vol. 10, 741.
5. Royal Commission on the Ancient and Historical Monuments of Scotland, 7. 9th Report, the Outer Hebrides, Skye, and the Small Isles.
6. P.S.A.S., Vol. X, 741.
7. Capt. Burnaby, O.S., Lewis, 1848-52, Antiquity No. NB6 SE1.
8. Mac Gille Chaluim, S.G., 15 Feb., 1952.
9. A. MacBain, Highland News, 18 April, 1896.

THE NORSE

1. D. A. Mackenzie, Scotland, the Ancient Kingdom, 204.
2. Palsson and Edwards, Landnamabok Saga, 23, 24.
3. Snorri Sturlason, The Olaf Sagas, Everyman's Edition, Vol. 2, 230.
4. P. A. Munch, The Chronicle of Man, 5
5.   Ibid.
6. G. Henderson, The Norse Influence on Celtic Scotland, 34.
7. Heimskringla Saga, op. cit., 261.
8.   Ibid.
9. W. Sacheverell, An Account of the Isle of Man, 33.
10.   Ibid.   262.
11. D. Gregory, History of the West Highlands and Islands of Scotland, 7.
12. P. A. Munch, op. cit., 16.
13. W. Sacheverell, op. cit., 16.
14.   Ibid.   53.
15. Fraser, The Wardlaw MS., 40, 41.

THE MACLEODS

1. Cosmo Innes, Origines Parochiales, Vol. II, 382.
2.   Ibid.
3. W. C. Mackenzie, History of the Outer Hebrides, 93.
4. Cosmo Innes, op. cit., 382.
5. A. Mackenzie, History of the MacLeods, 287.
6. Capt. Burnaby, op. cit., O.N.B. 21A 24.
7. A. Mackenzie, op. cit., 287.
8. A. Morrison, The MacLeods, Section Four, The MacLeods of Lewis, 1-13.
9. W. J. Watson, Scottish Verse from the Book of the Dean of Lismore, 56.
10. Cosmo Innes, op. cit., 382.
11. A. Mackenzie, op. cit., 294.
12.   Ibid.   294.
13.   Ibid.   299.
14. Collectanea de Rebus Albanicis, 383 (n).
15. Highland Papers, Vol. II, 282, 383.
16.   Ibid.   267.
17.   Ibid.   267.
18. Collectanea de Rebus Albanicis, 39.
19. Highland Papers, Vol. II, 267.
20.   Ibid.   268.
21.   Ibid.   268, 269.
22.   Ibid.   268, 269.
23.   Ibid.   269.
24.   Ibid.   272-274.
25. W. F. Skene, Celtic Scotland, Vol. III, 429.

26. Acts of the Parliament of Scotland, Vol. IV, 138.
27. P. C. R., Vol. V, lxxvi.
28.   Ibid.   364.
29.   Ibid.   462, 463.
30.   Vol. VI, 422.
31.   Vol. XIV, cxxiii-cxxx.
32.   Ibid.   lxxxi-lxxxii.
33.   Vol. VI, 422.
34.   Ibid.
35.   Vol. XIV, cxxiii-cxxx.
36.   Vol. VI, 422.
37. Sir R. Gordon, The Earldom of Sutherland, 271.
38. P. C. R., Vol. VI, 422.
39. Sir R. Gordon, op. cit., 273.
40. P. C. R., Vol. VI, 420.
41.   Ibid.   Vol. IV, 420.
42.   Ibid.   Vol. VI, 545.
43.   Ibid.   Vol. VII, 54.
44.   Ibid. 87, 88.
45. Highland Papers, Vol. II, 275.
46.   Ibid.   276.
47.   Ibid.   276.
48.   Ibid.   276.
49.   Ibid.   277.
50. I. F. Grant, The MacLeods, 206.
51. P. C. R., Vol. IX, 13, 14.
52.   Ibid.   xxxi.
53. A. Nicolson, Gaelic Riddles and Enigmas, 68.
54. P. C. R., Vol. IX, 579.
55.   Ibid.   579.
56. Sir R. Gordon, op. cit., 275.
57. P. C. R., Vol. X, xxix.
58. Pitcairn's Criminal Trials, Vol. III, 244.
59.   Ibid.   247.
60. Highland Papers, Vol. III, 128.
61. S. G., The Final Adventures of Neil MacLeod, 11 May, 1974.
62. I. F. Grant, op. cit., 219.
63. Mac Gille Chaluim, Families of Lewis, S. G., 30 Dec. 1952.
64. P. C. R., Vol. X, 609.
65.   Ibid.   654.
66.   Ibid.   Vol. XIII, 83.
67. Highland Papers, Vol. II, 2nd Series, 265.
68.   Ibid.   265.

THE MACKENZIES

1. P. C. R., Vol. X, 817.
2. D. MacDonald, Tales and Traditions of the Lews, 92.
3. Macfarlane's Geographical Collections, Vol. II, 533.
4. Collectanea de Rebus Albanicis, 190, 191.
5. Highland Papers, Vol. II, 313.
6. P. C. R., Sec. Ser., Vol. II, 336.
7. M. Martin, A Description of the Western Islands of Scotland, 357.
8. P. C. R., Sec. Ser., Vol. III, 95.
9. D. MacDonald, op. cit., 154.
10. Capt. Burnaby, O.S., op. cit., NB 43SW 9.
11. Macfarlane's Geographical Collections, Vol. II, 215.
12. D. MacDonald, op. cit., 44.
13. Anon. A History of the Lews, 778.
14. The Scots Peerage, Vol. VII, 504.
15. A. Mackenzie, The Prophecies of the Brahan Seer, 67.
16. The Scots Peerage, op. cit., 513.
17. Morison and Macrae, Highland Second Sight, 157.
18. The Scots Peerage, op. cit., 513.

19. Morison and Macrae, op. cit., 158.
20. GD. 46/6/100.
21. The Scots Peerage, op. cit., 573.
22. Major H. Davidson, The 78th Highlanders, 5.
23. The Scots Peerage, 513.
24.   Ibid.   513.
25.   Ibid.   513.
26. O.S.A., Vol. XIX, 252.
27. M. Martin, op. cit., 168.
28. P. White, The Present State of the Scotch Fisheries, 48.
29. J. L. Buchanan, Travels in the Highlands and Western Isles, 34.
30. Morison and Macrae, op. cit., 165.
31. Lord Teignmouth's Reminiscences, Vol. I, 351.
32. GD 46/1/128.
33. GD 46/17/Vol. 83.

THE MATHESONS

1. A. Mackenzie, The Celtic Magazine, 1882, Vol. VII, 489, 490.
2. GD 46/4/263.
3. S.C.E., 1841, 178.
4. Crofters Commission Report, 1884, App. A, 207.
5. Capt. Burnaby, op. cit., O.N.B., 72, 27B, 109.
6.   Ibid.   109.
7.   Ibid.   10, 14, 20.
8. Highlands and Islands Commission, op. cit., 208.
9.   Ibid.   3307.
10. H.R.B., 1849, 7.
11. Crofters Commission Report, 1884, 1084.
12.   Ibid.   3307.
13. A. Mackenzie, op. cit., 496, 497.
14. Crofters Commission Report, 1884, 1091, 1098.
15. H.R.B., 1849, 15.
16. Crofters Commission Report, 1884, 3305.
17. Sir J. McNeill Report, 1851, App. B. 150.
18.   Ibid.   App. B. 149.
19. Crofters Commission Report, 1884, 3306.
20.   Ibid.   App. xxxix, 154.
21. A. Mackenzie, op. cit., 201.
22. Crofters Commission Report, 1884, 1091, 1098, 1102.
23.   Ibid.   1084.
24.   Ibid.   1092.
25.   Ibid.   1090.
26. A. Mackenzie, op. cit., 499.
27.   Ibid.   499.
28. Brand Report, 1902, lxxi.
29. J. N. MacLeod, Bardachd Leodhais, 72, 73.
30. Rules and Regulations of the Lews Estate, 1879, 2.
31.   Ibid.   2.
32.   Ibid.   2.
33.   Ibid.   4.
34.   Ibid.   4-12.
35.   Ibid.   12.
36. A. Mackenzie, op. cit., 503.
37. Crofters Commission Report, 1884, 1073.
38.   Ibid.   App, XLIV, 196.
39.   Ibid.   1063.
40. Brand Report, op. cit., lxiii.
41.   Ibid.   lxxvi.
42.   Ibid.   lxxvi.
43. SC 33/4/6.
44. AF 67/59.

45. Brand Report, op. cit., lxiii.
46.   Ibid.   xlvii.
47.   Ibid.   li, lii.
48.   Ibid.   liii.
49.   Ibid.   liii.

THE PEOPLE

1. Lewis' Topographical Dictionary of Scotland, Vol. II, 176.
2. A. Mitchell, The Past in the Present, 55.
3. N.S.A., Ross and Cromarty, 147.
4. Census of Scotland, Vol. I, 15.
5. N.S.A., op. cit., 147.
6. O.S.A., Vol. IV, 315.
7. J. L. Buchanan, op. cit., 56.
8.   Ibid.   100.
9. M. Macleod, Luerbost and Edinburgh.
10. N.S.A., op. cit., 165.
11.   Ibid.   165.
12.   Ibid.   165.
13.   Ibid.   140.
14. O.S.A., Vol. XIX, 260.
15. GD 46/13/52 (4).
16. O.S.A., Vol. XIX, 252, 253.
17.   Ibid.   253.
18. N.S.A., op. cit., 123.
19. M. Martin, op. cit., 201.
20. N.S.A., op. cit., 116.
21. M. Martin, op. cit., 88, 92.
22. GD 46/17/Vol. 16.

HOUSING

1. J. Macdonald, General View of the Agriculture of the Hebrides, 94.
2. N.S.A., op. cit., 128.
3. GD 46/1/150.
4. GD 46/17/Vol. 79.
5. N.S.A., op. cit., 129.
6. N.S.A., op. cit., 164.
7. J. L. Buchanan, op. cit., 91.
8. A. Mitchell, op. cit., 54.

HOUSEHOLD INDUSTRIES

1. W. F. Skene, op. cit., Vol. III, App. III, 429.
2. A. Mitchell, op. cit., 4.
3. A. Goodrich Freer, Outer Isles, 387.
4. E. Dwelly, Gaelic Dictionary, 601.
5. M. Martin, op. cit., 129.
6. Mactalla, op. cit., 9, 16 August, 1901.
7. State of the British Fisheries, Third Report (1795), 158.
8. O.S.A., Vol. XIX, 259, 285.
9.   Ibid.   244, 269.
10.   Ibid.   278.
11. GD 46/13/168.
12. W. R. Scott, Report to the Board of Agriculture of Scotland, 55
13. O.S.A., Vol. XIX, 285.
14. T.G.S.I., Vol. XII, 408.

AGRICULTURE

1. J. Macdonald, op. cit., 808.
2. O.S.A., Vol. XIX, 275.
3. J. L. Buchanan, op. cit., 149: J. Macdonald, op. cit., 814.
4. J. Handley, Scottish Farming in the Eighteenth Century, 100.
5. T. Pennant, A Tour in Scotland and the Hebrides, Vol. II, 274.
6. Cosmo Innes, op. cit., 385-389.
7. I. F. Grant, Highland Folkways, 12.
8. N.S.A., op. cit., 167.
9. W. F. Skene, op. cit., Vol. III, App. III, 428-431.
10. Crofter and Cottar (Napier Commission), 194.
11.   Ibid.   194.
12. Sheriff Nicolson, A Collection of Proverbs, 8.
13. J. Macdonald, op. cit., 174.
14. N.S.A., op. cit., 166.
15. J. Macdonald, op. cit., 177.
16. N.S.A., op. cit., 166.
17. J. Macdonald, op. cit., 100.
18. R. Martin, Balallan, Lewis.
19. E. Dwelly, op. cit., 262.
20.   Ibid.   262.
21. O.S.A., Vol. XIX, 248.
22.   Ibid.   266.
23.   Ibid.   285.
24. N.S.A., Vol. VII, 187.
25. O.S.A., XIX, 250, 266, 277, 285.
26.   Ibid.   277.
27. W. C. Mackenzie, op. cit., 170.
28. J. L. Buchanan, op. cit., 147.
29. Rules and Regulations of the Lewis Estate, Rule 13, 8.
30.   Ibid.   Rule 12, 8.
31.   Ibid.   Rule 2, 4.
32. W. C. Mackenzie, op. cit., 170.
33. E. Dwelly, op. cit., 519.
34. M. Martin, op. cit., 244.
35. I. F. Grant, op. cit., 113.
36. E. Burt, Letters from the North, Vol. I, 89.
37. N.S.A., op. cit., 164.
38. W. Anderson Smith, Lewisiana, 16.
39. M. C. MacLeod, Pamphlet on the Settlement of the Lake Megantic District, Quebec.
40. Bell, Law Dictionary, 240, 241, 256.
41. Duncan Macdonald, Balallan, Lewis.
42. GD 46/13/178(1).
43. GD 46/1/526.
44. GD 46/1/539.
45. GD 46/17/Vol. 71.

ANIMAL HUSBANDRY

1. C.D.B., Report on Livestock and Agriculture, 65.
2. Crofter and Cottar, op. cit., App. A, 469.
3. O.S.A., Vol. XIX, op. cit., 245, 266, 276, 284.
4. E. Dwelly, op. cit., 235.
5. GD 46/17/Vol. 43.
6. I. F. Grant, op. cit., 71.
7. J. Handley, op. cit., 69.
8. C. A. Morrison, Balallan, Lewis.
9. J. Walker, op. cit., 60, 61.
10. The Scotsman, 14 Aug., 1976.
11. GD 46/1/526.
12. GD 46/1/526.
13. GD 46/1/520.

14. GD 46/17/Vol. 58.
15. GD 46/1/134.
16. O.S.A., Vol. XIX, 245.
17. J. Macdonald, op. cit., 447.
18. O.S.A., Vol. XIX, 267.
19. J. Macdonald, op. cit., 460.
20. E. Dwelly, op. cit., 289.
21. Murdo Macleod, Luerbost and Edinburgh.
22. GD 46/17/Vol. 53.

KELP

1. Brand Report, op. cit., lxxxi.
2. Ibid.
3. J. L. Buchanan, op. cit., 157.
4. GD 46/17/Vol. 3.
5. W. F. Skene, op. cit., 373.
6. Brand Report, op. cit., xxxiii.
7. GD 46/17/Vol. 13.
8. Ibid.
9. GD 46/17/Vol. 58.
10. GD 46/17/Vol. 75.
11. N.S.A., op. cit., 134.
12. Ibid.
13. J. L. Buchanan, op. cit., 56.
14. Ibid. 159.
15. GD 46/17/Vol. 79.
16. GD 46/17/Vol. 6.
17. J. L. Buchanan, op. cit., 157.
18. T.G.S.I., Vol. XII, 406.
19. J. Macdonald, op. cit., 801.
20. T.G.S.I., Vol. XII, 407.
21. J. Macdonald, op. cit., 801.
22. Ibid. 802.
23. GD 46/17/Vol. 80.
24. Ibid.
25. GD 46/17/Vol. 59.
26. GD 46/13/132.
27. N.S.A., op. cit., 154, 165.
28. Sir J. McNeill Report, 1851, 105.

FISHING

1. Sir D. Monro, op. cit., 522.
2. N.S.A., op. cit., 133.
3. W. F. Skene, op. cit., 429.
4. MacFarlane's Geographical Collections, op. cit., Vol. II, 185.
5. T.G.S.I., Feb. 1900, 127.
6. Crofters Commission Report 1884, 1032.
7. T.S.G.I., Feb. 1900, 127.
8. Ibid. 128.
9. P. White, op. cit., 50.
10. O.S.A., Vol. XIX, 256.
11. Ibid. 265.
12. Ibid. 275.
13. Ibid. 282, 288.
14. Crofters Commission Report, 1884, 951.
15. Ibid. 176.
16. Ibid. 176.
17. GD 46/1/153.
18. GD 46/17/Vol. 62.
19. Ibid.

20. GD 46/17/Vol. 63.
21.   Ibid.
22. AF 38/133/2 (12).
23. GD 46/17/Vol. 75.
24. GD 46/13/530.
25.   Ibid.
26. Crofters Commission Report, 1884, 951.
27.   Ibid.   952.
28.   Ibid.   3314.
29. GD 46/17/Vol. 13.
30. Lewisman, Vol. I, Feb. 1889.
31. GD 46/12/147 (2).
32. P.C.R., Vol. II, 534.
33. Ibid. Vol. VI, 169.
34. Ibid. Vol. IX, 13.
35. Ibid. Vol. VII, 89.
36. Ibid. Vol. IV, Sec. Ser., 12.
37. J. R. Elder, The Royal Fishery Companies of the Seventeenth Century, 42.
38.   Ibid.   61.
39. P.C.R., Vol. VI, Sec. Ser., 620.
40. M. Martin, op. cit., 358.
41.   Ibid.   356.
42.   Ibid.   356.
43. P. White, op. cit., 55.
44. W. Mackay, An Inverness Merchant of the Olden Time, 17.
45.   Ibid.   12.
46. T.G.S.I., 20 Feb., 1900, 17.
47.   Ibid.   135.
48.   Ibid.   129.
49. P. White, op. cit., 50.
50. N.S.A., op. cit., 161.
51. O.S.A., Vol. XIX, 283.
52. P. White, op. cit., 46.
53. Oban Times, 18 May, 15 June, 1867.
54. Crofters Commission Report, 1884, 1120.
55. Oban Times, 25 March, 1876.
56.   Ibid.
57. Oban Times, 23 Sept., 1876.
58. The Scotsman, 20 Aug., 1859.
59. Lord Advocate's Papers, Box. 19.
60. Fishery Board of Scotland, Seventeenth Report, 210.
61.   Ibid.   Eighteenth Report, 226.
62. J. P. Day, op. cit., 276.

THE CHURCH

1. D. Maciver, op. cit., 82.
2. M. Martin, op. cit., 106.
3.   Ibid.   106.
4. A. MacBain, op. cit., 106.
5. Cosmo Innes, op. cit., 381.
6. Collectanea de Rebus Albanicis, 6.
7. H. Scott, Fasti Ecclesiae Scoticanae, Vol. 7, 199, 208.
8. A. MacBain, op. cit., 1896.
9. H. Scott, op. cit., 199, 200, 205, 206.
10.   Ibid.   203, 204, 207, 208.
11. M. Martin, op. cit., 100.
12. H. Scott, op. cit., 205.
13. M. Macphail, Oban Times, 1 July, 1898.
14. CH 2/473/1, 11-13.
15.   Ibid.   17.
16. M. Martin, op. cit., 107.
17.   Ibid.   90.
18. GD 46/17/Vol. 63.

19. GD 46/12/36 (1).
20. CH 2/473/2, 121.
21. W. Ewing, Free Church Annals, Vol. I, 1.
22.   Ibid.   39, 40.
23. Sir James Graham, Disruption Worthies of the Highlands, 150.
24. GD 46/12/48 (2).
25. M. Macphail, Oban Times, 3 June, 1899.
26. CH 2/473/2, 208.
27. T. Brown, Annals of the Disruption, 651.
28.   Ibid.   653.
29. W. Ewing, op. cit., Vol. II, 236-238.
30.   Ibid.
31.   Ibid.
32. AF 67/253.

THE ARMED SERVICES

1. T.G.S.I., An Econ. History of the Hebrides, Feb. 1900, 127.
2. Scots Magazine, Nov., 1778.
3. I. D. Duff, S.G., 9 Aug., 1955.
4. J. S. Keltie, History of the Scottish Highlands, Vol. IV, 545.
5. The Scots Peerage, op. cit., 573.
6. W. James, The British Navy in Adversity, 385.
7. GD 46/6/104 (1).
8. GD 46/6/22.
9. GD 46/6/23.
10. GD 46/6/25.
11.   Ibid.
12. Crofters Commission, 1884, 3310.
13. Col. A. J. Mackenzie, The Old Soldiers of Uig, S.G., 29 July, 1955.
14. GD 46/17/Vol. 3.
15.   Ibid.
16. GD 46/17/Vol. 15.
17. General D. Stewart, Sketches of the Highlanders, Vol. II, 189 (n)
18.   Ibid.
19. Major Davidson, op. cit., 1.
20.   Ibid.   96.
21.   Ibid.   98.
22.   Ibid.   108.
23.   Ibid.   108.
24.   Ibid.   115.
25. Col. A. J. Mackenzie, op. cit., 5 Aug., 1955.
26. Oban Times, 24 April, 1875.
27. J. S. Keltie, op. cit., 696.
28.   Ibid.   682.
29. GD 46/6/100.
30. GD 46/6/Vol. 13.
31. GD 46/6/38.
32.   Ibid.
33. GD 46/6/108.
34. Kerr and Grimble, The R.N.V.R., 17.
35. Oban Times, 23 Sept., 1876.
36. CE 86/4/3: Oban Times, 23 Sept. 1876.
37. S.G., 4 May, 1954.
38. S.G., 24 Dec. 1970.
39. GD 46/11/Vol. 44.

PERIODS OF SCARCITY

1. M. Martin, op. cit., 86.
2. O.S.A., Vol. XIX, 259.
3. GD 46/13/170.
4.   Ibid.

5. GD 46/13/175 (1).
6. GD 46/17/Vol. 47.
7. M. McNeill's Report, 1888, 98.
8. GD 46/17/Vol. 75.
9. Edinburgh Courant, 12 May, 1836
10. GD 46/13/199 (4).
11. GD 46/13/199 (5).
12. GD 46/13/199 (6).
13. Ibid.
14. A.C.E., 178.
15. Poor Law Enquiry Commission for Scotland, 375.
16. Ibid. 375.
17. Ibid. 381.
18. An Sgeulaiche, Vol. 2, Oct. 1909, 139, 141.
19. Brand Report, op. cit., xvi.
20. Ibid.

SMUGGLING

1. M. Martin, op. cit., 86.
2. I. Macdonald, Smuggling in the Highlands, 55.
3. GD 46/6/101.
4. Ibid.
5. GD 46/17/Vol. 40.
6. GD 46/17/Vol. 13.
7. GD 46/17/Vol. 15.
8. GD 46/17/Vol. 52.
9. GD 46/17/Vol. 58.
10. SC 33/5/3.
11. GD 46/17/Vol. 44.
12. GD 46/1/527.
13. GD 46/1/530.
14. N.S.A., op. cit., 140.
15. Inverness Courier, 14 Nov., 1827.

LAW AND ORDER

1. J. Anderson, Orkneyinga Saga, op. cit., 5(n).
2. P.S.A.S., 1878, 507.
3. S.G., 13 May, 1964.
4. Mrs C. Macdonald, North Tolsta, Lewis.
5. SC 33/3/1
6. Ibid.
7. Ibid.
8. H.R.B., Report on the Outer Hebrides, App. B., Aug. 1849.
9. SC 33/5/2.
10. SC 33/5/3.

EDUCATION

1. P.C.R., Vol. V, 270.
2. Ibid. Vol. X, 270.
3. Collectanea de Rebus Albanicis, 8.
4. P.C.R., July 26, 1616.
5. Ibid. July 26, 1616.
6. Macfarlane's Geographical Collections, Vol. II, 215.
7. CH 2, August, 1743.
8. Ibid. August, 1750.
9. Hyndman Report, 1760, 59.
10. CH 2, 1774.
11. J. Kerr, Scottish Education, 181.

12. H. Hunter, S.S.P.C.K. in the Highlands, 14.
13. J. Kerr, op. cit., 184.
14. O.S.A., Vol. XIX, 269.
15. GD 46/12/21.
16. O.S.A., Vol. XIX, 243.
17.   Ibid.   243.
18.   Ibid.   243.
19. GD 46/12/142.
20. O.S.A., Vol. XIX, 243.
21.   Ibid.   243.
22. GD 46/12/21.
23. C.S.S., First Report, 12.
24.   Ibid.   13.
25.   Ibid.   14.
26. Ibid. Fifth Report, 59.
27. Ibid. First Report, 47.
28.   Ibid.   48.
29. Ibid. Second Report, 3.
30.   Ibid.   9.
31.   Ibid.   33.
32.   Ibid.   33.
33.   Ibid.   34.
34.   Ibid.   34.
35. Ibid. Third Report, 13.
36. Ibid. Fourteenth Report, 38.
37. Ibid. Sixteenth Report, 32.
38. Ibid. Eighteenth Report, 35.
39. Ibid. Twenty-ninth Report, 7 Feb., 1840.
40. GD 46/12/149.
41. General Assembly's Education Report, Vol. I, 1.
42. J. Kerr, op. cit., 193.
43. N.S.A., op. cit., 139, 150, 155, 168.
44. GD 46/12/145.
45. T. Brown, op. cit., 314.
46.   Ibid.   323.
47. Free Church Blue Book, Education Report, App. II, 25.
48.   Ibid.   App. I, 11.
49. T. Brown, op. cit., 683.
50. L.H.A., First Report, 42.
51. Ibid. Sixth Report, 2.
52. Sheriff Nicolson, The State of Education in the Hebrides, 91.
53. CH 2/473/4, 129.
54. L.H.A., Thirtieth Report, 6.
55.   Ibid.   7.
56. Ibid. Thirty-third Report, 12.
57. Ibid. Sixth Report, 3.
58. J. P. Day, op. cit., 28.
59. J. Wilson, Tales and Travels of an Inspector, 142.
60. J. P. Day, op. cit., 161.
61.   Ibid.   162.
62. W. J. Gibson, History of the Nicolson Institute, MS., 4.
63.   Ibid.   5.
64.   Ibid.   5.
65.   Ibid.   5.
66. Dr J. L. Robertson, S.E.D. Report, 1911, 24.
67. L.H.A., Thirty-second Report, 13.
68.   Ibid. 1882, 13.
69. J. P. Day, op. cit., 169.
70. Dr D. J. Macleod, S.E.D. Report, 1911-13, 69, 70.
71. Dr J. L. Robertson, Ibid. 1911, 24.

EVICTIONS

1. W. F. Skene, op. cit., 429.

2. Act of Sederunt, 1756.
3. GD 46/17/Vol. 49.
4. GD 46/17/Vol. 11.
5. GD 46/17/Vol. 80.
6. Crofters Commission, 1884, 190, 1140.
7. GD 46/17/Vol. 4.
8. SC 33/5/2.
9. GD 46/17/Vol. 67.
10. R. Martin, Balallan.
11. GD 46/17/Vol. 66.
12. GD 46/17/Vol. 60.
13. GD 46/1/538.
14. GD 46/1/530.
15. GD 46/17/Vol. 64.
16. GD 46/17/Vol. 68.
17. Crofters Commission, 1884, 1080.
18.   Ibid.   1063.
19. GD 46/1/128.
20. Crofters Commission, 1884, 1064.
21. Capt. Burnaby, O.S., op. cit., 1850, O.N.B., 45 D, 130.
22. Crofters Commission, 1884, 1156.
23.   Ibid.   1157.
24.   Ibid.   973.
25.   Ibid.   931.
26.   Ibid.   1140-1142.
27.   Ibid.   1135.
28. GD 46/17/Vol. 76.
29. Brand Report, op. cit., 55-59.
30.   Ibid.
31. Crofters Commission, 1884, 161.
32.   Ibid.   885.

EMIGRATION

1. Edinburgh Courant, July, 1773.
2. D. Whyte, A Dictionary of Scottish Emigrants to the U.S.A., 230, 300.
3. GD 46/17/Vol. 71.
4. S.C.E., 1841, 174, 175.
5. Cuairtear nan Gleann, 1 Feb., 1843.
6. S.C.E., 1841, 176, 177.
7.   Ibid.   97.
8. M. C. MacLeod, op. cit.
9. Crofters Commission, 1884, 163-174.
10. The Scotsman, 21 Sept., 1888.
11. Murchadh Cam, MacTalla, 16 June, 1899.
12. D. Morrison, Bragar and U.S.A.

LAND AGITATION

1. Crofters Commission, 1884, 995.
2.   Ibid.   196.
3. N. Macdonald, Breasclete, Lewis.
4. Crofters Commission, 1884, 908.
5.   Ibid.   904.
6. Dr D. Macdonald, Gisla, op. cit., 147.
7. Crofters Commission, 1884, 893.
8. N.S.A., op. cit., 166.
9. SC 33/5/6.
10. Crofters Commission, 1884, 1143, 1144.
11.   Ibid.   1144.
12.   Ibid.   152.
13.   Ibid.   152.

14.   Ibid.   1144.
15. The Scotsman, 2 Dec., 1887.
16.   Ibid.   17 Jan., 1888.
17.   Ibid.   12 Jan., 1888.
18.   Ibid.   10 April, 1891.

THE LEVERHULME PERIOD

1.   AF 67/252.
2.   AF 67/248.
3.   Ibid.
4.   AF 67/268, 1-11.
5.   AF 67/278.
6.   AF 67/250.
7.   Ibid.
8.   AF 67/254.
9.   AF 67/252.
10.   Ibid.
11.   Ibid.
12. AF 66/104.
13. AF 67/254.
14.   Ibid.
15.   Ibid.
16.   Ibid.
17.   Ibid.
18.   Ibid.
19.   Ibid.
20.   Ibid.
21. AF 67/255.
22. AF 67/254.
23.   Ibid.
24. AF 67/105.
25. AF 67/258.
26. AF 66/105.
27.   Ibid.
28. AF 67/254.

DESERTED ISLANDS

1.   Capt. Burnaby, O.S., op. cit., O.N.B. 136.
2.   Sir D. Monro, A Description of the Western Isles of Scotland, 522.
3.   Ibid.   523.
4.   Ibid.   523.
5.   Capt. Burnaby, O.S., O.N.B., 136.
6.   M. Martin, op. cit., 100.
7.   Ibid.   100.
8.   Ibid.   102.
9.   Ibid.   103.
10.   Ibid.   104.
11. O.S.A., Vol. XIX, 271.
12. J. MacCulloch, The Highlands and Western Isles, 1815, Vol. III, 317.
13.   Ibid.   315, 316.
14.   Ibid.   317.
15.   Ibid.   319, 320.
16. Capt. Burnaby, O.S., op. cit., O.N.B., 136.
17. O.S.A., Vol. XIX, 271.
18. SC 33/5/4.
19. GD 46/17/Vol. 70.
20. W. C. Mackenzie, The Book of the Lews, 249.
21. Sir D. Monro, op. cit., 514.
22. M. Martin, op. cit., 105.
23. Capt. Burnaby, O.S., O.N.B., 134.
24. O.S.A., Vol. XIX, 276.

25. Capt. Burnaby, O.S., op. cit., O.N.B., 135.
26. M. Martin, op. cit., 97-99.
27. Northern Lighthouse Board, Flannan Isle Lighthouse Pamphlet.
28. Sir D. Monro, op. cit., 515.
29. Cosmo Innes, op. cit., Vol. II, 386.
30. Macrae, Revivals in the Highlands in the 19th Century, 86.
31. G.S.S., Twenty-third Report, 1833, 10.
32. Census of Scotland, 1861.

INDEX

Fuel, 194

Gaelic, 16, 111, 156, 157, 177, 179
Gall-Gaidheil, 18
Gallipoli, 122, 138
Galloway, 18
Gallows Hill, 135
Galson, 13, 40, 43, 46, 48, 161, 176
Games, 51
Gannets (Gugas), 55
Laird's Dyke, 33
Garrabost, 24, 37, 43, 48, 87, 133
Garry, 13, 15
Garynahine, 80
Gas Company, Stornoway, 39
Gaugers, 130-132
Gearraidh Chruaidh, Castle Grounds, 37
General Assembly Schools, 149
George I, King, 141
George IV, King, 87
Geriah, 36, 117
Gestation Rhyme, 82
Gibson, William J., 157
Gillanders, Alexander, 117
Gillanders, George, 37, 85, 131
Glanadh a' Bhaile, 80
Glasgow, 31, 43, 133
Glenelg, Synod of, 110, 145, 149
Glenshiel, Battle of, 35, 116
Goat Island, 34, 136
Godfrey Crovan, 20
Godfrey the Black, 21
Godfrey Donn, 19, 20, 22
Olaf the Red, 20
Gordon, Police Superintendent, 175
Government-sponsored Settlements in Canada, 168, 169
Gradanadh, 75
Graddan Meal, 75, 89
Grammar School, the, Aberdeen, 154
Gravir, 37, 48, 152, 159, 174, 177
Great Seal, the, 30
Great War, the, 51
Gress, 14, 34, 48, 56, 78, 79, 87, 93, 99, 104, 107, 147, 161, 178, 179
Grimersta, 22, 56
Grimshader, 22, 37, 98, 136
Groningen, Holland, 122
Ground Leave, 100
Ground Officers, 34, 74, 90, 97, 159, 172

Habost, Ness, 14, 135
Hacklete, 168
Halidon Hill, Battle of, 23
Hallowe'en, 110
Hakon the Good, King of Norway, 18, 19

Harlaw, Battle of, 23
Harold the Fairhaired, King of Norway, 18
Harvesting, 73
Hastings, Battle of, 19
Haversford, Battle of, 18
Hay, Sir George, 30
Hebrides, the, 15, 18, 20-23
Hebridean Sheep, 52, 84
Heimskringla Saga, 19
Helm, Dundas, 116
Herring Fishery Board, 106
Highlands and Islands, 27, 126, 141, 145, 146, 155
Highlands and Islands Commission, (Napier Commission), 45
Highlands and Islands Development Board, 106
Highlands and Islands Works Act, 48, 100, 105
Highland Society of Scotland, 83
Highland Relief Board, 40, 46
Highland Relief Committee, 42
Highland Relief Society, 129
Hillock of Evil Counsel, the, 15
Holm, 104, 133
Holm, the Beasts of, 122
Horse-hair, 93
Housing, 39
Hood, Admiral Sir Samuel, 37
Hood, Lady, 37
(See Mrs James Alexander Stewart Mackenzie)
Hudson Bay Company, 55, 86, 157, 168
Humberston, Col. Thomas Mackenzie, 36, 116
Hunting, 14
Huntly, Earl of, 24
Hyderabad, 160
Hypothec, 41

Iceland, 15, 18, 84
Illegal Trawling, 106
Illicit Distilling, 44, 125, 130, 132
India, 116
Indian Mutiny, 117, 120
Illiteracy, 146
Ingemund, 19
Innes, Charles
Insecurity of Tenure, 57
Inverkirkaig, 135
Iolaire, H.M.Y., Disaster, 122, 123
Iona, 15, 20, 107, 140
Ionian Isles, 38
Iorram, 26
Ireland, 15, 18, 19, 107
Islay, 133

218